THE GREENING

THE ENVIRONMENTALISTS' DRIVE FOR GLOBAL POWER

LARRY ABRAHAM

WITH

FRANKLIN SANDERS

First Hardcover Printing 1993

First Paperback Printing 1994

ISBN 0-9626646-2-6

Library of Congress Card Catalog Number 91-70520

Dauphin Publications Reprint Edition 2015

ISBN 978-1-939438-35-5

Support *The Abraham Project*, and help spread the news of freedom from the New World Order. Donations welcomed.

www.NoneDare.com

Acknowledgments

When an author undertakes the task of writing a book about a social or political condition which affects as many people as *The Greening* does, the problem is never one of finding material, rather, it is deciding which documentation best relates to the story. It is to this keen sense of "what is important" and "what is not" that I owe a great debt of appreciation to many people.

First, of course, is my brilliant collaborator, Franklin Sanders. Without his contribution and determination this volume would have never been concluded.

Next is my publisher, partner, and good friend, Chip Wood, who refused to let me "keep going," knowing well that writing a book is like constructing a building – you have to stop somewhere.

Invaluable were the faxed and mailed tidbits from my colleagues, especially Gary North, and my own subscribers to *Insider Report*.

I wish also to express appreciation to the Kroening brothers, Steve and Bob, who never revolted during the many edits and rewrites, and who tirelessly and professionally typeset and edited this manuscript.

And finally, for my beloved Sherry, who has plowed through enough issues of the *New York Times*, *Time* magazine, the *Washington Post*, and all the other liberal media on my behalf to satisfy for an eternity any purgatorial requirements demanded by a just God.

Dedication

To all those independent-minded loggers, miners, farmers, businessmen, and businesswomen who, under the most vicious of assaults, continue to develop the resources and produce the products which make life worth living. And most especially to the memory of my father who typified in his own life this very indefatigable spirit.

TABLE OF CONTENTS

INTRODUCTION

Over the past 30 years I have observed, chronicled, and opposed numerous onslaughts which would reduce the sovereignty of the individual and add to or increase government's power.

Without exception, every one of the projects and pro-grams subjected to this scrutiny was touted as "necessary" or "vital." Some were even presented as "life-saving" or "life-threatening." And to be sure, each "crusade" contained two common denominators: (1) a grain of truth about the concern, and (2) a well-organized minority which helped create "the appearance of popular support" for same.

Edmund Burke observed, all too accurately, "The people never give up their liberties but under some delusion." What was true in 1784 is even more applicable today, given the impact of instantaneous and worldwide media coverage. The delusions which lead people to give up their liberties always produce the same result: bigger and more powerful government.

Another factor – one which many prefer to ignore or suppress – leaps out at us as well. The late George Washington University Professor of Law, Arthur Selwyn Miller, identified this factor in his book, *The Secret Constitution and the Need for Constitutional Change*. He wrote, "Those who formally rule take their signals and commands not from the electorate as a body, but from a small group of men (plus a few women). This group will be called the Establishment. It exists even though that existence is stoutly denied. It is one of the secrets of the American social order." Professor Miller adds, "A second secret is the fact that the existence of the Establishment – the ruling class – is not supposed to be discussed."

In this study, Franklin Sanders and I will set out to document, and I believe prove, that in the name of "preserving the environment" or "stopping pollution," the greatest surrender of liberty in all human history is well underway. It will transfer heretofore undreamed-of power not to "the people" or "the electorate as a body," but rather to what Professor Miller called "a small group of men" or "elite Establishment." The implications of this transfer are almost beyond calculation.

I must also point out and emphasize that our quarrel is not with those millions of people who are legitimately concerned about the earth's environmental well-being or the various components of these concerns, *i.e.*, "ozone depletion," "the greenhouse effect," "acid rain," "endangered species," "population explosion," plus countless other causes of varying focus. Nor is this the time or place to evaluate the *validity* of those arguments, although the public debate should be free to weigh that validity without phony data and propagandistic manipulation. Each of these "concerns" has promoters as well as antagonists, and considering what's at stake here, that is as it should be.

No, our concern is how "The Greening" juggernaut is steamrolling all opposition, silencing critics by a feigned moral and intellectual superiority, and, in the process, transferring global wealth and power on an unprecedented scale. It is also my sincere hope that even the most fervid and dedicated among the "green" movement will pause to consider how their dedication is being directed, used, and misused in ways as sinister as they are subtle.

On the more practical side of what is outlined here – and let's not be coy about it, either – are the billions and billions of dollars being spent and the fortunes being made. What's happening in the "environmental" movement is not a zero-sum game. There are winners and losers on a vast scale and we will identify those in both categories.

Finally, I hope and pray that those people of goodwill who read this book will use their wealth and influence to preserve what is mankind's most precious, precarious, and endangered environmental condition: *liberty*.

- Larry Abraham
Wauna, Washington,
January 1993

CHAPTER 1

THE GREENING

IS BORN

At first it all seemed so right. Who would not want clean air, nice parks and preserves, abundant and contaminant free water? At first we were shocked at the wanton slaughter of elephant herds for their ivory, appalled at the foul water used by the people struggling for existence in the barrios of Mexico City or the bowels of Calcutta, disgusted by the tearing away of precious topsoil to snatch a few more tons of ore from the earth, repulsed by the smog layers covering our cities, so that the very act of breathing became hazardous to our health.

At first, many welcomed the young and idealistic who were willing to dedicate themselves to saving the earth. We applauded their selfless zeal to work for a "cleaner environment."

Then slowly, ever so slowly, a new realization started coming into focus. Factories were being closed, huge tracts of land were declared "off limits," multimillion-dollar projects were stopped in their tracks, and thousands of jobs were lost, to protect a little fish, or a whooping crane, or an owl no one had heard of before. It reached the point where you couldn't even hope to build a home beside a babbling brook, without worrying about "wetlands" or other interminable red tape.

What was happening in America? The gentle, green face of conservation and preservation was turning into a nightmare ogre of "ecology" and "environmental activism." Whole armies of refugees from the '60s were no longer marching for "peace." They were marching *against* something – and their enemy was *man the despoiler*. And as their forces grew, their targets included jobs, factories, farms, forests, anything and anywhere man wanted to change nature.

The Marxist college professors, who in the past extolled the virtues of everything Soviet, had now become experts in ecology. And just as before, they found the enemy right here at home – middle-class Americans and the businesses they had built.

Huge foundations bulging with millions of tax-exempt dollars poured forth their largesse to anyone who pointed an accusing finger at the "greedy businessman" who in the "pursuit of profit" threatened the "ecological balance." Politicians at every level rushed to become the champion of every "green" cause, no matter how outlandish. Whole new "threats" to our existence were put forth as absolute and unchallengeable facts. Global warming, ozone holes, population explosions, species extinction, all were the new H bombs just waiting to explode and "destroy life on the planet as we know it."

In a rush to meet these "threats," Earth Days were proclaimed, TV specials produced, textbooks rewritten, and emergency conferences convened from one end of the earth to the other. Self-appointed "guardians of the land" rushed from one international soiree to another, to declaim on the need to "preserve the environment" and to condemn the works of man.

Predictably, with all this new awareness came thousands of new laws, regulations, and proclamations at every level of government, from the lowest city and hamlet to the UN itself.

Finally, some of the victims of this runaway juggernaut began to realize what was happening, and to speak out. What at first seemed so benign and so right is now touching, or about to touch, everyone, everywhere. "Touching" is the wrong word. "Smashing" is more appropriate. The real goal is nothing less than to control natural resources worldwide. The Insiders of Environmentalism realize –

even if many innocent bystanders do not – that the wealth of the world consists of the things men take from the earth, and *they want to control it all.*

Thanks to the unholy alliance between the international Establishment and socialist revolutionaries, they just might succeed. For what is now being unleashed in the name of "saving the earth" is nothing less than the most historic grab for power in all of human history.

World Peace and Environmentalism

Over the next 15 years, the U.S. federal budget for environmentally-related expenditures will replace and surpass defense spending in both size and economic impact. I use 15 years as an arbitrary number only, electing to be overly conservative. In all probability, it will take far less time for this dramatic "change in priorities" to occur.

At the end of June 1990, Senate Armed Services Committee Chairman Sam Nunn proposed shifting substantial Defense Department and intelligence resources to ecological programs. Nunn was joined by committee members Al Gore, Tim Wirth, Jeff Bingaman, and Jim Exon in calling for the creation of a "Strategic Environmental Research Program." Earlier in the same year, February 26th to be exact, Secretary of State James Baker, speaking before the National Governors' Association in Washington, D.C., pledged "the greening of our foreign policy" and the full integration of environmental concerns into all its aspects.

On September 26,1990, German Foreign Minister Hans- Dietrich Genscher spoke before the United Nations, describing some of the "historic responsibilities" that would be part of German reunification. *The Week in Germany* reported, "The minister emphasized as well the importance of environmental protection, saying that the two German states are aware that 'a policy for safeguarding the environment is also a policy for safeguarding world peace.'"

Day after day media and politicians around the world repeat this same theme: "National and international security depends on ecological security." The message is clear: World peace and the ecological agenda must be viewed as one and the same. And lest you believe that this "linkage" is just the overly enthusiastic result of political rhetoric, let me demonstrate otherwise. The first piece of evidence to support this hypothesis is quite lengthy in its presentation, but when you finish I believe you will agree it was worth the time and space.

What if Peace Breaks Out...Green Peace?

In 1967 a little book of just over 100 pages was published by Dial Press. The thoroughly innocuous title was *Report from Iron Mountain on the Possibility and Desirability of Peace*. Leonard C. Lewin, who wrote the introduction, de-scribes the circumstances of the book's publication as follows:

"John Doe," as I will call him in this book for reasons that will be made dear, is a professor at a large university in the Middle West. His field is one of the social sciences, but I will not identify him beyond this. He telephoned me one evening last winter, quite unexpectedly; we had not been in touch for several years. He was in New York for a few days, he said, and there was something important he wanted to discuss with me. He wouldn't say what it was. We met for lunch the next day at a midtown restaurant.

He was obviously disturbed. He made small talk for half an hour, which was quite out of character, and I didn't press him. Then, apropos of nothing, he mentioned a dispute between a writer and a prominent political family that had been in the headlines. What, he wanted to know, were my views on "freedom of information"? How would I qualify them? And so on. My answers were not memorable, but they seemed to satisfy him. Then quite abruptly, he began to tell me the following story:

Early in August of 1963, he said, he found a message on his desk that a "Mrs. Potts" had called him from Washington. When he returned the call, *a man* answered immediately, and told Doe, among other things, that he had been selected to serve on a commission "of the highest importance." Its objective was to *determine, accurately and realistically, the nature of the problems that would confront the United States if and when a condition of "permanent peace" should arrive, and to draft a program for dealing with this contingency.* The man described the unique procedures that were to govern the commission's work and that were expected to extend its scope far beyond that of any previous examination of these problems.

Considering that the caller did not precisely identify either himself or his agency, his persuasiveness must have been of a truly remarkable order. I entertained no serious doubts of the *bona fides* of the project, however, chiefly because of his previous experience with the excessive secrecy that often surrounds quasi-governmental activities. In addition, the man at the other end of the line demonstrated an impressively complete and surprisingly detailed knowledge of Doe's work and personal life. He also mentioned the names of others who were to serve with the group; most of them were known to Doe by reputation. Doe agreed to take the assignment – he felt he had no real choice in the matter – and to appear the second Saturday following at Iron Mountain, New York. An airline ticket arrived in his mail the next morning.

The cloak-and-dagger tone of this convocation was further enhanced by the meeting place itself. Iron Mountain, located near the town of Hudson, is like something out of Ian Fleming or E. Phillips Oppenheim. It is an underground nuclear hide-out for hundreds of large American corporations. In Iron Mountain's underground depository beneath the concrete and steel of lower Manhattan, there are amounts of stored precious metals, and numerous corporate lockers. One custodian says that they also maintain a lodge-like facility up on the Hudson River. Most of them use it as an emergency storage vault for important documents. But a number of them maintain substitute corporate headquarters as well, where essential personnel could presumably survive and continue to work after an attack. This latter group includes such firms as Standard Oil of New Jersey, Manufacturers Hanover Trust, and Shell.

I will leave most of the story of the operations of the Special Study Group, as the commission was formally called, for Doe to tell in his own words. At this point it is necessary to say only that it met and worked regularly for over two and a half years, after which it produced a Report. It was this document, and what to do about it, that Doe wanted to talk to me about.

The report, he said, had been suppressed – both by the Special Study Group itself and by the government inter-agency committee to which it had been submitted. After months of agonizing, Doe had decided that he would no longer be party to keeping it secret. What he wanted from me was advice and assistance in having it published. He gave me his copy to read, with the express understanding that if for any reason I were unwilling to become involved, I would say nothing about it to anyone else.

Why Insiders Love War

Lewin then describes how he came to understand fully why Doe's associates didn't want their work product publicized and why the real author of the Report had to use the trite but necessary *nom de plume* of John Doe. Lewin writes that the Special Study Group concluded:

Lasting peace, while not theoretically impossible, is probably unattainable; even if it could be achieved it would almost certainly not be in the best interests of a stable society to achieve it.

That is the gist of what they say. Behind their qualified academic language runs this general argument: war fills certain functions essential to the stability of our society; until other ways of filling them are developed, the war system must be maintained – and improved in effectiveness.

Lewin concludes his introductory comments: "I should state, for the record, that I do not share the attitudes toward war and peace, life and death, and survival of the species manifested in the Report. Few readers will. *In human terms, it is an outrageous document. But it does represent a serious and challenging effort to define an enormous problem. And it explains, or certainly appears to explain, aspects of American policy otherwise incomprehensible by the ordinary standards of common sense.* What we may think of these explanations is something else, but it seems to me that we are entitled to know not only what they are but whose they are." [Emphasis added.]

A short time after the book was published, a popular guessing game of "Who is Doe?" sprang up amid the govern-mental and academic *literati*. By 1969 John Kenneth Galbraith, the Harvard economist and Insider *par excellence*, admitted his involvement and vouched for its authenticity, but never, to this very day, disclosed the identities of the other members of the research team.[1]

With this background, let's now extract just a few of the most startling revelations from *Report from Iron Mountain* as they pertain to the current hysteria on the "environment" and the "end of the Cold War." As we do, remember we are quoting verbatim from a document published in 1967 which was the result of a project started in 1963. The Special Study Group said:

> Our work has been predicated on the belief that some kind of general peace may soon be negotiable. The de facto admission of Communist China into the United Nations now appears to be only a few years away at most. [It was four years, to be exact.] It has become increasingly manifest that conflicts of American national interest with those of China and the Soviet Union are susceptible of political solution... It is

---

1 I first wrote about the Report from Iron Mountain as a special report to the readers of my monthly newsletter, Insider Report, in 1989. Since that time a whole new debate has arisen about J.K. Garbraith's authorship. So that the readers of this volume can determine for themselves, the original assessment, I have included as the Appendix, an article from the SCP Journal by the scholar Brooks Alexander who has recently researched all of the original book reviews at the time the Iron Mountain Report first burst on the scene. His analysis is scholarly, thoughtful, and very timely.

not necessary, for the purposes of our study, to assume that a general detente of this sort *will* come about...but only that it *may*.

In Section 5, entitled "The Functions of War," the *Report* states, "As we have indicated, the pre-eminence of the concept of war as the principal organizing force in most societies has been insufficiently appreciated."

The Special Study Group then explains how war, or the threat of war, is very "positive" from government's perspective because it allows for major expenditures, national solidarity, and a "stable internal political structure." They state, 'Without [war], no government has ever been able to obtain acquiescence in its 'legitimacy,' or right to rule its society." They further state, "Obviously, if the war system were to be discarded, new political machinery would be needed at once to serve this vital sub-function. Until it is developed, the continuance of the war system must be assured, if for no other reason, among others, than to preserve whatever quality and degree of poverty a society requires as an incentive, as well as to maintain the stability of its internal organization of power."

Before moving into a discussion of what could possibly serve as a substitute for the positive aspects of war, Doe writes, "Whether the substitute is ritual in nature or functionally substantive, *unless it provides a believable life-and-death threat it will not serve the socially organizing function of war.*" [Emphasis added.]

A Substitute for War

Then in Section 6, "Substitutes for the Functions of War," Doe, writing for the Special Study Group, outlines the economic necessities which must be applied:

> Economic surrogates for war must meet two principal criteria. They must be "wasteful," in the common sense of the word, and they must operate outside the normal supply-demand system. A corollary that should be obvious is that the magnitude of the waste must be sufficient

to meet the needs of a particular society. *An economy as advanced and complex as our own requires the planned average annual destruction of not less than 10 percent of gross national product....* [Emphasis is definitely added.]

Please read this incredible revelation a second time, and maybe even a third, for this admission will help you understand Lewin's following comment and 40-plus years of contemporary history: "[I]t explains, or certainly appears to explain, aspects of American policy otherwise incomprehensible by the ordinary standards of common sense."

It also aids mightily to unravel the untouchable mystery of "bi-partisan" foreign policy, against all political odds remaining consistent through one administration after another. Regardless of any differences debated during campaigns, each post-World War II President, once installed, pursued a policy indistinguishable from his predecessor, Republican or Democrat.

After exploring a whole range of "substitute" possibilities, such as a war on poverty, space research, even "the credibility of an out-of-our-world invasion threat," the Special Study Group reports and Doe recites:

It may he, for instance, that gross pollution of the environment can eventually replace the possibility of mass destruction by nuclear weapons as the principal apparent threat to the survival of the species. Poisoning of the air, and of the principal sources of food and water supply, is already well advanced, and at first glance would seem promising in this respect; it constitutes a threat that can be dealt with only through social organization and political power. *But from present indications it will be a generation to a generation and a half before environmental pollution, however severe, will be sufficiently menacing, on a global scale, to offer a possible basis for a solution.* [Emphasis added.]

I hope you didn't skim over the preceding paragraph. It explains, with almost unbelievable boldness, that *environment concerns* would be an almost perfect replacement for war, but it would take a generation or a generation and a half (that is, 20 to 30 years) to bring this about. Remember, we are talking about a report completed about 1967.

The time frame is now complete, as evidenced by an article in the March 20, 1990 *Seattle Post-Intelligencer*. The front-page headline reads, "Pollution 'a ticking time bomb,' conference warned." Datelined Vancouver, B.C., the article starts, "Environmental destruction is a 'ticking time bomb' that poses a 'more absolute' threat to human survival than nuclear annihilation during the Cold War, former Norwegian Prime Minister Gro Harlem Brundtland told an international environment conference here."

It then continues, "The conference, Globe '90, was launched yesterday amid warnings that pollution and over-population are threats that require resources previously committed to the arms race."

I'll have more to say about Globe '90 and other such conferences later. Now let's continue with *Report from Iron Mountain* and its revelations.

In the section, "Substitutes for the Functions of War," it concludes:

However unlikely some of the possible alternate enemies we have mentioned may seem, *we must emphasize that one must be found*, of credible quality and magnitude, if a transition to peace is ever to come about without social disintegration.

Then they say, "It is more probable, in our judgment, that such a threat *will have to be invented*, rather than developed from unknown conditions." [The emphasis once again is definitely added.]

Doe, a.k.a. Galbraith, then summarizes, "What is involved here, in a sense, is the quest for William James' 'moral equivalent of war.'"

All I can say is the "quest" has indeed been successful; the "equivalent of war" has been formed. But "moral" it will never be!

It is also worth noting that in his section entitled, "Back-ground Information," Doe said, "The general idea...for this kind of study dates back at least to 1961. It started with some of the new people who came in with the Kennedy Administration, mostly, I think, with McNamara, Bundy, and Rusk." All three earned the sobriquet "Insider" many times over.

Earth Day -1970 -1990

Now let's shift the scene to April 22, 1970. On that day, with the approval of the Congress, President Richard M. Nixon declared the first Earth Day and in that same year established the Environmental Protection Agency. (A few more cynical types, familiar with how the Marxist-Leninists and their Insider buddies like to link dates, have pointed out that most biographers also cite April 22 as V.I. Lenin's birthday. Not wanting to be *ultra*-conspiratorial, I'll use April 23 for Lenin's birthday, as some others do, and not try to draw any ominous conclusions. Just thought you might be interested.)

Now, finally "a generation and a half" later, the whole world geared up for Earth Day 1990. April 22 was a very big day. My final tally showed that 107 countries worldwide were involved in a planet-wide recognition of this Green Gala. In anticipation of the global festivities, the media had been beating the drums for months ahead of time.

In a front-page feature in the Sunday, January 28, 1990 *Seattle Times*, reporter Bill Dietrich said, "Environmentalists are hoping history is about to top itself with a[n]...Earth Day celebration...involving more than 100 countries and 100 million people. The goal is to make the '90s the 'Decade of the Environment.'"

And how does this fit with the *Report from Iron Mountain?* Just two citations from the same *Seattle Times* piece make the point:

"Government, business, and consumers have spent up to a trillion dollars, by Department of Commerce count, to clean the environment...The U.S. seems to find three new environmental hazards for each one it conquers." And: "Twenty years after Earth Day, those of us who set out to change the world are poised on the threshold of utter failure only to find ourselves now on the verge of losing the war?" That particular lament was uttered by none other than Dennis Hayes, the founder of the original Earth Day.

In a moment of surprising candor, Ken Weiner, Jimmy Carter's Deputy Director of the Council for Environmental Quality and now a Seattle attorney, admitted Hayes is more than half right: "The Environmental movement is recognizing its issue is being taken away by the establishment. It has been said war is too important to be left to the generals. Some are wondering if environment quality is too important to be left to the environmentalists."

As the jubilant contestants on "Family Feud" would say, while clapping hands and jumping up and down, "Good answer, good answer!" So let's quickly do a recap on the environment and see if it fits the "Substitute for the Function of War" so desperately sought by the Special Study Group in the *Report from Iron Mountain*:

1) We have a "war";
2) It involves "everyone - everywhere";
3) It is "urgent";
4) It has already required the spending of "a trillion dollars" with much more to come;
5) It's "international." And most frightening of all;
6) You ain't seen nothin' yet.

A think-tank proposal like *Report from Iron Mountain is one thing. A concrete plan for its implementation, however, is of an entirely different magnitude.*

In exactly the same month and year as the first Earth Day, April 1970, an article appeared in the most important Insider policy-setting publication on earth. Writing in *Foreign Affairs*, the quarterly journal of the Council on Foreign Relations, no less a personage than George F. Kennan presented what he entitled "To Prevent A World Wasteland...A Proposal." His opening paragraph set the tone for what would follow:

> Not even the most casual reader of the public prints of recent months and years could be unaware of the growing chorus of warnings from qualified scientists as to what industrial man is now doing – by overpopulation, by plundering of the earth's resources, and by a precipitate mechanization of many of life's processes – to the intactness of the natural environment on which his survival depends.

> "For the first time in the history of mankind," UN Secretary-General U Thant wrote, "there is arising a crisis of *worldwide proportions* involving developed and developing countries alike – the crisis of human environment...It is becoming apparent that if current trends continue, *the future of life on earth could be endangered.*" [Emphasis added.]

Before we juxtapose Kennan's "Proposal" with the *Report from Iron Mountain*, a few words about the man himself are essential. Among the policy planners of international statecraft, George F. Kennan is an icon of unparalleled proportion. In their book *The Wise Men – Six Friends and the World They Made*, Walter Isaacson and Evan Thomas include Mr. Kennan in their pantheon of Establishment heavyweights, which also included John J. McCloy, Dean Acheson, Robert Lovett, Charles "Chip" Bohlen and Averell Harriman.

Kennan is universally recognized as the "father of containment," the policy now being accorded the "strategy" for "Cold War victory." As a former Ambassador to the USSR and head of the State Department's Policy Planning staff, Kennan not only led the team for 40 years of foreign policy – he created it.

Writing under the provocative *nom de plume* "X" in the very same journal, *Foreign Affairs*, Mr. Kennan coined the word "Containment" in his July 1947 article entitled "The Sources of

Soviet Conduct." It was this policy which provided the Soviets "super-power" status, divided the world into "bilateral" power blocks and led to the expenditure of trillions of dollars for "national defense."

It is becoming increasingly obvious that "Soviet Containment" was more "Soviet Preservation" than anything else. Preservation of a totalitarian system which would have collapsed of its own, years ago, were it not for the "super-power" status given it by George Kennan and his Establishment colleagues. But regardless of what may have been the true nature of the Soviet "threat," no one can deny that at least 10 percent of GNP was spent to "contain" it.

I'll have much more to say about the Establishment in the next chapter, so let us now turn back to Kennan's April '70 assessment and "proposal." Remember as we do that this very man who gave us the "Cold War" will be offering a replacement for it, per the *Report from Iron Mountain*. Let me quote verbatim its most salient points:

> But it is also clear that the national perspective is not the only one from which this problem needs to be approached. Polluted air does not hang forever over the country in which the pollution occurs. The contamination of coastal waters does not long remain solely the problem of the nation in whose waters it has its origin. Wildlife – fish, fowl and animal – is no respecter of national boundaries, either in its movements or in the sources from which it draws its being. *Indeed, the entire ecology of the planet is not arranged in national compartments; and whoever interferes seriously with it anywhere is doing something that is almost invariably of serious concern to the international community at large...*

> The first of these [functions] would be to provide adequate facilities for the collection, storage retrieval and dissemination of information on all aspects of the problem. This would involve not just assembling the results of scientific investigation but also keeping something in the nature of a register of all conservational activities at international, national, regional and even local levels across the globe. The task here is

not one of conducting original research but rather of collecting and collating the results of research done elsewhere, and disposing of that information in a manner to make it readily available to people everywhere...

A second function would be to promote the coordination of research and operational activities which now deal with environmental problems at the international level.

A third function would be to establish international standards in environmental matters and to extend advice and help to individual governments and to regional organizations in their efforts to meet these standards....

The fourth function that cries out for performance is from the standpoint of the possibilities in international (as opposed to national or regional) action, the most important of all. In contrast to all the others, it relates only to what might be called the great international media of human activity: the high seas, the stratosphere, outer space, perhaps also the Arctic and Antarctic – media which are subject to the sovereign authority of no national government. It consists simply of the establishment and enforcement of suitable rules for all human activities conducted in these media. It is a question not just of conservational considerations in the narrow sense but also of providing protection against the unfair exploitation of these media, above all the plundering or fouling or damaging of them, by individual governments or their nationals for selfish parochial purposes. *Someone, after all, must decide at some point what is tolerable and permissible here and what is not; and since this is an area in which no sovereign government can make these determinations, some international authority must ultimately do so.*

For all of these purposes, the first step must be, of course, the achievement of adequate international consensus and authorization in the form of a multilateral treaty or convention. But for this there will have to be some suitable center of initiation, not to mention the instrument of enforcement which at a later point will have to come into the picture.

What is needed here is a watchdog; and the conscience and sense of duty of the watchdog must not be confused by contrary duties and undertakings. It may be boldly asserted that of the two purposes in question, conservation should come first. The principle should be that one exploits what a careful regard for the needs of conservation leaves to be exploited, not that one conserves what a liberal indulgence of the impulse to development leaves to be conserved.

What is lacking in the present pattern of approaches would seem to be precisely an organizational personality –part conscience, part voice – which has at heart the interest of no nation, no group of nations, no armed force, no political movement and no commercial concern, but simply those of mankind generally, together – *and this is important - with man's animal and vegetable companions, who have no other advocate*...

The process of compromise of national interests will of course have to take place at some point in every struggle against environmental deterioration at the international level...

All of this would seem to speak for the establishment of a single entity which, while not duplicating the work of existing organizations, could review this work from the standpoint of man's environmental needs as a whole, could make it its task to spot the inadequacies and identify the unfilled needs, could help to keep governments and leaders of opinion informed as to what ought to be done to meet minimum needs, could endeavor to assure that *proper rules and standards are established wherever they are needed, and could, where desired, take a hand, vigorously and impartially, in the work of enforcement of rules and standards.*

This entity, while naturally requiring the initiative of governments for its inception and their continued interest for its support, would have to be one in which the substantive decisions would be taken not on the basis of compromise among governmental representatives but on the basis of collaboration among scholars, scientists, experts, and perhaps also something in the nature of environmental statesmen and diplomats – but true international servants, bound by no national or political mandate, by nothing, in fact, other than dedication to the work at hand...

One can conceive, then, by an act of the imagination, of a small group of advanced nations, consisting of roughly the ten leading industrial nations of the world, including communist and non-communist ones alike, together (mainly for reasons of their maritime interests) with the Scandinavians and perhaps with the Benelux countries as a bloc, constituting themselves something in the nature of a club for the preservation of natural environment, and resolving, then, in that capacity, to bring into being an entity – let us call it initially an Environmental Agency – charged with the performance, at least on their behalf, of the functions outlined above.

It may be argued that under such an arrangement the participating institutions from communist countries would not be free agents, would enjoy no real independence, and would act only as stooges for their governments. As *one who has had occasion both to see something of Russia and to disagree in public on a number of occasions with Soviet policies, the writer of this article is perhaps in a particularly favorable position to express his conviction that the Soviet Academy of Sciences, if called upon by its government to play a part in such an undertaking, would do so with an integrity and a seriousness of purpose worthy of its great scientific tradition, and would prove a rock of strength for the accomplishment of the objectives in question.*

The agency would require, of course, financial support from the sponsoring governments. There would be no point in its establishment if one were not willing to support it generously and regularly; and *one should not underestimate the amount of money that would be required.*

And finally, the father of the Cold War offers a vision in the name of "environmentalism" which will foretell the end of that phase of world history and usher in the next:

Not only the international scientific community but the world public at large has great need, at this dark hour, of a new and more promising focus of attention. *The great communist and Western powers, particularly, have need to replace the waning fixations for the cold war with interests which they can pursue in common and to everyone's benefit.* For young people the world over, some new opening of hope and creativity is becoming an urgent spiritual necessity. Could there, one wonders, be any undertaking better designed to meet these needs, to relieve the great convulsions of anxiety and ingrained hostility that now rack international society, than a major international effort to restore the hope, the beauty and the salubriousness of the natural environment in which man has his being? [All emphases added.]

So, there we have it. First an "idea" in 1963-67 which would usher in a "substitute for war," then a blueprint for making it happen. If you go back and analyze both the *Report from Iron Mountain* and Kennan's "Proposal" of 1970, you will quickly see that these two paragons of Establishment wisdom laid the base for most aspects of what is now operational under the mantle of "environmentalism."

So it was that The Greening was given birth, first as an idea, then as a reality.

Last comes the consummation. In 1991 the Trilateral Commission published Jim MacNeill's book, *Beyond Interdependence: The Meshing of the World's Economy and the Earth's Ecology*. MacNeill called for the environmental strait jacket to be snugly and finally fitted on the shoulders of the world at the Rio Earth Summit in June 1992.

The Wise Men Consummate:
Beyond Interdependence

Beyond Interdependence: The Meshing of the World's Economy and the Earth's Ecology comes with a foreword fresh from the pen of Insider David Rockefeller. He sets the tone for the tome. Environmental issues are "rightly moving onto the central policy agenda" and we all feel the need for a "new synthesis." (The more Insider hogwash changes, the more it remains hogwash.)

Rockefeller is not the only worthy with a preliminary word. Maurice Strong (the "Guardian of the Planet," the "Wizard of the Baca") wrote the introduction. Strong was executive secretary of the first eco-summit, the 1972 Stockholm Conference on Human Environment which Kennan was joyously anticipating in 1970. In the last 20 years, whenever the UN groupies were planning to harness the rest of us with Green chains, millionaire Maurice Strong has been there, either as the chairman or a member of the committee.

Jim MacNeill authored *Beyond Interdependence*, with the help of European Pieter Winsemius and Japanese Taizo Yakushiji for window dressing. MacNeill was executive secretary of the World Commission on Environment and Development (the "Brundtland Commission"). That UN group brought forth a less-than-charming turgidity called "Our Common Future." Not much to anyone's surprise, the Brundtland Commission report warned that the world was coming to an end. Moreover, the West is guilty of hogging all the resources and must send them overseas under the direction of a benevolent world government.

The End is Near

Introducing *Beyond Interdependence*, Strong tells us that "the world has now moved beyond economic interdependence to ecological interdependence – to an intermeshing of the two. This interlocking...is the new reality of the century, with profound implications for the shape of our institutions of governance, national and international." Decisions must be made that "will literally determine the fate of the earth."

So what was the purpose of the 1992 Rio Earth Summit? It was to have the political capacity to produce the basic changes needed in our national and international economic agendas and in our institutions of governance to ensure a secure and sustainable future for the world community. "By the year 2012, these changes must be fully integrated into our economic and political life..." Someone was setting deadlines. Someone was busy planning your future and the big payoff was to come at the Rio Summit in 1992.

MacNeill gives us further warning of Rio's significance. "The primary purpose of this conference is to launch a global transition to sustainable development." This shift will follow the well-known pattern of fascist *partnership*. The Earth Summit was to involve "not only representatives of most governments, but also of hundreds of major industries and thousands of non-governmental organizations (NGOs)."

Sustainable Growth

MacNeill hammers our eyelids numb with "sustainable growth," the obnoxious buzzword spawned in the Brundtland Commission report. It is Insider jargon for Green de-industrialization, global cartelization of natural resources, and international control of the world's economy. The "world's last chance" is here.

All this fits the *Iron Mountain* pattern perfectly. Now is the appointed time to substitute the environmental crusade for war. The "credible threat" of communism has at last openly collapsed into the pitiable farce it always was. *The unthinkable has happened:* **peace has arrived.**

"Sustainable growth" is a new synonym for *Iron Mountain's* "stability," i.e., perpetuating Insider control. Economically, it fits the *Report's* recommendation: wasteful outside the normal supply-demand framework and wasteful enough to squander at least 10% of the West's gross national product. Conditions for "sustainable development" include:

(1) growth sufficient to meet human needs,
(2) a more equitable distribution of wealth among nations,
(3) democracy and human rights,
(4) an economic system able to generate surpluses on a sustainable basis (the Establishment's counterfeit "free market" and "privatization").

(5) international central planning,

(6) preserving resources (global control of all natural   resources), and

(7) reducing population.

Following the Pattern

Beyond Interdependence serves up the pure milk of its Iron Mountain mother. Environmentalism pays off here as the perfect substitute for war. MacNeill is willing to start small, say $20 to $50 billion (cash) a year, only about 0.2% of world GNP. Don't worry. The waste will grow, and de-industrialization will take care of the rest of the world's "surplus." Central planning will be necessary, perpetuating the fascist *partnership* between government and Insider business while eliminating a lot more of the surplus – and a lot more of the competition.

We Need Lots of Dough

Lest the new international bureaucrats lack money to waste, MacNeill recommends *environmental taxes* to account for environmental costs. (These have already been implemented in the European Community.) "Taxation for revenue is obsolete," former New York Federal Reserve Chairman Beardsley Ruml observed almost 50 years ago. In a world of central bank fiat money created out of thin air, taxes nowadays are strictly for social control. Of course, these would be world taxes. Remember how much fun America's IRS affords? Just *imagine* what a blast the UN's version will be!

The Green GNP

MacNeill also recommends a "Green GNP" which would factor so-called hidden environmental costs into national economic accounting. Environmental experts will estimate the cost of using natural resources. GNP figures are already speculative, since no government can keep up with the vast multitude of economic transactions in any country. Inserting these subjective figures will render GNP figures such complete guesswork that they would be totally useless.

Never mind economic common sense. The Green GNP is indispensable to central planning and control of the world's economy. The environmental "credible threat" must take over all economic activity, including international trade. Even agriculture must be shifted from the developed to the developing nations. MacNeill also introduces the concept of "shadow ecologies." These are the ecologies of the developing nations affected by the environmental "shadow" of the West. Yes, this is impossible to define objectively, but it is also a perfect rationale for unlimited global economic control.

The End of National Sovereignty

Politically, MacNeill teaches that environmental inter-dependence means the end of national sovereignty. It will provide the "external necessity" for a world government with new laws and regulations aplenty. At the Rio summit, world leaders were "begin[ning] to re-shape our international institutions for an age of total interdependence."

The Same Old Hash

What "credible threat" does MacNeill dish up? The same old worn-out menu of eco-hoaxes: overpopulation, ozone hole, global warming, deforestation, bio-diversity, acid rain, rising sea levels, soil degradation, *ad nauseam*. The childishness of eco-propaganda reveals how profoundly the Insiders disdain us peasants. They are arrogantly certain that their media blackout has spiked all exposure of the Eco-hoax, and confidently believe that even the most intelligent *peónes* have swallowed it. When you own all the newspapers, you can afford to be contemptuous.

MacNeill demands a new "global bargain." On every page he longs for what bureaucrats call "enforcement provisions with real teeth. Economic sanctions will be used against the new Green sinners ("alternate enemies"). Consider the object lessons in sanctions recently served up for South Africa and Iraq. Those exercises were only a warm-up for the New World Order. "Societal resistance must be expected to increase sharply as the costs of action go up and proposed policy changes have more drastic impacts on everyday life. Politicians will have to make 'bargains' between electorates who want action and interest groups that resist it."

Redefining National Security

Sociologically, MacNeill assures us that environmentalism is the "moral equivalent of war." *"National security" must be redefined to include protection against all environmental threats.* For global ecology's sake we must re-shape institutions and control everything, including those "destabilizing elements" and resisting "interest groups" who want to run their own lives as *they* see fit. Although MacNeill doesn't mention it, the new Mother Earth religion is also gaining ground every day. Green pharisaism tyrannizes and annoys every free spirit on the planet. There's plenty of Green guilt to go around.

There are Too Many of You

Ecologically, MacNeill repeatedly reminds us that we cannot reach true environmentalism and "sustainable development" without population control. Governments are not doing enough to reduce population, but surely MacNeill and his global associates will not lack suggestions. Every year abortion alone already kills three times as many Americans as World War II. Decency blushes to guess what infanticide and euthanasia also contribute to population reduction.

Culturally and scientifically, environmentalism is fast becoming the new determinant of values. MacNeill heartily prefers "sustainable development" to economic growth. At the same time, he assures us the environment can easily replace war as the prime motivator of scientific advancement. "Industrialized nations should also collaborate to fund institutes to develop efficiency innovations." If followed to their logical consequence, however, MacNeill's Green ideas may very well usher in the end of all scientific progress and completely de-industrialize the world economy. In his book *Green Rage: Radical Environmentalism and the Unmaking of Civilization*, Eco-radical Christopher Manes admits that deeply primitivist activists oppose industrial civilization itself.

The Super-Agency Again

Finally, the *Iron Mountain* pattern would not be complete unless MacNeill and associates demanded a new international environmental Super-agency. He wants an "Earth Council" (Get it, Earthlings and Planetary Citizens?) as a "new form of governance to guide the planet through the next turbulent decades." Or maybe he'll call it the "World Environment and Development Forum." For a planetary bureaucrat, life is full of tough decisions like that.

Beyond Interdependence does not forget our old friend, "piecemeal functionalism." "There have been few indications that major nations are prepared to relinquish any, let alone a substantial, part of their sovereignty to an international body. Yet, these same nations have accepted a steady encroachment on their sovereignty by the forces of economic interdependence. This erosion will accelerate as a result of ecological interdependence and its rapid meshing with economic interdependence." This is the *classic* European Iron and Steel Community strategy, piecemeal functionalism at its best.

The Insiders are still advancing on all fronts. In case piecemeal functionalism fails, they can fall back on the new Super-agency. "Some...take an incremental approach, building on existing institutions. Other recommendations foresee more fundamental change involving some *pooling of national sovereignty*." (For a plain-spoken Canadian, this boy is handy with one-world euphemisms.)

The UNCED Agenda

It all happened at UNCED in Rio, June '92. The agenda includes:

(1) adopting an "Earth Charter" setting out new principles for government relations and an agenda for the 21st century;

(2) adopting an "agenda for action 'Agenda 21'" - "Most importantly, the agenda will designate the national and international agencies that will bear responsibility for the first phase of implementation, tentatively set for the last seven years of this century,"

(3) possible signing of new treaties, on global warming, deforestation, and bio-diversity;

(4) forming new international institutions of control.

Cheer up. The eco-Nazis love you and have a wonderful plan for your life. "2012 should see a new global partnership expressed in a revitalized international system in which an Earth Council... maintains the interlocked environmental and economic security of the planet." George Orwell worded it much more plainly in 1984, his nightmare novel of a totalitarian future. "If you want a picture of the future, imagine a boot stamping on a human face forever." A Green boot, that is.

Conclusion

If these plans all leave you feeling somewhat less than secure, you're not alone. From the *Report from Iron Mountain* through Kennan's "Proposal" to *Beyond Interdependence* and the Rio Earth Summit, the pattern does not vary. The Insiders have chosen environmentalism as the perfect substitute for war. Forget any legitimate concern for the earth's environment or human well-being. This is the pre-meditated design of arrogant power-brokers so hardened to human feelings that in this century alone they have already consigned millions of men, women, and children to desperation and death. Even our most charitable impulses cannot avoid the unbelievable conclusion. These megalomaniacs genuinely *believe* they are the destined elite worthy to rule the world. Environmentalism is merely the ratty, ragged rationalization designed to hoodwink the world into accepting their rule.

The Insiders will use the environmental crusade to control government and economy far into the future. Environmentalism is, unfortunately, no passing fad, but already-adopted, long-range policy at the highest national and international levels. The Rio eco-summit was the Big Green Payoff for establishing international control. Although environmentalism is childishly maudlin, morally stunted, and scientifically baseless, politically it is the "new reality."

Like previous Insider efforts at world government, this, too, will fail. It is simply another Tower of Babel, another lofty scheme raised up against the True Ruler of this world. Interpreting Nebuchadnezzar's dream, the prophet Daniel comforted us as well, directing our minds to the *unseen reality.*

"And, in the days of those [Roman] kings shall the God of Heaven set up a kingdom which shall never be destroyed: and the kingdom shall not be left to other people, but it shall break in pieces and consume all these kingdoms, and it shall stand forever" (Daniel 2:44).

Environmentalism as we now see it, robust and growing, had an extraordinary parentage – Establishment all the way. Planned Parenthood should be "Green" with envy.

CHAPTER 2

ESTABLISHING THE ESTABLISHMENT

Before going further into the various plans, programs, and objectives encompassed in The Greening, it is essential that we pause to establish the Establishment. In the introduction, I quoted from the late Arthur Selwyn Miller about what he called a "small group of men" or "elite establishment." The existence and world view of this group is central to everything which follows. As Aldous Huxley wrote in *Brave New World Revisited*, "This Power Elite directly employs several millions of the country's working force in its factories, offices, and stores, controls many millions more by lending them money to buy its products, and through ownership of the media of mass communications, influences the thoughts, the feelings and the actions of virtually everybody." In using the opprobrious term "Power Elite," Huxley was citing Professor C. Wright Mills. Huxley then concluded his own thoughts, "To parody the words of Winston Churchill, never have so many been manipulated so much by so few."

There is an incredible irony to the subject of the "elite." Anybody who writes on the subject without offering a socialist or elitist solution is accused of "being an advocate of conspiracy theory." We are vilified as "anti-intellectual," "simplistic," "reactionary," and even "fascist." Yet even a cursory survey within every segment of society proves that "everybody" believes that "they" (however undefined) are "running the show."

My own experience leads me to conclude that there are three groups that, each for different reasons, deny the existence of a Power Elite, and in so doing completely miss the essence of what issues are being pushed and why. They are: (1) So-called liberal intellectuals (except when they were haranguing their students about the "military-industrial complex"); (2) "responsible Republicans"; and (3) the actual practitioners of the power.

The "liberal intellectuals" are a sad joke. This type is most often found teaching undergraduate students, frequenting the monthly meetings of the local bar association, leading the local teachers' union, or milling about the cloakrooms of Congress and state legislatures. Never reading anything other than the liberal polemics of their "pop culture" heroes, they seem almost immune to anything insightful. They also have another common trait: an unfailing belief that it is government – the state – that is best suited to solve the problems we face.

The "responsible Republicans" are best evidenced by those who enjoy the symbiotic relationship with Big Business or who are part of Big Business itself. Put off by populist arguments, they find their intellectual rallying cry in the words of former Secretary of Defense Charles Wilson, who once commented, "What's good for General Motors is good for the country." Most willingly call themselves conservatives; and more than a few of them head, or orbit around, prestigious organizations in Washington, D.C., which provide "think-tank" solutions to whom should run the apparatus of Big Government. They see themselves as movers and shakers, consider themselves well-read, and usually heap scorn on such "conspiratorialists" as ourselves.

The "liberal intellectuals" rush to support the Jimmy Carter, Mike Dukakis, and Bill Clinton types, the "responsible Republicans" champion a George Bush, and both are too arrogant to recognize that the Power Elite has been giving them both a perpetual Hobson's choice. The practitioners, or "wise men," as they prefer to be called, by necessity must deny their own existence. Motivated by what they see as *realpolitik*, they are quick to acknowledge their central role in private but are loathe to "fess up" in public, since they are well aware of the indignation that revelation could inspire. So in an atmosphere of what has been called "an open conspiracy," they hold their international meetings, publish their little-read journals, write their strategic books, fund their think-tanks, elect pliable politicians at every level, and quietly go about building what they have called for generations a New World Order, confident that their role and identity will be deflected by their unconscious allies in groups (1) and (2).

Time and time again we've been asked something like, "If such a thing existed how could so many people keep it a secret?" The answer is – they don't. If you are waiting for banner headlines in the *New York Times* or the *Washington Post* to announce "Worldwide Plot Uncovered," you'll wait in vain. But for those who read anything other than the popular press, the evidence is voluminous, readily available, and even acknowledged by the practitioners themselves. Please note, we are not talking about the books and articles written over the years by those on the so-called Right, although there are many good ones. No, we are referring here to the scores of books written by people who understand how our world really works because *they are part of the control apparatus.*

As we write, we are virtually surrounded by volumes which carry the same underlying theme – *that the modern world in general and the American government in particular, are directed by a small group of like-minded elitists who serve an ongoing agenda.* Here are just a few of the books we mean: *Tragedy and Hope*, by Carroll Quigley; *Elites in American History*, volumes II and III, by Philip H. Burch, Jr.; *Ritual Politics and Power*, by David I. Kirtzer; *The Wise Men*, by Walter Isaacson and Evan Thomas; *The Alliance*, by Richard J. Barnet; *The Politics of War*, by Walter Karp; *The Secret Constitution and the Need for Constitutional Change*, by Arthur S. Miller; *Report from Iron Mountain*, edited by Leonard C. Lewin; *The New Industrial State*, by John Kenneth Galbraith; *Walter Lippmann and the American Century*, by Ronald Steele; *The House of Morgan*, by Ron Chernow; *Imperial Brain Trust*, by L.H. Shoup and W. Minter; *The Powers That Be*, by G.M. Domhoff; *Kissinger*, by Walter Isaacson; *The Chairman*, by Kai Bird; and *Power Shift*, by

Alvin Toffler. The discerning reader will recognize immediately that not one of these authors could even remotely be considered a man of the Right, or what we would today call a "conservative." On the contrary, and without exception, each of these books is written by someone who considers himself to be a "liberal" or at the very least "an objective scholar."

As to the question of "secrecy," a few brief excerpts from two of the aforementioned works will make my point abundantly clear.

In his monumental history of the past century, *Tragedy and Hope*, the late Harvard and Georgetown professor and Bill Clinton mentor, Carroll Quigley, had this to say:

> I know the operations of this network because I have studied it for twenty years and was permitted for two years in the early 1960s to examine its papers and secret records. I have no aversion to it or most of its aims and have for much of my life been close to it and too many of its instruments. I have objected, both in the past and recently, to a few of its policies. But in general, my chief difference of opinion is that it wishes to remain unknown and I believe its role in history is significant enough to be known. [Emphasis added.]

That is from page 950 of this 1300-page, eight-pound tome. Gary Allen and I quoted extensively from *Tragedy and Hope* in the writing of our *None Dare Call It Conspiracy* in 1972, and Dr. Cleon Skousen wrote a lengthy popular review of it called *The Naked Capitalist*, which itself became a book. It is this same professor Quigley, whom Bill Clinton cited in his acceptance speech at the Democratic National Convention in July of 1992. As a student at Georgetown, young Bill adopted Quigley's worldview and proceeded to follow the road to political power.

But here is an excerpt from a book which is equally important yet not one conservative in a thousand knows of it: *The Secret Constitution and the Need for Constitutional Change* by Arthur S. Miller. Note again what Miller had to say about this "open" conspiracy:

In other words, those who formally rule take their signals and commands not from the electorate as a body but from a small group of men (plus a few women). This group will be called the establishment. *It exists even though that existence is stoutly denied. It is one of the secrets of the American social order. A second secret is the fact that the existence of the establishment, the ruling class, is not supposed to be discussed.* [Emphasis added.]

Now in each instance we have cited men of recognized and much-heralded academic achievement who by and large are writing for what they believed was a limited audience. They didn't expect nor did they want Mike Wallace and the "60 Minutes" camera crew to do a probing interview on this subject for the masses on Sunday night. As Miller states, it "is not supposed to be discussed." While both Miller and Quigley used the word "secret," they knew full well that it was only the public at large that was to be kept in the dark. The truly well-informed "know" even though "that existence is stoutly denied."

There is another unspoken message that you will find throughout the books listed above. It is one of both arrogance and pride. It can be summarized in an attitude which whispers, "We know what's going on, the people who are making the rules know what's going on, and it's not important for anybody else to know."

If the consequences of their actions were not so tragic, it would almost be amusing to see how many on both the Right and the Left love to ridicule those like myself, or other more deserving scholars, who have taken the time to look beyond the obvious. This book is not the place to chronicle every aspect of this "open conspiracy," but some specifics are in need of elaboration.

Well before World War I, there existed what Quigley called, "the Anglo-American establishment." This view is amply supported by Miller, Mills, and the others cited above. More recently, scholars on both sides of the Atlantic have picked up the same evidence and added some of their own. In *The Making of an Atlantic Ruling Class,*

Netherlands-born lawyer and political scientist, Kees van der Piyl, from the University of Amsterdam, writes: "The vanguard of this quest for Anglo-Saxon unity was a secret society, The Round Table. It had been founded in 1891 by Cecil Rhodes, the conquistador of the mineral riches of Southern Africa, and the journalist, William T. Stead. Both had been pupils of the Oxford professor John Ruskin."

The Dutch scholar then goes on to describe the post- World War I aspects of this nexus. "At the end of World War One, the Anglo-American connection was symbolically reinforced by the creation of the Institute of International Affairs by American and British delegates at Versailles."

The U.S. branch of the Institute was called the Council on Foreign Relations (CFR) and was officially founded in 1921. Prior to the formation of the CFR, a tight reciprocity existed between the Round Table group in the U.K. and the Carnegie Endowment for International Peace in the U.S., and once the Council was formed most, if not all, of the Carnegie Trustees comprised its original board of directors.

Dominating the leadership of the U.S. Establishment was the Wall Street lawyer for both Andrew Carnegie and J.P. Morgan, Elihu Root. Root was both chairman of the Carnegie Endowment and the first honorary chairman of the CFR. Orbiting Root were Morgan bank partners John W. Davis (CFR president 1921-33), Dwight Morrow, Thomas Lamont, and Henry P. Davison, along with other legal powerhouses such as Paul Cravath, Norman Davis, Russell Leffingwell, and Root's special protégé, Col. Henry L. Stimson.

Van der Piyl, writing on this concentration of financial power, says, "American investment bankers, led by J.P. Morgan, from an early date developed an awareness of the value of the Atlantic economy reciprocity, and were soon transcending the 'Atlanticism' of the Rhodes/Milner Group in Britain." As one observer has written, "It was Wall Street... which first discerned the potential of a widening Atlantic Community"

Partisanship has little or nothing to do with how this continuing influence is exerted. Republicans and Democrats, liberals and conservatives, come and go from the Oval Office, yet the policy-making positions remain firmly in the grasp of the Establishment. Professor Miller put it very succinctly when he wrote, "A third secret is implicit in what has been said – that there is really only one political party of any consequence in the United States, one that has been called the 'Property Party.' The Republicans and the Democrats are in fact two branches of the same (secret) party." "Secret" is *his* word, not mine, although I heartily agree with his choice. Alvin Toffler, in his latest book, *Power Shift*, identifies this consortium as "the Invisible Party" and agrees with Miller that partisan politics has little or no bearing on the wielding of this all-encompassing "power."

One oblique acknowledgment of this nexus is usually expressed in the favorable phrase "bipartisan foreign policy." But this is very misleading when we examine the proponents of the "policy" in question. In foreign affairs the continuity is dramatic. With the exception of James Byrnes, every Secretary of State since the founding of the CFR has been a member. Every UN Ambassador, every CIA Director, every National Security Advisor (except the defrocked Admiral Poindexter), also meets this same criterion. What isn't as widely known is how this influence is also exercised in key domestic posts. This continuity is never more in evidence than the transition from Bush to Clinton.

From Benjamin Strong at its creation up to and including Alan Greenspan today, all chairmen of the Federal Reserve have been CFR stalwarts. The same can be said of the World Bank, and with only two exceptions in 70 years, the Secretary of the Treasury. In the "private sector" of media, banking, multinational corporations, and the academy, the list is every bit as impressive. And it should come as no surprise that both John Kenneth Galbraith, a.k.a. John Doe, and George F. Kennan have been members of the CFR for most of their lives. As we shall soon see, this same "elitist" control now exists within the environmental movement as well, especially as it relates to the giant foundations and public-policy groups.

CHAPTER 3

THE GREENING OF THE REDS

To place The Greening in perspective, we must examine in part the "end of the Cold War." Just as the Special Study Group was planning the protracted future in the U.S., other "generation or generation-and-a-half" plans were being discussed half a world away. Any thorough retrospective demands an examination of a possible fit. What Doe (Galbraith) didn't mention in the *Report from Iron Mountain* was that if the "Cold War" was to come to an end and if "peace breaks out," surely the adversary, i.e., the Soviet Union, might have something to say about it. In a three-part series which appeared in *Insider Report* during the summer of 1989, I called this metamorphosis "The Greening of the Reds."

I was referring at that time to the so-called "democratic" revolution in China; the power-sharing and elections in the Soviet Union; the elections in Poland, Hungary, and throughout Eastern Europe; the collapse of East Germany and the re-unification of Germany; the general disunity in NATO; and the "conversion" to anti-communism by the radical and establishment Left in this country. By the fall of 1991, we watched this process of "democracy" reshape even the Soviet Empire itself. We are living through a dialectic that has been brilliantly and patiently designed to mislead the world, and more specifically, the American people.

If I am right, what you are witnessing is nothing less than the beginning of the final stages of the drive toward a New World Order. It's clever; it's powerful; it's believable; and it's working. *But most important to our present point, it's Green.*

In a previous chapter we quoted Secretary of State James Baker pledging to commit U.S. foreign policy to the Green agenda. Corollary to that was the program of Mikhail Gorbachev and his colleagues. Writing in the *New York Times* of August 14, 1991, syndicated columnist Flora Lewis began an article entitled "Gorbachev Turns Green" with these words: "Soviet diplomacy is preparing a dramatic leap in the concept of 'new world order' that will leave President Bush in the primeval sludge if he doesn't move." She continued, "Mikhail Gorbachev gave Mr. Bush a hint to his thinking at their Moscow meeting, proposing that next year's UN conference in Rio de Janeiro on the environment be held at the summit level. European leaders at the London Group of Seven [meeting held July 1991] also urged the U.S. to be ready with firm commitments." True to her love affair with internationalism and Big Government, Flora Lewis enthused, "Moscow's new idea is not only an astonishing reversal of Soviet attitudes about international relations; it *goes beyond accepted notions of the limits of national sovereignty and rules of behavior.*" [Emphasis added.]

Here's the "astonishing" Soviet plan as revealed by Lewis: "Foreign Ministry officials say they are working on a plan for a global code of environmental conduct. Moscow suggests a convention for all states to sign. It would provide for the World Court to judge states."

Lewis can hardly contain herself as she gushes, "This is a breathtaking idea, beyond the current dreams of ecology militants. It is meant to show that the Soviets really take seriously their 'integration' in the world economy. *And it is that the environment be its topic for what amounts to global policy.*" [Emphasis added.]

Picking up the line of ho w national borders must come down to accommodate The Greening, Lewis says, "Environmental problems ignore borders, and the convention would draw the consequences on the basis of laws applied to all." She concludes with the following scolding: "The U.S. is lagging woefully in this aspect of leadership. Mr. Bush said he intended to be the 'environmental President.' But as things are going, he risks being the environmental outcast, with Mr. Gorbachev far ahead by the Rio meeting."

Since Lewis wrote the above, not one thing has happened to deter the eco-globalist movement. All the new personalities on the world stage have embraced Gorbachev's proposals including Yeltsin, Clinton, and Gore. As the West danced on the grave of communism and Gorbachev himself resigned from the Communist Party, the international aspects of eco-control advanced at an even more rapid pace. But, as I said at that time, "We will stake our reputations on the assertion that when the UN Conference on the Environment is held in Brazil in June of 1992, the 'uncommunists' of the 'Commonwealth of Independent States' from the 'defunct' Soviet Union will be there offering the plan that Flora Lewis called 'memorable,' 'astonishing,' and 'breathtaking.'"

My reputation is still intact. The Gorbachev proposals of August 1991, which Flora Lewis so ardently described, were jot and tittle the outcome of Rio's Earth Summit. If anything is "astonishing" about Flora Lewis's piece, it is how the old Gorbachev "plan" coincides perfectly with what George F. Kennan proposed in his April 1970 article in *Foreign Affairs*.

The Hidden Picture

Now let's go a couple steps further in this analysis. I do not always look behind every silver lining for the dark cloud I'm convinced must be there. Nor does my good friend and collaborator Franklin Sanders. In the age-old struggle between freedom and slavery, we welcome "good news" as much as the next person. It is just that we have spent too many years and plowed through too many thousands of volumes not to recognize a carefully arranged deceit when one is presented to us. Those of you who read *None Dare Call It Conspiracy*, or its sequel, *Call It Conspiracy*, will remember my using the following metaphor:

Most of us have had the experience, either as parents or youngsters, of trying to discover the "hidden picture" within another picture in a children's magazine. Usually you are shown a landscape with trees, bushes, flowers, and other bits of nature. The caption reads something like this: "Concealed somewhere in this picture is a donkey pulling a cart with a boy in it. Can you find them?" Try as you might, usually you could not find the hidden picture until you turned to the page further back in the magazine which revealed how cleverly the artist had hidden it from us. If we study the landscape we realize that the whole picture was painted in such a way as to conceal the real picture, and once we see the "real picture," it stands out like the proverbial painful digit.

We believe the picture painters of the mass media are artfully creating landscapes for us which deliberately hide the real picture. In this book we will show you how to discover the hidden picture in the landscapes presented to us daily through newspapers, radio, and television. Once you see through the camouflage, you will see the donkey, the cart, and the boy who have been there all along.

Those paragraphs were written back in 1971. They were the result of my trying to find a way to explain to people just how confusing world events can be – until you see the real picture. I first developed that metaphor in 1969 while giving a three-hour lecture, which ultimately became the basis for *None Dare Call It Conspiracy*. How that lecture evolved into the runaway best-seller Gary Allen and I authored is an interesting story, but one that is better left for another time and place.

My point today is (and was then) that in the real world of mega-power politics, we are being deceived on a scale so massive it is almost beyond human comprehension. I must grudgingly admit that my use of a "green" and natural landscape as part of the deception was totally coincidental, but its current application is more appropriate than ever.

Some Ancient Stratagems

This whole strategy isn't anything new, except to the extent that television and other sophisticated communications techniques make it more compelling and effective. As long-time readers of my newsletter, *Insider Report*, know, I have for years encouraged serious students of politics to become familiar with Sun Tzu and his classic work, *The Art of War*. This treatise, which was written nearly 2,500 years ago, contains the blueprint for all that is being done to us today, as the Insiders pursue their age-old dream of a New World Order.

Quoted below are just a few examples of Sun Tzu's stratagems. As you read them, reflect on what you are constantly exposed to every day of your life.

(1) All warfare is based on deception.
(2) When the enemy is divided, he is destroyed.
(3) When he is united, divide him.
(4) To subdue the enemy without fighting is the acme of skill.
(5) Those skilled in war subdue the enemy without battle.
(6) When able to attack, seem unable; when active, seem inactive.
(7) When near, make the enemy believe you are far; when far away, make him believe you are near.
(8) If weak, pretend to be strong and so cause the enemy to avoid you; when strong, pretend to be weak so that the enemy may grow arrogant.

Sun Tzu knew, as do his more modem practitioners, that painting false pictures for the purpose of deception is a key part of the "ultimate weapon." Power-seekers know all about the strategies of deception; it is as essential to them as votes to a politician. An important book on this subject was written in 1989 by the brilliant investigative reporter, Edward Jay Epstein. He has even called his book *Deception*, and it is one that I highly recommend. In it he says:

First, the victim's leadership has to be in a state of mind to want to accept and act on the disinformation it receives from its own intelligence. This might not happen unless the disinformation fits in with the adversary's prevailing preconceptions or interest – which is, at least in the case of the United States, not difficult to determine. Angleton [James Angleton, former CIA head of counter-espionage] suggested that Lenin showed he understood this principle when in 1921 he instructed

Dzerzhinsky, his intelligence chief, in creating disinformation to "ML them what they want to hear."

Second, the victim has to be in the state of mind in which he is so confident of his own intelligence that he is unwilling to entertain evidence, or even theories, that he is or can be duped. This kind of blanket denial amounts to a conceit, which Angleton claimed could be cultivated in an adversary... [to leave] a nation defenseless against deception.

The CIA's late superspy, James Angleton, was fond of saying, *"Deception is a state of mind – and the mind of the state"* [Emphasis added.]

For another example of this strategy at work - but one that is far removed from the world of international geo-politics – rent a video of that classic Paul Newman/Robert Redford movie, "The Sting." They were indeed masters of deception.

And in fact, "The Sting" wasn't all that different from the international machinations we've been discussing. If you'll remember, essential to the success of that con game was what James Angleton called the "feedback channel" – a way to successfully disseminate false but believable information back to the "mark," or in this case, the person who was to be stung.

A Series of *Glasnosts*

Describing all of the ramifications of what's been going on right before our eyes for the past five years would take volumes of no small proportions. There is a desperate need today for just such a study, but in the meantime, consider just a few facts and juxtapose them with the principles of deception and the "art of war" that we've been describing. In a special report I wrote in July 1990 (which became the basis for this book), I postulated the following:

Mikhail Gorbachev was the central figure in a massive PR campaign, the results of which framed the policy of our government and others into "preserving his leadership role" and "helping him to succeed."

In my original special report of 1989, I wrote:

If, by the time you read this, Mr. Gorbachev is no longer a major player on the world stage of geopolitics, the results of his sponsorship and PR will be inherited by his successor of even more "liberal" worldviews.

The report went on to chronicle:

Gorbachev's *glasnost* was actually the sixth one we've experienced since Lenin's day. As Epstein pointed out and my own studies confirmed, they were:

(1) *The New Economic Policy* (NEP), *Spring* 1921-1929. At that time, Lenin said, "*Glasnost* is a sword which heals the wound it inflicts."

(2) *The Soviet Constitution*, 1936-1937. This was the time of what Stalin called "reconstructions," or "perestroika."

(3) *The Wartime Ally*, 1941-1945. Stalin was known as "Uncle Joe." After Yalta, FDR's close advisor, Harry Hopkins, wrote of the Soviets, "there wasn't any doubt that we could live and get along with them peacefully for as far into the future as any of us could imagine." The British Foreign office concluded, "The old idea of world revolution is dead."

(4) *De-Stalinization under Khrushchev,* 1956-1959. Remember when Khrushchev pounded his shoe on the podium at the UN – and later declared, "We spit in your face and you call it dew"?

(5) *Detente*, 1970-1975. As Epstein writes, "The central theme was that the Soviet government...had no interest in adhering to the Leninist Doctrine of class warfare."

And finally there is:

(6) *The Deception Occurring Right Now And Its Consequences...*

In each period of glasnost the Corporate Marxists from the West fell over each other in their rush to bail out the Soviets with money, technology transfers, and credit – all guaranteed by the U.S. taxpayers, and sold under the name of "containment."

This "deception by *glasnost*" was never limited to the USSR or its new union. On the contrary, to the list above could be added Tito of Yugoslavia, Dubcek of Czechoslovakia, Mao of China, plus a fist of lesser lights like Nasser or Ortega. At one time or another, each had his own *glasnost* – and his own sponsors among the Insiders of Corporate Marxism.

In every case, the methodology of deception was the same: A brutal tyrant was portrayed as something else. The "art of war" was applied to the West's "state of mind" and became "the mind of the state."

Masters of Deceit

Here are some further points to keep in mind as we attempt to untangle the deception being foisted upon us:

* Dissidents such as the late Andrei Sakharov and Lech Walesa were never really anti-sodalist or exponents of competitive capitalism at all. They sought to preserve the power structure by calling it "non-communist," declaring a so-called "market socialism," and providing a new face. These men represent carbon copies of a ploy used many years ago, during Lenin's first *glasnost*, the New Economic Policy. Then the so-called "democratic opposition" was called "the Trust," and it was later proved to have been created and directed by the Party itself.

* The "student revolution" in China and the Tiananmen Square turkey-shoot started while Gorbachev was there and was encouraged by Communist Party leaders. In the process, it identified all the real anti-communists, who were promptly marked for extinction. The numbers executed in this ploy may never be known.

* All the TV news and newspaper commentaries were using anti-communist rhetoric of the type they would have scorned only a few years before as "simplistic" or "early Reagan" rhetoric. But at no time did they call for breaking diplomatic relations or imposing South Africa-style economic sanctions on Deng's China or Ceaucescu's Romania. Our money and trade would "mellow" them.

* Without a single exception I can remember, every expert interviewed (and sometimes doing the interviewing) was a familiar CFR/Trilateral type, such as Henry Kissinger, William Hyland, John Chancellor, Dan Rather, Ted Koppel, Orville Schell, Flora Lewis, or Betty Bao Lord (wife of elite Insider Winston Lord, our immediate past ambassador to China). Many of these very same people, plus CFR academics, were even present during the four-day "coup" of August 1991. Stephen B. Cohen of Princeton, Zbigniew Brzezinski of Columbia, and Marshall Goldman of Harvard joined their CFR colleagues Jack F. Matlock and Robert Strauss, former and current ambassadors to the Soviet Union, respectively, to explain to the viewing public the "historic" events taking place.

* Did you notice, by the way, that in all those thousands of hours ground out by ABC, NBC, CBS, and CNN, not once was a truly anti-communist analyst the subject of those in-depth interviews?

* In almost every instance, from China to Red Square and all stops in between, the news coverage was written and arranged for Western and especially U.S. audience's – not for Soviet domestic consumption.

* Simultaneous to all of the above, the "Green Movement" has taken over the role of radical socialism from Euro-Communism and is being pushed by everyone from David Rockefeller to the Red Brigade.

The message is increasingly clear: The "preservation of the environment" is a basis for "worldwide cooperation," regardless of ideology. It is even more acceptable if done under the banner of "democracy." Nobody, including Gorbachev, believes "you can trust a communist" anymore.

Placing all of these seemingly disconnected events and developments in context, it could be that while the world has focused on the "breakup" of communism, the stage is being set for another dose of control even stronger, but one which will be accepted by all as "necessary."

As Mr. Gorbachev said in his "inaugural speech" on March 17,1990, *"major decisions are being prepared that will spell not only anew step in improving Soviet-American relations but also an important contribution to our two countries consolidating positive tendencies in the entire world politics."* [Emphasis added] Obviously, he wasn't kidding.

While the world sang funeral dirges over the grave of communism, the reality was the emergence of what can now be called "The Greening of the Reds."

CHAPTER 4

SEEING THE WORLD THROUGH GREEN GLASSES

Almost 500 years ago, Niccolo Machiavelli observed, "Men in general make judgments more by appearances than by reality, for sight alone belongs to everyone, but under-standing to a few." This keen theoretician of statecraft understood then what every smart political operative before and since has recognized and applied. Machiavelli's 20th- century counterpart, Henry Kissinger, put it this way: "Perceptions *become* reality."

As we observe the world around us, our constant struggle is to make the distinction between what the author of *The Prince* called "appearances" and what events mandate must be reality. This is no easy task under the best of circumstances. In modem times it has become almost impossible. When we put our common sense against the tidal waves of misinformation flooding out of the major media, too often we capitulate to what appears to be an overwhelming consensus. Time and time again, on issue after issue, this mental surrender occurs.

The "creation of the appearance of popular support" is at the center of all contemporary political activity. This technique is so all-pervasive that it leads even the most rational among us to conclude, even in the face of the most outlandish proposals, "I must be the only one who feels this way." Our opposition to some preposterous scheme seems to be unique, with the result that we shrug our shoulders and accept what we are told is "the wisdom of the majority," or the all-conclusive, argument-ending trump-card, "world opinion."

Our innate desire to believe the best strengthens this seductive mind-set. We have been nurtured on happy endings and the vision of the "good guy" riding off into the sunset, having righted all wrongs. It goes against our nature to believe the worst, to assume we are being deceived, to be always on guard against deception. Every power seeker from Sun Tsu to Clinton knows this implicitly. "Tell them what they want to hear," Lenin admonished Felix Dzerzhinsky.

Clear and Present Danger

During the Reagan years, and even more so in his successor's term, the soothing voice of the Great Communicator worked its magic on the unspoken concerns of the West, and the American people specifically. The ritual of keeping alive the Reagan rhetoric has become for Conservatives something akin to the custom of the Bunyoro tribesmen of Uganda. When the king died and his heir emerged, he would return to his father's corpse and remove the jawbone. The new king would then bury the jawbone with full ceremonies. Later, a house would be built over the spot for the dead king's regalia – with the rest of his body being unceremoniously discarded. The tomb housing the royal jawbone would long be venerated.

Another modem nation which follows this practice was profiled in a September 8, 1991 segment on "60 Minutes" – Room 19. In this report, a Russian journalist revealed how the Communist Party had Lenin's brain under "study" hoping to find a way of "duplicating" his brilliance. Also behind the doors of Room 19 were cuttings of Stalin's brain. One can only speculate as to whether or not C.S. Lewis knew of Room 19 when he portrayed the "Supreme Intelligence" as the "brain-power" source for global strategy in his novel *That Hideous Strength*. The "head" was precisely that – a head.

Now don't judge me or Mr. Reagan too harshly by these amusing comparisons. He did much to deserve our gratitude, just as, I am certain, the late lamented Bunyoro king did for his constituents

(Lenin doesn't qualify). But the fact remains that venerated jawbones do little to cast the spotlight of reality on our *clear and present danger.*

And just what is that danger? Planned over decades, it has been built on the corpses of millions of innocents. The ultimate goal has been described by the Insiders themselves as the creation of a New World Order (a term which has lately become an ever-present cliché, thanks to Mr. Bush). As I pointed out in the previous chapter, the most important current strategy in that design can be summarized as "The Greening of the Reds." Let me cite a few recent, and not so recent, news items and articles to illustrate my point.

* *The New York Times*, December 8, 1989, text of Gorbachev's speech at the United Nations: "International economic security is inconceivable unless related not only to the world's environment but also to the elimination of the threat to the world's environment...Let us also think about setting up within the framework of the United Nations a center for emergency environmental assistance."

* *Facts on File*, March 24, 1989, "Greens Emerge – the Ecologists Party, or Greens, Won Over 1,800 City Council Seats Across France."

* *New York Times*, June 18, 1989, Flora Lewis's column, headline: "Red-Green Tide in Germany."

* *Seattle Post-Intelligencer* news service, June 20, 1989, headline: "The Green Parties Post Big Gains in Euro-Parliament."

* Reuters, June 23, 1989, dateline: Stockholm, Sweden. "Socialists indicated yesterday that their red flag of the future will have broad bands of green as left-wing parties embrace environmental politics. 'Issues such as safeguarding our environment, international resource management and protection... are going to dominate our common future,' Austrian Chancellor Franz Vranitzky told the triennial meeting of Socialist International. The threat to the environment was the top theme at the three-day

meeting of 81 socialist and Social Democratic parties. 'This is our new mission,' said Swedish Environment Minister Birgetta Dahl. Speaker after speaker stressed that left-wing parties had to adapt to the *new reality* [emphasis added] if socialism was to keep step with the times. [I will have more to say about the "new reality" shortly.] They also indicated that traditional concerns such as security and global disarmament were less compelling in an atmosphere of East-West rapprochement. 'Conventional conflicts [are] no longer the main threat to humanity/ said Hans-Jochen Vogel, Chairman of the West German Social Democratic Party."

* *Seattle Post-Intelligencer*, July 12, 1989, Editorial headline: "Greening of the Soviets. Bowing to environmentalists, the Soviet Parliament this week fired the timber minister Mikhail Busygin. It is seen as evidence of the governmental lobbies' growing strength in this new era of Soviet reform."

* *ABC News Special Report*, July 13, 1989, Paris. Head-line: "Paris Environment Takes Center Stage at Economic Summit Meeting."

Since I outlined these specific citations in the July 1989, *Insider Report*, not a single day passes without some dispatch or news items carrying the same theme. An Op-Ed piece in the *New York Times* of March 27, 1990, is typical of this barrage. It was headlined, "From Red Menace to Green Threat." The writer, Michael Oppenheimer, co-author of *Dead Heat: The Race Against the Greenhouse Effect*, writes, "Global warming, ozone depletion, deforestation, and over-population are the four horsemen of a looming 21st century apocalypse...As the cold war recedes, the environment is becoming the No. 1 international security concern." My files are bulging with variations on this same theme coming from every point on the compass. Are you getting the impression that there may be a trend here?

The "New Reality"

And just what is this "new reality" to which the Reds referred? This phrase keeps popping up in some very interesting and diverse places. In the Summer 1988, *Foreign Affairs* (the quarterly publication of the Council on Foreign Relations), Henry Kissinger and Cyrus Vance co-authored a lengthy piece for the incoming and yet-to-be-determined President. It was called, "Bipartisan Objectives for American Foreign Policy."

Within this presumptuous 22-page epistle, Messrs. Kissinger and Vance used the phrase "new realities" three times – without once defining what they mean. Mr. Gorbachev, in the aforementioned UN speech six months after the Kissinger-Vance article, used the phrase "newly emerging realities" – again, without explanation. Now the same phrase appears in the meetings of the Socialist International in Stockholm, Sweden.

Since these "wise men" don't reveal what their "new reality" is based on, let me tell you what it encompasses.

* It means abandoning the old face of communism, and embracing the Corporate State.

* It means the merging of State Socialism and Corporate Marxism which, in turn, will build a New World Order [their phrase, not mine] of monetary and political establishments.

* It means transferring the world's major resources to massive eco-holding companies (the working reality of what the architects of the policy call the World Conservation Bank, or WCB).

All around the world the move is on to transfer the rain forests, the deserts, the jungles, the plains, and even private property to a consortium of foundations, international agencies, and councils, all of which are interlocked through directorships and agenda.

In almost every state of America – I can think of no exception - local environmental groups are pushing ahead with their plans to seize ownership of some of the most productive and beautiful areas of our planet. The same thing is happening in other parts of the globe: Africa, South and Central America, Europe, Australia, New Zealand, Canada, and even Asia. Always and everywhere, there is some local crisis or pending catastrophe to justify their move. In my home state of Washington in the Pacific Northwest, the beneficiary of this concern is the spotted owl. In Montana it is the timber wolf. In Nebraska, the whooping crane. In Africa the elephant takes center stage. (In the case of the spotted owl, the leader of the Sierra Club was quoted as saying, "If the spotted owl did not exist, we would find it necessary to genetically engineer one.")

Add to this the so-called threat to the ozone, the green-house effect, acid rain, and countless other real or ersatz environmental concerns, and you have the prescription for a worldwide control mechanism awesome in scope and power.

The Plan Behind it All

Standing astride this environmental juggernaut like a colossus is the same group of Insiders who have been playing God with people's lives since before World War I. Thanks to their "internationalism" and "balance of power" schemes, the 20th Century has proved to be the bloodiest in all human history. Yet these so-called "wise men" finance tyranny, replace governments, elect presidents and prime ministers, and, in general, act as the unelected rulers for a world gone crazy.

Once again, let's be specific. This is the economic and political cartel represented in Britain by membership in the Royal Institute for International Affairs, in the United States in the Council on Foreign Relations, and internationally in such groups as the Bilderberger Group, the Club of Rome, and more recently, the Trilateral Commission.

Now I know that, in some circles, singling out these organizations and the men or women who lead them is not viewed as "responsible." We are supposed to believe that all of this "greening" is the result of some overnight worldwide consensus. But any objective examination of reality takes us directly to the doorsteps of the above organizations, and being responsible demands being truthful. More than likely, the same people who label us irresponsible secretly feel the same way about our country's Founding Fathers. After all, those irresponsible rebels accused Parliament of a *conspiracy* to extort money from the Colonies.

As we examine such foundations (which we will anon) as the World Wildlife Fund, the Heritage Trust, the Nature Conservancy, the National Wildlife Federation, The Sierra Club, the World Wilderness Congress, Conservation Inter-national, the Center for Earth Resource Analysis (to name but a few), what do we find? Not so strangely, key members of the Insider institutions cited above are leading or directing every one of them. This doesn't take into consideration the UN organizations which are, at the very least, directed by deep red socialist's tinned green.

Are we to believe that only radical leftists, mega-bankers and Corporate Marxists are concerned about our environment? Or could it be that there is another agenda afoot – a "new reality"?

Allow me to quote briefly from a letter I received in the mail not long ago. It starts:

Dear Investor,

I'd like you to prepare yourself for a mild shock of a most rare and welcome kind.

There is indeed a group that has quietly "bought up" acres and acres of wild land in your state.

But not for condominiums or shopping centers, golf courses or industrial parks, not for strip mining or highways or parking lots.

Not for profit or private gain at all.

For love, for life, for the preservation of this exquisitely beautiful planet of ours for the benefit of future generations of *all* its inhabitants.

This letter continues for four more pages, bragging about the various activities of the organization whose letterhead it bears, "The

Nature Conservancy." They boast, "We own and manage a national system of more than 1,000 sanctuaries." This is the very same group that, along with Citicorp, Chase Manhattan, and Bank of America, is up to its ears in debt-for-nature swaps in Costa Rica, Ecuador, Guatemala, and even the state of California. (And let me add, they are only one of the groups involved in these debt-for-nature swaps now being played out throughout South and Central America.)

The scope of these programs is vast and growing. One was a $9 million Ecuador foreign debt exchange for such priority targets as part of the Ecuadorian Andes and Galapagos National Park. The World Wildlife Fund and Nature Conservancy bought this debt for twelve cents on the dollar. Earlier that same year (1989), the ubiquitous Nature Conservancy announced a debt-swap deal with the Bank of America for a foreclosed property in California called the Dye Creek Ranch/Preserve. It includes 40,000 acres of redwoods and an option on another 2,900 acres.

In April of 1989, Brazilian president José Sarney was up in arms over what was being planned for his country and the 1.9 million square miles of the Amazon Basin. An Associated Press dispatch from Rio earlier in April said that Sarney's speech was "marked by a strongly nationalist tone [as] Sarney raised Brazil's century-old battle cry, 'A Amazonia e nossa [the Amazon is ours].'" The article went on to report that, concerned about "national sovereignty, Sarney ruled out debt-for-nature swaps, financial arrangements under which Brazil would retire discounted dollar debt in return for contributing in local currency to Brazilian environmental projects." Then comes the punch line, revealing all who joined the big banks in putting the pressure on Sarney. The article states, "Last Friday as Sarney presided over a meeting of Latin American environmentalists in Brasilia, Mostafa Tolba, an Egyptian diplomat representing the United Nations Commission on Environment and Development, chided him for opposing the debt-for-nature swaps."

Poor Sarney was getting hit by traffic going both ways. Here was a Third World bureaucrat in the UN giving a Brazilian president a dressing down because he won't give up sovereignty within his own country to the big banks and their greenie front groups. In June 1990, Sarney quietly announced that he was dropping his opposition to these plans, but it didn't save his political career. He was removed from office a year later. For Sarney, a "new reality" was a career ender. This same Mostafa Tolba is now the Executive Director for the United Nations Environment Program (UNEP); was a featured speaker at Globe '90, the giant eco-conference held in Vancouver, B.C., in March 1990; and helped preside over the 1992 UNEP conference in Brazil.

In his speech at Vancouver, Tolba said, "The Cold War is dwindling...Environment has rocketed to the top of the world political agenda.... [W]e need a global partnership – dynamic, innovative and highly interconnected.... [W]e have no choice but to curb the wasteful consumption by the rich and lift the status of the poor...[M]ore bilateral and multi-lateral assistance is needed. Much more. We are talking hundreds of billions."

And get a load of this part of his conclusions. "We need shifting of resources from destruction to building – from arms to protecting our environment. We need to think of new sources. I am advocating *The Users Fee* – a fee for using the environmental resources like air" [Emphasis added.] Who says you can't raise big money out of thin air? This, too, is a "new reality."

Back in the U.S.A.

Over the past few sessions of Congress, a bill titled the American Heritage Trust Act has been gently pushed within the halls of Congress. In its first year alone this bill would appropriate a minimum of $1 billion to be used in the purchase of private taxpayers' property and lock it away under the guise of preserving our heritage. Not so coincidentally, utilization of these funds would be available to "private non-profit organizations...qualified for exemption from income taxes under Section 501(c) (3) of the Internal Revenue Code...." That's bureaucratese for Foundations.

These monies will be extended as matching funds to the various states rushing to take advantage of such a windfall.

The ramifications of tax dollars pushing this scheme could run into volumes, but before we move on, consider these few statistics. In just the eleven western states of the U.S., wilderness areas now account for 86,474,870 acres. Federal agencies have recommended another 20,256,780 acres for wilderness designation. And further "studies" for possible inclusion would add up to 133,653,459 more acres. In countries like Brazil and Australia, the lockup numbers are not measured in acres, but in *square miles*.

To help put it all in perspective and grasp this "new reality," let me recall for you what occurred in Denver, Colorado, in September 1987. When the Fourth World Wilderness Congress gathered there, many delegates were surprised to find that something called the "Denver Declaration for Worldwide Conservation" had already been written for them. World Wilderness Congress founder Dr. Ian Player said at the time, "The declaration is the most important in the history of conservation. It's our new Magna Carta." Whatever happened to the genteel custom of understatement?

Point Four of the Declaration reads, "Because new sources of funding must be mobilized to augment the expansion of conservation activities, a new international conservation banking program should be created to integrate international aid for environmental management into coherent common programs for recipient countries based on objective assessments of each country's resources and needs."

Bailing out the Banks

Notwithstanding the flowery language, there is a big payoff to all this. Up to 30 percent of the world's wilderness land mass is proposed to be set aside for wilderness areas. That's over 12 billion acres, with who knows what kind of natural resources underneath. Title to this land would be vested in a "World Wilderness Trust."

This plan was unveiled to the more than 1,500 people from 60 countries who attended the World Wilderness Congress. And lest you think this was just a group of ineffectual whale lovers and fern fanciers, let me disabuse you of that notion right now. Hosting and attending were such well-known "greenies" as David Rockefeller of Chase Manhattan, Baron Edmund de Rothschild of the 200-year-old international banking family, and then – U.S. Treasury Secretary James Baker. With that kind of clout, who says it's not easy being green?

Here's how the "World Conservation Bank Fact Sheet" explained the group's plan. The World Conservation Bank would finance, directly and through syndicated and co-financing arrangements:

(1) The preparation, development, and implementation of national conservation strategies by developing country governments;

(2) The acquisition/lease of environmentally important land for preservation of biological diversity and watersheds;

(3) The management and conservation of selected areas.

And, "Plans for the World Conservation Bank (WCB) propose that it act as intermediary between certain developing countries and multilateral or private banks to transfer a specific debt to the World Conservation Bank, thus substituting an existing doubtful debt on the bank's books for a new loan to the WCB [the debt-for-nature swaps]. In return for having been relieved of its debt obligation, the debtor country would transfer to the WCB natural resource assets of 'equivalent value.' Or, developing country debts under foreign assistance programs, which have little hope of repayment, could be retained in-country and applied toward conservation, reforestation, or rural agricultural programs through WCB."

In other words, the mega-banks' bad loans which are not now collateralized would be sold at *full nominal value* to the World Conservation Bank, instead of their presently discounted value on the open market (as low as 6 to 25 cents on the dollar). The WCB would "buy" the loan from the existing holder and the debtor country would have to collateralize the loan with wilderness areas. If the debtor failed to pay, the WCB, or whoever its stockholders happen to be, would end up with vast tracts of land and everything below it.

Now you see why I've been warning for years that the mega-banks were just not going to fail. The fix is in. What was proposed in Denver was the "Proposal" of Kennan over twenty years ago and of The Iron Mountain Study Group in the early '60s. That has now become a "new reality." With the momentum of events as cited above, the whole world is now turning "green" – led, as we shall see, by the "wise men" of the New World Order.

The name of the game is the creation of world banks, regional currencies, multinational trusts, giant foundations, land expropriations, and massive transfers of natural resources – the cartelization of the world's natural resources – which will ultimately evolve into transfers of natural sovereignty and what Flora Lewis reported and cited above as "global policy."

CHAPTER 5

ENVIRONMENTAL STATESMANSHIP MEANS FOLLOW THE MONEY

This volume chronicles the environmental onslaught we are now facing. It is sweeping across us like a gigantic tidal wave. Like a tidal wave, it was created and launched by forces not easily seen, but whose existence and intent we can definitely document.

The whole panoply shows conclusively how every facet of the Left (along with many movements considered main-stream) is now cooperating in the promotion of a single *worldwide program*. The ultimate objective is to gain control of most of the world's resources.

This amalgam of groups and organizations includes the United Nations, the old and "new" Russia, multinational banks and corporations, scores of tax-exempt foundations, the Socialist International, most of the governments in the world, the Green Parties of Europe, Congress, the Clinton Administration, and radical street revolutionaries in every country. The last time so many groups and forces united on one issue was more than four decades ago. Then, as now, the rallying cry was "war."

Solving the Debt Crisis

What I didn't emphasize in the previous chapters is how this whole movement is bound together with the subject of "debt." Immediately prior to his remarks about the "world's environment" in his UN speech, Gorbachev said this:

The Soviet Union favors a substantive discussion of ways to settle the debt crisis at multilateral forums, including consultations under the auspices of the United Nations among heads of government of debtor and creditor countries.

In virtually *every* instance where international efforts to protect the environment are discussed, juxtaposed with it you'll find the subject of *debt*. Tolba and Brundtland both linked debt to the environment in their Globe '90 speeches.

Not wishing to miss the chance to have his country's debt "forgiven," Costa Rican president and Nobel Peace laureate Oscar Arias added his plea. In a column entitled "For the Globe's Sake, Debt Relief," which appeared in the Op-Ed section of the *New York Times*, July, 1989, Arias first decried the "destruction of tropical forests" and the loss of "animal and plant species." He then proffered the following solution to this worldwide crisis:

Debt for nature swaps should be encouraged by both developed countries and *multilateral development banks*. [Emphasis added.] These swaps should be expanded from commercial to bilateral obligations so that old loans requiring foreign exchange could be earmarked in local currency for environmentally sound projects.

Sound familiar? Arias then concluded by calling for a massive surrender of national sovereignty:

Efforts to negotiate global treaties that recognize as common resources our shared elements – such as the atmosphere, the oceans, and bio-diversity – should be encouraged and expedited. Actions to mitigate global environment problems cannot wait for a new international economic order.

Did you get that? Mr. Arias was in such a hurry to have the debt and environment problems solved he said we can't wait for the "new international economic order" to be established. It had to be done now!

And You Pay For It

Recall that in the last chapter we brought to your attention a mischievous piece of legislation that had been introduced in Congress, the American Heritage Trust Act. This bill would provide federal matching funds to states for the purchase of "environmentally threatened areas" in the United States. It is an add-on to what was proposed and passed in the mid-70s.

Well, the ink wasn't even dry on the new proposal when two self-appointed champions of the eco-system held a press conference in Seattle. Former Senator Daniel J. Evans, a Republican, and former Congressman – now Governor Mike Lowry, a Democrat, joined together to announce the formation of something called the "Washington Wildlife and Recreation Coalition."

And what is the first order of business of this new coalition? To win approval for a $500 million bond offering – the money to be used, along with matching funds provided under the federal program, to push the eco-land grab.

All of this is no idle "Liberal" dream, either. The coalition's member organizations include some 20 different groups, not the least of which are The Nature Conservancy and Sierra Club. (Evans's long-time directorship in the debt-for-nature swap mothership, The Nature Conservancy, was not mentioned at the press conference.)

Residents of the state of Washington should remember the facts all too well when it comes to the politics of Evans and Lowry. Dan Evans has been a political lackey for Rockefeller interests for over 25 years. He was such a faithful lapdog of the Establishment, in fact, that he was invited to the founding meeting of the Trilateral Commission in 1973.

Mike Lowry's politics were so far to the Left that he was rejected in his Senate bid in 1988 – at the very same time 53 percent of the Washingtonians voted for another left-wing Democrat named

Michael Dukakis. But by 1992, Lowry had softened his image and "moved to the center," and a coalition of liberal forces propelled him into the Governor's mansion after a very close race.

Two weeks after the original Evans/Lowry announcement, Elliot Marks, vice president of The Nature Conservancy and its Washington State director, announced that he was assuming the presidency of the coalition. Marks said the Washington group "was following the lead of California and other states that recently approved bond issues for wildlife...California to the tune of $976 million." Some of the other states he mentioned were Minnesota, Maine, Rhode Island, and New Mexico. Similar programs are now being pushed in every one of the fifty states.

Does it not strike you as a little strange that in underdeveloped countries the name of the game is to *eliminate debt* by swapping lands and resources, while here in the good ol' U.S. of A. the game plan requires the exact opposite. Here, we're supposed to jump with joy over the prospect of *increasing* debt and levying new taxes to pursue the very same environmental agenda!

You may be wondering who is going to supply the "hundreds of billions" and pay the "user fees" for the air; remember Mr. Tolba's comments about "wasteful consumption by the rich." You, gentle reader, are the fatted calf, and it's your slaughter that will supply the lucre for these plans and programs.

Worldwide Orchestration

All across this country and all around the globe, the people who are being most directly affected either have no say in what is being done, or are made to feel that they are "greedy," "uncaring," and "despoiling holdouts" in an ecology-conscious world. As a woman from Missouri told me on the phone, "Mr. Abraham, the people up in St. Louis don't seem to care about what's being done to us here in the Ozarks." No, ma'am, I'm afraid they don't, but you are going to pay for it just the same – as will the people in Seattle, Los Angeles, New York, or Minneapolis.

How many people in Madagascar (yes, I said Madagascar) had any say while their government queued up at the World Wildlife Fund to swap $2,111,111.12 of its bad paper and untold thousands of its acreage to Banker's Trust and others in a debt-for-nature exchange?

This whole environmental power play is a PR masterpiece. Everywhere we turn, we find another angle being promoted. For example, in a recent issue of their customer newsletter, Bank of America ran a column headlined "Thanks for All Your Support." In it they boasted that "Sales of B of A's cause-related series of special checks – featuring whales, pets, and endangered species – have raised more than $157,000 for five non-profit organizations. This success is due to the continued interest and support of our customers...for each order of checks and/or matching leather checkbook cover ordered, we make a 50 cent donation to the corresponding organization."

Isn't that sweet? While B of A customers got a warm and fuzzy feeling penning their checks over the face of a little red fox or the torso of a blue whale, they also helped raise $63,000 for the Nature Conservancy, whose 1992 budget grossed over $180 million. But, the more significant aspect of such programs lies in the fact that Bank of America customers are having what behavioral scientists call a "consciousness raising experience" – they are being Greened.

Evidence of a more cerebral aspect of this P.R. program, or "consciousness raising," lies in the number of Eco-books being pumped off the presses. Over the past three years only diet books and cookbooks have surpassed the eco-related tomes within the non-fiction category. Most of these "quickie" volumes are churned out to appeal to the unsophisticated reader whose head is easily turned by an appeal to the emotions. Serious scholarship is as rare as a cocktail reception at a Baptist convention.

However, there are those few, which, while not widely promoted, are intended to set agendas for The Greening. One such book is

Ozone Diplomacy – New Directions in Safeguarding the Planet. The author, Richard Elliot Benedick, was Ambassador and chief U.S. negotiator during a series of meetings which started in 1985 at Geneva and culminated 30 months later. Those meetings led to the signing of the Montreal Protocol on Substances That Deplete the Ozone Layer.

Mostafa K. Tolba, the Executive Director of the United Nations Environment Program, said of *Ozone Diplomacy*, "This book is a welcome overview of how common obstacles have been handled and how future ones may be addressed as the fight to save our planet Earth intensifies." Establishment gadfly and CFR mainstay Elliot L. Richardson enthuses, "This timely book gives a balanced and illuminating picture of a precedent-setting negotiation that has been justly described as 'the beginning of a new era in environmental statesmanship.'" A few excerpts will show why the international power elite love *Ozone Diplomacy*.

On page one, Benedick says of the September 16, 1987 signing, "By their action, the signatory countries sounded the death knell for an important part of the international chemical industry, with implications for billions of dollars in investment and hundreds of thousands of jobs in related sectors." Bad news for chemical companies? Not so, according to Mr. Benedick. *He later shows how the Chemical Manufacturers Association directly participated in drafting the Protocol.* Obviously not everyone is going to be a loser in this mega-shift within the chemical industry.

Not without significant interest is the fact that Mr. Benedick was, as he says, "fortunate to be assigned by the Department of State as a senior fellow of The World Wildlife Fund and The Conservation Foundation."

He also writes, "Although the State Department regularly sends career diplomats to think-tanks and to university faculties of political science, economics, or government, this was the first such appointment to a private environmental organization – perhaps a

symbol of the coming of age of environment in our foreign policy?"
During his "assignment" Benedick worked with William K. Reilly,
who was to become Mr. Bush's EPA administrator. Topping his list
of grateful acknowledgments are then Secretary of State George
Schultz (CFR) and Deputy Secretary of State John Whitehead (also
CFR), the former head of the powerful banking firm of Goldman-
Sachs. As I keep trying to make clear, The Greening is very, very
powerful.

Considering how much money and power is bound up in the
enforcement of the Montreal Protocol, one would think that a total
examination of the truth or falsehood of ozone depletion theories
would have dominated the meetings. Not according to the chief U.S.
negotiator and the man whom most agree made it happen. Here's
what he writes, "'Politics,' Lord Kennet stated in special hearings on
the accord in the British House of Lords a year later, 'is the art of
making good decisions on insufficient evidence.'" Benedick waxes
eloquent, "Perhaps the most extraordinary aspect of the treaty was its
imposition of substantial short-term economic costs to protect
human health and the environment against unproved *future dangers
– dangers that rested on scientific theories rather than on firm data.*
[Emphasis added.]

Can you believe this? By his own admission "billions of dollars"
and "hundreds of thousands of jobs" are being given the "death
knell" by "improved future dangers." And this is what the UNEP
director calls "the beginning of a new era of environmental
statesmanship." But never you mind. If the name of the game is to
purposefully waste 10 percent of the world's gross national product
as the Iron Mountain crew proposed, then why let a simple matter of
truth or prudence stand in your way? "The Planet must be saved"
regardless of who gets hurt or who pays.

One more glimpse of how much money is going to be spent on
questionable environmental concerns can be found in the Flora
Lewis article from the *New York Times* of August 14, 1991, quoted

above. She says, "A remarkable *New York Times* report on a scarcely known but huge U.S. military program to start cleanup of damage done by American forces and military industry in the last 30 years suggests the enormous scope of what needs to be done. The whole project is expected to last 30 years and cost $400 billion."

Unquestionably, the most widely promoted book on the environment has been *Earth in the Balance*, by then candidate and now Vice President A1 Gore.

In the televised debate between Dan Quayle and Gore, Quayle cited Gore's own book to make his point about how the Clinton-Gore team would use taxpayer monies to support radical environmentalism. Quayle said Gore was advocating the expenditure of up to $100 billion. Gore vociferously denied that charge and the next day the national media did their best to berate Quayle and support Gore.

I'll let you be the judge, as we quote directly from pages 304 and 305 of *Earth in the Balance*. The chapter is entitled "A Global Marshall Plan":

Charles Maier points out that the annual U.S. Expenditures for the Marshall Plan between 1948 and 1951 were close to 2 percent of our GNP. A similar percentage today would be almost $100 billion a year (compared to our total nonmilitary foreign aid budget of about $15 billion a year.)

Yet the Marshall Plan enjoyed strong bipartisan support in Congress. There was little doubt then that government intervention, far from harming the free enterprise system in Europe, was the most effective way to foster its healthy operation. But our present leaders seem to fear almost any form of intervention. Indeed, the deepest source of their reluctance to provide leadership in creating an effective environmental strategy seems to be their fear that if we do step forward, we will inevitably be forced to lead by example and actively pursue changes that might interfere with their preferred brand of laissez-faire, nonassertive economic policy.

Nor do our leaders seem willing to look as far into the future as did Truman and Marshall. In that heady postwar period, one of Marshall's former colleagues, General Omar Bradley, said, "It is time we steered by the stars, not by the lights of each passing ship." This certainly seems to be another time when that kind of navigation is needed, yet too many of those who are responsible for our future appear to be distracted by such "lights of passing ships" as overnight public opinion polls.

In any effort to conceive of a plan to heal the global environment, the essence of realism is recognizing that public attitudes are still changing – and that proposals which are today considered too bold to be politically feasible will soon be derided as woefully inadequate to the task at hand. Yet while public acceptance of the magnitude of the threat is indeed curving upward – and will eventually rise almost vertically as awareness of the awful truth suddenly makes the search for remedies an all-consuming passion – it is just as important to recognize that at the present time, we are still in a period when the curve is just starting to bend. Ironically, at this stage, the maximum that is politically feasible still falls short of the minimum that is truly effective. And to make matters worse, the curve of political feasibility in advanced countries may well look quite different than it does in developing countries, where the immediate threats to well-being and survival often make saving the environment seem to be an unaffordable luxury.

It seems to make sense, therefore, to put in place a policy framework that will be ready to accommodate the worldwide demands for action when the magnitude of the threat becomes clear. And it is also essential to offer strong measures that are politically feasible now – even before the expected large shift in public opinion about the global government – and that can be quickly scaled up as awareness of the crisis grows and even stronger action becomes possible.

With the original Marshall Plan serving as both a model and an inspiration, we can now begin to chart a course of action.

As you pay your taxes for all of the above, please try and remember to "Have a nice day." It won't be easy.

CHAPTER 6

ECO-PROPHETS

Setting out to examine just a few of the better-known names in the environmental movement, we uncovered some tantalizing coincidences. First there is the HYPE phenomenon. Although the personalities we examined were not chosen for educational or personal background, amazingly enough 14 out of 20 (70%) were members of HYPE – the Harvard-Yale-Princeton-Elite. Thirteen of the 17 either graduated from Harvard, Princeton, or Yale, or have taught there. If you throw in Stanford and Berkeley, you have covered all but three of our eco-stars. Coincidence?

We also turned up traces of – how shall we say it delicately – *cronyism*. One environmentalist promotes the other, advancing careers and cronies in incestuous tandem. Environmental groups award prizes to these eco-stars to confer on them the necessary prestige. Their work for environmental groups, regardless of any near-total lack of scientific training, qualifies them as "experts" in the eyes of the media. These experts then introduce their protégés as experts. How do they become experts? Why, they head up some environmental foundation or institute *which they founded*!! Environmentalists, it seems, sign each other's credentials.

These folks have also mastered the art of grantsmanship. Large foundations fund the private organizations which the environmentalists found, and the grant money is then used to attract members and media attention. In the meantime, an enormous interest group has been built up: the environmental Establishment and everyone who earns his living from it.

The persons presented below are not necessarily the most important names in the environmental movement, but each is well-known or important in his own right. As you read through this list, keep in mind the interlocks of organization, education, and background – and other interesting coincidences.

DAVID ROSS BROWER Born July 1, 1912, Berkeley, California.

Education: University of California at Berkeley.

Organizational Connections: Sierra Club; Friends of the Earth (founder); Earth Island Institute (founder and now head); Friends of the Earth International; Trustees for Conservation; Citizens Committee for Natural Resources; Natural Resources Council of America; North Cascades Conservation Council; Rachel Carson Trust for Living Environment; League of Conservation Voters; Earth Island Limited, London; Environmental Liaison Center, and the Spirit of Stockholm Foundation.

In 1973 former Secretary of the Interior Stewart ("Mo") Udall described militant environmentalist David Brower as "the most effective single person on the cutting edge of conservation in this country." As Executive Director of the Sierra Club for 17 years, Brower tried to turn the "posy picking hiking society" into a radical environmental mass movement. Brower adopted an aggressive stance against the "plunderers of the earth" and "fought them with the 'all is fair' attitude of nature's true patriot using fair means or foul in what to him is a transcendent cause."

"The 'foul' means, in the view of his opponents, included alarmist, 'exaggerated' full-page newspaper messages" aimed at arousing public opinion. Brower's marketing talents flourished at the Sierra Club, where from the Sierra Club Press in the 1960s flowed 20 expensive volumes of landscape photographs. From 1952, when Brower became executive director of the Sierra Club, to 1969, membership increased tenfold (from 7,000 to 70,000) and the budget rose from $75,000 to $3,000,000.

Brower gathered other eco-vigilantes and together they attacked such diverse targets as the mining, lumber, and utility industries, the Bureau of Reclamation, and the ever-busy Army Corps of Engineers. Dam-stopping was their forte, but they also helped pass the Wilderness Act of 1964, an important forerunner piece of environmental legislation. Brower's biography (*Current Biography*, 1973) brags that "in the late 1960s alone they blocked seven billion dollars' worth of construction projects" they considered a threat to the natural environment.

Matters finally came to a head with the more conservative elements of the Sierra Club. In the spring of 1969 the Board of Directors ousted Brower on "charges that he had led the club into issues foreign to its region and its immediate concerns and that he was an extremist." (Hart, *Companion to California*, 1978.)

In 1969, Brower founded the Friends of the Earth (FOE), the express purpose of which was to be a political-activist group lobbying for environmental legislation and campaigning for eco-candidates. Later Brower apparently became too radical even for Friends of the Earth and left to found the Earth Island Institute, where he remains.

Brower, who believes that messages can be transmitted between animal species by tone of voice, claimed in John McPhee's 1971 book about him (*Encounters with the Arch- Druid*), that he learned to talk to chickens as a child. He grew up climbing, walking, and hiking in the Berkeley hills, and became a collector of rocks and minerals, discovering at age 15 a new species of butterfly. A loner, according to published biographies, after two years Brower dropped out of the University of California and worked in a candy factory for several years. About this time he began to make long trips through the Sierra Wilderness, and was sponsored into the Sierra Club in 1933 by photographer Ansel Adams.

Brower lost his candy factory job in 1935 and went to work with the park service in Yosemite National Park. A year later he became publicity manager, and in his six-year tenure at that position he perfected his publicity and mountaineering skills.

In 1941, Brower became an editor at the University of California Press, which took his story onto a rather remarkable track. With no apparently proven talent or future, he was sponsored into the Sierra Club by a famous photographer. At Yosemite, he sharpened what were apparently natural skills as a publicist. Then, although he dropped out of college, he was hired as an editor at the University of California Press.

From 1943 to the end of World War II, Brower was in the Army's Tenth Mountain Division, instructing troops. After the war he returned to the University of California Press. In 1947 he helped prepare the Sierra Club Handbook, and from that success he eventually moved to the Executive Directorship in 1952.

When Brower founded FOE (now with worldwide branches) he was initially subsidized with a $100,000 grant from the Ford Foundation and $80,000 from Robert O. Anderson, then board chairman and CEO of Atlantic Richfield. (Doesn't it seem, well, *awkward* that the head of one of the largest oil companies would fund the organization most viciously opposed to the Alaska pipeline?) Brower's announcement of FOE's formation noted that "The earth needs a number of organizations to fight the disease that now threatens the planet, 'cirrhosis of the environment.'" FOE was instrumental in organizing the first Earth Day, April 22, 1970.

Brower is also a zealous population controller and a promoter of "small is beautiful." In a well-worn speech, he asserts that "6 percent of the world's population uses 60 percent of the world's resources, and 1 percent of the 6 percent uses 60 percent of the 60 percent." This kindly butterfly-fancier favors "bringing population under control by some kind of coercion, such as punitive taxation." (*Current Biography*, 1973.)

McGEORGE BUNDY Born March 30, 1919, Boston, Massachusetts.

Education: Dexter School, Brookline, MA; Groton School; A.B., Yale.

Organizational Connections: Harvard; NYU; Council on Foreign Relations (CFR); Ford Foundation; The Population Council; Skull and Bones.

Once described as "the brightest man in America," McGeorge Bundy is an Insider's Insider. His father served as secretary to Justice Oliver Wendell Holmes, and then did two stints in Washington under Henry L. Stimson. McGeorge himself co-authored Stimson's memoir *On Active Service in Peace and War* (1948).

After graduating from Yale in 1940, Bundy became a junior fellow at Yale in 1941. He entered the army as a private but emerged as a captain. As an intelligence officer, he participated in planning Operation Overload (France) and Operation Husky (Sicily). While in London he attended Fabian socialist Harold Lasky's Tuesday soirees.

After the war Bundy helped Stimson write his memoirs, then consulted on the administration of the Marshall Plan, and finally worked for the CFR as a political analyst of the Marshall Plan. In 1949 Bundy returned to Harvard, eventually becoming Dean of the Graduate School in 1953.

Although a self-professed Republican, Bundy organized a committee for Kennedy, and was rewarded with a National Security Council seat as coordinator of military and political planning. After Kennedy's death he stayed with Lyndon Johnson until 1966, when he became president of the Ford Foundation (1966-1979), the perfect position for bankrolling the environmental movement.

Bundy is now chairman of The Population Council, which lobbies for depopulation around the globe and funds antifertility research. It is also worth recalling that Doe/ Galbraith in *Report from Iron Mountain* speculated that the Study Group "started with some of the new people who came in with the Kennedy Administration, mostly, I think with McNamara, Bundy, and Rusk."

HELEN BROINOWSKI CALDICOTT Born in Melbourne, Australia, August 7, 1938.

Education: University of South Australia, Children's Hospital Medical Center, Boston; facility, Harvard Medical School.

Organizational Connections: Physicians for Social Responsibility, Royal Australian College of Physicians, Women's Action for Nuclear Disarmament (founder).

Pediatrician, mother, and self-styled "world citizen" (how global can you get?), Caldicott has been an anti-nuclear and environmental activist since the early 1970s. She was active in banning French atmospheric nuclear testing in the South Pacific as well as the Australian export of uranium, and has been in the forefront of the war against nuclear power. After moving to the U.S., Physicians for Social Responsibility became her primary organizational vehicle, although it was nearly defunct when she arrived.

In 1966, Caldicott became associated with Harvard Medical School, but resigned in 1980 to join the cystic fibrosis clinic at Boston Children's Hospital Medical Center. Most of her time was spent spreading alarmist propaganda about the supposed carcinogenic and mutagenic effects of radiation from nuclear technology. She is probably the most vocal member of the nuclear disarmament and anti-nuclear power community, as well as an outspoken feminist. In 1989, America got a break when Caldicott moved back to Australia.

BARRY COMMONER Born May 28, 1917 in Brooklyn, New York.

Education: B.A., Columbia, 1937; M.A., Harvard, 1938; Ph.D., 1941; Faculty, Washington University (St. Louis), Queens College.

Organizational Connections: Center for the Biology of Natural Systems, Queens College; Soil Association of England; AAAS Committee on Environmental Alterations; American Cancer Society; St. Louis Committee for Nuclear Information; St. Louis Committee for Environmental Information; Scientists' Institute for Public Information; Citizens' Party Candidate for Presidency, 1980; American Association for the Advancement of Science (AAAS), American Institute of Biological Sciences, American Society of Naturalists, National Parks Association, environmental advisor to Jesse Jackson's campaigns.

On the February 2, 1970 cover of *Time* magazine, Dr. Barry Commoner was billed as the "Paul Revere of ecology." He is also that rarest of Green life-forms: a well-known environmentalist who is actually a scientist.

Commoner majored in biology at Columbia, where he championed left-of-left causes such as that of the Spanish Loyalists. He received an MA at Harvard and then a doctorate in biology in 1941. That same year he began teaching biology at Queens College. In 1942, he joined the Naval Reserve, and as a lieutenant was assigned as a naval liaison officer with the Senate Committee on Military Affairs.

In 1947, Commoner joined Washington University in St. Louis. Grants from the Rockefeller Foundation, the American Cancer Society, the National Foundation for Infantile Paralysis, and Lederle Laboratories funded his virus research – primarily on the tobacco mosaic virus (TMV).

In the early 1950s, Commoner was already insisting "that scientists had a moral obligation to play a role in public affairs and to keep the populace well informed about the potentially disastrous effects of science and technology on man's habitat." (*Current Biography*, 1970.) About the same time he helped found the St. Lords Committee for Nuclear Information, an anti-nuclear group branded as subversive by some critics.

Commoner was one of the very earliest environmental alarmists. In 1968, he told *Time* magazine, "There is now simply not enough air, water, and soil on earth to absorb man-made poisons without effect. If we continue in our reckless way, this planet before long will become an unsuitable place for human habitation." He has also ridden the anti-population bandwagon, and in January 1970, told a meeting of the American Association for the Advancement of Science that by the year 2000 the world would contain between six and eight billion people, the maximum that its food system could sustain, suggesting population be stabilized through the redistribution of goods.

In a March/April 1990 interview in *Mother Earth News*, Commoner maintained (in the face of the facts and contrary conclusions from many other reputable scientists) that all the government efforts to "clean up the environment have not worked, and that pollution levels have either been just slightly improved, or gotten worse." Commoner's proffered solution to the failure of government controls? Why, more controls, of course, but controls aimed at changing the technology of production by transferring decision-making from private to government hands.

In the same interview Commoner also complains that the environmental movement has split into two groups, with the old-timers cozying up to the industries they are supposed to try to eliminate. The "old-line groups in Washington live by the control strategy. Their bread and butter are legislation and standards. More recently, they're negotiating with corporations as to what levels of pollution are acceptable. You have, for example, the head of the worst waste management company in the country...on the board of directors of the National Wildlife Federation...[N]o way you can do that and function very well. The cutting edge of the environmental movement now is the grass-roots groups."

Noteworthy is that Commoner not only understands but advocates the collaboration of the environmental movement with the civil rights, feminist, and peace movements. In his view, all must work for the same end: socialism – although he tactfully avoids using the ugly S-word itself.

PAUL RALPH EHRLICH Born May 29, 1932 in Philadelphia.
Education: A.B., University of Pennsylvania, 1953; A.M., University of Kansas, 1955, Ph.D., 1957. Presently teaches biology at Stanford.
Organizational Connections: American Academy of Arts and Sciences; (AAAS); California Academy of Sciences; Society for the Study of Evolution; Society for Systematic Zoology; American

Society of Naturalists; Lepidopterists Society; American Museum of Natural History; Center for the Study of Democratic Institutions; International Association for Ecology; Zero Population Growth (founder).

Here's a quick but fundamental lesson about the nature of the environmental movement. One of the key propagandists for population control, Paul Ehrlich, is not a demographer at all, but a specialist in – butterflies. Here's an example of his demographic expertise: in 1968, when Ehrlich published his first population jeremiad, *The Population Bomb*, the peak in U.S. population growth had been passed exactly ten years before. It continued to drop, first to, and then through, the replacement rate. Unique in American history, this fact was well known to U.S. demographer's – but Ehrlich has never been deterred by facts. He simply ignores them.

In 1973 (the year the U.S. population growth rate fell through the replacement rate), Ehrlich predicted that by 1990, 65 million Americans would be dead – starved by the effects of overpopulation. Uncannily, Ehrlich missed the number of Americans with eating problems by only five million – except that 60 million was the number of Americans reported in 1990 to be *dieting due to overeating*. If the environmental movement were not so serious, Ehrlich would be the perfect lead in the comic opera, *Monsieur Butterfly*.

After obtaining his doctorate, Ehrlich worked at the University of Kansas studying parasitic mites (perhaps sensing a spiritual empathy) on a fellowship from the National Institutes of Health. In 1959, he joined the facility at Stanford University, where he became a full professor of biology in 1966.

A prolific if hilariously inaccurate writer, in 1967 Ehrlich asserted in the British magazine *New Scientist* that "the battle to feed humanity is over" and predicted that "somewhere between 1970 and 1985 the world will undergo vast famines." He has also compared the "uncontrolled multiplication of people to cancer, advocates tying

U.S. food aid to population control enforcement in developing countries, and discouraging [sic] U.S. population growth through such devices as luxury taxes on diapers and baby foods." (*Current Biography*, 1970.)

It was radical environmentalist and fellow butterfly-lover David Brower (whom we've already met) who suggested that Ehrlich publish *The Population Bomb*, which was in fact published by the Sierra Club with Ballantine Books in 1968.

Ehrlich lets his imagination run wild in a sort of mathematical spasm, arguing that if growth were maintained at the present rate for the next 900 years, there would be 60 million billion people on earth, or about 100 persons for each square foot of the earth's land and sea surface. (There will be even more if none of them die.) With truistic exactitude at once laughable and brutal, Ehrlich asserts, "The world's population will continue to grow as long as the birth rate exceeds the death rate...There are two kinds of solutions to the population problem. One is a 'birth rate solution' in which we find ways to lower the birth rate. The other is a 'death rate solution' in which ways to raise the death rate – war, famine, pestilence – find us."

Ehrlich helped found Zero Population Growth, which advocates legalized abortion, government support of birth control, tax incentives for smaller families, and a maximum of two children per family. Good as his prophetic word, Ehrlich had himself spayed in 1953 after the birth of his only daughter.

DAVE FOREMAN Born in 1947 in Albuquerque, New Mexico.
Education: University of New Mexico.
Organizational Connections: The Wilderness Society, Earth First! (Co-founder).

Don't let the beard, red flannel shirt, and stocking-cap fool you – Dave Foreman is no backwoods yokel. A 1972 campaign for the reclassification of the Gila Primitive Area in New Mexico brought him to the attention of The Wilderness Society. In early 1973, he began working for them as South-western Issues Consultant and eventually became Southwest representative. In January 1978, Foreman moved to Washington to serve as the Society's chief lobbyist, although he remained in that position little more than a year.

As a teenager, Foreman campaigned for Barry Goldwater. At San Antonio Junior College he formed a chapter of the conservative Young Americans for Freedom, then went on to the University of New Mexico to become the chairman of Students for Victory in Vietnam.

After graduation in 1968, Foreman went to Marine Corps Officer Candidate School, where he lasted 61 days. Of that, 31 days were spent in the brig for insubordination and AWOL. He received a general discharge as undesirable.

Foreman represents the logical extreme of environmentalism which Establishment environmentalists want to pretend doesn't exist. "A human life has no more intrinsic value than an individual grizzly bear life. If it came down to a confrontation between a grizzly and a friend, I'm not sure whose side I'd be on. But I do know humans are a disease, a cancer on nature."

Foreman's complaint about Washington was that the environmentalists were "being lobbied more effectively them [they] were lobbying," i.e., that the government officials they dealt with were on the side of mining, timber, and livestock industries. Dissatisfied, he "finally came to the conclusion that the environmental movement, and the Earth, needed people who had the guts to say what had to be said without compromising even before opening their mouths. To answer that need, we decided to form a group that would consciously not try to gain political credibility that would consciously not try to become part of the political establishment. Our group would operate outside the political system and make it known that we had fundamental differences with the world views of the political/industrial establishment." *Mother Earth News*, January/February 1985.)

The result was the founding of Earth First! in 1980 (the exclamation point doesn't indicate our surprise: it's part of the name). "Foreman saw that if Earth First! adopted the conventional bureaucratic structure of a large corporation, the group would inevitably assume the corporate values it was struggling against. Instead, Earth First! was conceived as a movement of autonomous grass-roots activists. It had no officers, no bylaws, no constitution, and no nonprofit tax status. But the tiny group soon leapt into the headlines with a series of guerrilla-theater actions and demonstrations." (*Omni*, November 1986.)

"Demonstrations" includes far more than picketing and protesting. "In practicing what Earth First! co-founder Dave Foreman calls 'a form of worship toward the Earth,' eco-guerrillas pour sand in the fuel tanks of logging equipment and drive spikes into the trees of old-growth forests, potentially ruining expensive lumber-mill saws [*and potentially injuring or killing irreplaceable lumber mill employees*]. They tear down power lines and pull up survey stakes; they sink whaling ships and destroy oil-exploration gear." (*Newsweek*, February 5, 1990.)

Foreman is the most visible member of a new breed of ultra-radical environmentalists – combination Jesuits, Zen Buddhists, Storm Troopers, KGB, and Grandpa McCoy – who really believe that snails are equal to human beings, that the Earth is sacred in the ancient pagan sense, that it is morally correct to endanger and even destroy human lives to save trees. They will literally stop at nothing in their religious crusade to save the Earth. On May 24, 1990, a car carrying two Earth First!ers and a bomb blew up in Oakland. In one case of tree spiking, when the saw band hit the spike, it broke and snapped back on the operator – fortunately with the blunt side. It only broke his jaw, knocked out several teeth, blinded one eye, and cut his jugular vein. The toothed side would have cut his head off.

In May 1989, Foreman was arrested by the FBI on conspiracy charges. Allegedly, Foreman and three others were plotting to topple power line transmission towers carrying lines to a pumping plant, and ultimately to cut lines to three nuclear power plants.

Foreman and his ilk will be lionized in the press. According to eco-debunker Dr. Petr Beckmann's Four Stages of Transmogrification, here's what we can expect. First, the media will give us breast-beating condemnation of eco-terrorism, while giving it plenty of what it needs most: publicity. In step two the media will say, "They are doing the right thing the wrong way." Step three is indirect legitimization, by presenting the thugs as victims. In the final stage all the eco-nazis' acts of violence will be fully blessed and they will be transmogrified to Full Heroes of the Ecology.

On August 13, 1991, in a plea bargain, Foreman pled guilty to one charge of conspiracy to commit property damage.

JAY DEE HAIR Born November 30, 1945, Miami, Florida.
Education: B.S., Clemson U., 1967, M.S. 1969; Ph.D. University of Alberta, 1975. Faculty: Clemson, University of North Carolina.
Organizational Connections: National Wildlife Federation; U.S. Department of the Interior; U.S. Department of Energy; National Petroleum Council; Natural Resources Council of America; Sol Feinston Environmental Awards Program; Global Tomorrow Coalition; Riggs National Bank; National Public Lands Advisory Council; National Wetland Policy Forum, National Groundwater Forum; National Nonpoint Source Institute; Keystone Center; Environmental Protection Agency; National Safety Council; Environmental Health & Safety Institute; International Union for Conservation of Nature and Natural Resources (IUCN).

According to many environmentalists, he is the High Priest of Co-option. Nevertheless, Jay Hair doesn't let it bother him. He has exploited his considerable marketing skills to expand the National Wildlife Federation into a $90 million a year, 970,000 member giant of the Washington environmental establishment. Hair is tall, photogenic, and a fountain of sound bites.

He grew up in rural Pennsylvania, graduated in biology from Clemson University in 1969, and served a tour in Vietnam as a reserve officer public health specialist. After Vietnam he finished a Ph.D. in biology at the University of Alberta. Later he taught at Clemson, then North Carolina State University.

Hair rose through the ranks of volunteers in the NWF, and in 1981, at age 35, the board elected him president. He then had to drag an overgrown rod and gun club into the mouth-foaming, posturing environmental mainstream, and has accomplished that with considerable marketing skill. Although at first his fellow Eco-establishmentarians accused him of being soft on Reagan, he was only biding his time until he knew which way the wind blew with the membership. When he learned by polling them that they rejected controversial Interior Secretary Watt, he quickly called for his resignation.

Similar stunts followed. His daughter developed a rare cancer in 1984, and Hair makes speeches explaining how her life was saved by a drug made from a rare flower from Madagascar. The only problem is that the plant is widely grown and the drug is lab-produced. Likewise Hair was the first Eco-establishment Fuehrer to arrive at Prince William Sound after the 1989 Exxon Valdez oil spill, earning wide network news exposure.

However, it is in the area of "partnership" between the environmental establishment and corporations that Hair has truly led the way. In 1982, he formed the Corporate Conservation Council, which embraces Asea Brown Boveri, Inc., AT&T, Browning-Ferris Industries, Ciba-Geigy Corp., Dow Chemical USA, Du Pont, Duke Power Co., General Motors Corp., Johnson & Johnson, 3M Co., Monsanto Co., Pacific Gas & Electric Co., Procter & Gamble Co., Shell Oil Co., USX Corp., Waste Management, Inc., and Weyerhaeuser.

From his association with this who's who of corporate power we can conclude that Hair understands how the Greening is played, and that environmentalism will be a useful tool of the corporate world, never a weapon against it.

DENIS ALLEN HAYES Born August 29, 1944, Wisconsin Rapids, Wisconsin.

Education: A.A., Clark College, 1964; B.A., Stanford University, 1969; J.D., Stanford, 1985.

Organizational Connections: Founder, Earth Day 1970; Smithsonian Institution; Illinois State Energy Office; Worldwatch Institute; Solar Energy Research Institute; Stanford University; Solar Lobby; Center for Renewable Resources; Sierra Club; American Institute of Public Service; Federation of American Scientists; Aspen Institute Energy Group; California Environmental Trust (director), American Solar Energy Society (director).

Denis Hayes may be the environmentalists' leading example of cronyism at its most effective. On July 26, 1979, Hayes was appointed head of the Solar Energy Research Institute, the "spearhead of the government's efforts to develop renewable forms of energy." (*Science*, October 24, 1980.) How could a 35-year-old without any formal training in science and engineering or any scientific credentials become head of a staff of 800 and a research budget of more than $120 million? Simple. Convince the Secretary of the Department of Energy that he's the "leading environmentalist of his generation." Appointed by Energy Secretary James R. Schlesinger (CFR), Hayes' placement was loudly supported by then-acting chairman of the Council on Environmental Quality, Gus Speth (CFR).

Hayes was the founder of Earth Day in 1970. At the ripe old age of 26 he became a trustee of Stanford University for two years (1971-72). Absent any scientific credentials, he was also a Visiting Scholar at the Smithsonian Institution, 1971-72, Director of the Illinois State Energy Office, 1974- 75, and a senior researcher at Worldwatch Institute, 1975-79.

Hayes only stayed at the Solar Energy Research Institute from 1979 to 1981. Then he became regent's professor at the University of California-Santa Cruz until 1982, and is still a consulting professor of civil engineering at Stanford University. In 1985 he graduated from law school at Stanford, and in 1986 joined a San Francisco law firm.

Hayes founded the Solar Lobby and was chairman of the board from 1978 through 1979. With all that activity, one could expect a number of eco-awards; he does not disappoint. In 1978 he won the award for outstanding public service from the U.S. Department of Energy. He received the Jefferson Medal from the American Institute of Public Service in 1979 and a Certificate of Outstanding Achievement from the American Solar Energy Society in 1985. The Sierra Club also garlanded him with the John Muir Award in 1985.

From the very beginning Hayes has been groomed for a public role. Keep your eye on this one.

AMORY BLOCH LOVINS Born Washington, November 13, 1947.

Education: Although listed as a "consultant physicist" in the 1979 World Future Society publication *The Future: A Guide to Information Sources,* Lovins attended Harvard without completing any degree. From there he went to Oxford where from 1969-71 he studied biophysics. In *Who's Who in the West* he claims an MA from Merton College. The "Dr." before his name refers to a string of honorary degrees.

Organizational Connections: University of California at Berkeley and Riverside; Rocky Mountain Institute; Friends of the Earth; AAAS; Lindisfarne Association; Federation of American Scientists.

Lovins is another example of instant stardom in Eco-land. In 1976 the Council on Foreign Relations journal *Foreign Affairs* published Lovins' article, "Energy Strategy: The Road Not Taken?" Fellow eco-star Paul Ehrlich immediately hailed this treatise "the most influential single work on energy policy written in the last five years." Real scientists were not so impressed. Nobel Prize-winning physicist Hans Bethe said, "He takes partial results of other people's work and leaves behind the numbers he doesn't like." "He's impressed a lot of people who don't know anything about energy and depressed a lot of people who do," says one oil executive. (*Newsweek*, November 14, 1977, p. 114.)

As the representative in Britain for Friends of the Earth, 1971-1984, Lovins ties back to David Brower. Could this account for his sudden rise to fame? Lovins and his wife Hunter masquerade as free marketers, promoting all sorts of soft energy devices along with their steadfast opposition to nuclear power. Lawyer and political scientist Hunter Lovins has less claim to scientific credentials than her husband. Both are now ensconced in a nonprofit foundation, the Rocky Mountain Institute in Old Snowmass, Colorado, with an annual budget of more than $1.2 million and a staff of 25.

Not bad for a boy who dropped out of Harvard.

JOHN MICHAEL McCLOSKEY Born in Eugene, Oregon, April 26, 1934.

Education: B.A., Harvard, 1956; J.D., University of Oregon, 1961.

Organizational Connections: Sierra Club, League of Conservation Voters; Commission on Environmental Law and Policy (International Union for Conservation of Nature – IUCN); President's Commission on Agenda for the 1980s; International Council on Environmental Law; Democratic Club; Explorers (NYC); Western Forest Environment Discussion Group; Mining Committee of the National Coal Policy Project; National Research Council; Ford Foundation's Energy Policy Project.

Another environmental superstar emerges from the David Brower Sierra Club kennel. From the time he graduated from law school, McCloskey was Northwest representative for the Sierra Club (1961-65, while Brower was executive director 1952-69). From 1965 to 1966 he was assistant to the president of the Sierra Club, conservation director, 1966-69, executive director 1969-85, acting executive director, 1986- 87, and chairman, 1985 to the present.

McCloskey has other environmental interlocks as well. He is on the board of directors of the League of Conservation Voters, and since 1978 vice-chairman of the Commission on Environmental Law and Policy of the IUCN. He was also a principal author of the United Nations' Charter for Nature. In the Carter Administration he was a member of the President's Commission on an Agenda for the 1980s (1979-80), and is now based in Washington with the Sierra Club.

Environmentalists reward their own. McCloskey has received the Sierra Club's John Muir Award (1979) and the California Conservation Council Professional Award (1969).

RALPH NADER Born Winsted, Connecticut, February 27, 1934.

Education: Gilbert School, Winsted; Woodrow Wilson School of Public and International Affairs, Princeton (A.B.), 1955; Harvard Law School, LL.B, 1958.

Organizational Connections: Public Citizen, Inc.; Center for Study of Responsive Law; Corporate Accountability Research Group; Public Interest Research Group; Tax Reform Research Group; Retired Professionals Action Group; Congress Watch; Citizen Utility Board; Buyers Up; League for Industrial Democracy (formerly Intercollegiate Socialist Society).

If John Muir is the patron saint of the environmental movement, Ralph Nader is the Ignatius Loyola. Although primarily considered a consumer rights advocate, Nader has been a powerful force in the environmental movement from its very inception, unsuccessfully trying to prevent the spraying of trees with DDT while he was an undergraduate at Princeton.

Although he comes from an ultra-Establishment educational background, Nader cultivates a frugal, monkish *persona*. His publicity maintains that he lives cheaply, wearing the same narrow-lapel suits and skinny ties he bought when he left the Army in 1958. He even claims that he is still wearing the 12 pairs of black socks he bought at the Army PX in 1958 (which by now probably need washing).

After he left Harvard Law School he spent six months in the Army as a cook at Fort Dix. In the early '60s he travelled widely in the Soviet Union, Africa, and South America as a freelance journalist for the *Atlantic Monthly* and the *Christian Science Monitor*. (How times change! In the 1968 *Current Biography* this excursion was listed as an "extensive tour, on his own, of Latin America, Europe, and Africa." In 1986 *Current Biography* reveals it was the Soviet Union, Africa, and South America.)

By 1964 Nader was restless in his small law practice in Hartford, Connecticut. His big break came when now U.S. Senator from New York Daniel Patrick Moynihan (CFR), then Assistant Secretary of Labor for policy planning, hired His Citizenship as a staff consultant on highway safety, already a Nader interest. Thus funded at the handsome 1964 stipend of $50 a day, Nader spent a year writing a legislative background document, "A Report on the Context, Condition and Recommended Direction of Federal Activity in Highway Safety" – and developing contacts in the press corps and Congress.

In November 1965, this report was published as *Unsafe at Any Speed*, which indicted the whole auto industry for its alleged lack of concern over safety. This established a pattern for Nader's hit and run tactics and his skillful use of the press. By the late '70s, however, Nader's influence was waning, having worn out the politicians who complained "they might vote with Nader a hundred times and then be called a 'tool of industry' for a single vote he considers anti-consumer."

To give the devil his due, Nader was instrumental in the passage of the Freedom of Information Act of 1974, an indispensable tool for prying information out of secretive and arrogant government agencies. But he was also behind passage of the Traffic and Motor Vehicle Safety Act (1966), Wholesome Meat Act of 1967, and other legislation regulating natural gas pipelines and underground coal mining, as well as the creation of the Environmental Protection Agency (EPA) and the Occupational Safety and Health Administration (OSHA, 1976).

For any free marketer, Nader's career must be viewed with bittersweet consternation. Although he professes to promote the benefit of the consumer and oppose monolithic corporate economic power, his thrust in court and Congress has been just the opposite. He inevitably champions the increased regulation that always stifles innovation and free entry into markets, and always results in a symbiosis between regulators and the regulated. In this fascist cartelization the one permanent sacrifice is the good of the consumer and the public. Nader has pushed a wide array of environmental issues, most especially opposition to the safest, cleanest, cheapest power generation known, i.e., nuclear power. A prolific writer, Nader may be temporarily eclipsed, but he is by no means dead.

WILLIAM KANE REILLY Born January 26, 1940 in Decatur, Illinois.
Education: B.A. Yale, 1962; J.D., Harvard Law School, 1965; M.S. in Urban Planning, Columbia, 1971.

Organizational Connections: Urban Policy Center; National Urban Coalition; Conservation Foundation; World Wildlife Fund; Winrock [Winthrop Rockefeller] International Institute for Agricultural Development; Clean Sites; Piedmont Environmental Council; Partners for Livable Places; Sol Feinston Group; American Farmland Trust; Natural Resources Council of America; German Marshall Fund; Habitat; Council for Environmental Quality; EPA.

William Reilly, Bush's head of The Environmental Protection Agency, is the quintessential apostle of business-government "partnership" in the environment. He has long urged "a new spirit of cooperation" among environmentalists, industry, and state and local governments.

Reilly has been in the avant-garde of the environmental establishment since there was one. In 1969, he was appointed associate director of the Urban Policy Center. In 1970 he joined the staff of The Council on Environmental Quality. Reilly cannily went back to Columbia for a master's degree in urban planning in 1971. Shortly thereafter, Reilly's Insider mentor, Laurence S. Rockefeller, appointed him executive director of the Rockefeller self-appointed Task Force on Land Use and Urban Growth in 1972. (Rockefeller's interest in conservation always seemed to pay off well. With uncanny foresight he always seemed to develop elite vacation resorts right next to areas the government later closed to the hoi polloi as wilderness. Pure luck and coincidence.)

In 1973, the comrades on the committee reported back that Congress should use a carrot-and-stick approach to impose a national land-use policy by giving aid to cooperative states and punishing the recalcitrant by withholding highway and other funds. Nice guy – if you don't eat his carrot he hits you with his stick.

That same year, Reilly became president of The Conservation Foundation, where the Rockefeller and Mellon foundations underwrote his work. In 1985 that foundation merged with the World Wildlife Fund (WWF) and Reilly became president. Interestingly, the WWF focusses on Latin America and the Caribbean, which has been a Rockefeller preserve for about 100 years. Under Reilly the WWF membership grew to 600,000 with a $35 million budget.

Beginning in 1982, Reilly began to criticize Reagan's environmental policy, calling for more government spending and "policy" rather than market environmental solutions. You can hardly name an eco-trip Reilly doesn't take: land- use control, wetlands, rain forests, pollution, endangered species, national park expansion, trace pollution, asbestos, and acid rain. Reilly even attacks that environmental blackguard, the family farmers. Obediently serving the needs of his Establishment banking constituency, Reilly has also pioneered "debt-for-nature" swaps with Latin American countries.

In October 1988, President-elect Bush appointed Reilly head of the EPA, on the recommendation of former EPA chief William Ruckelshaus. The environmental groups loved it, and Reilly lived up to his totalitarian promise. One of his early statements was, "The first requisite of an effective Superfund [cleanup] program is a clenched fist."

Reilly made good on Bush's promise, "no net loss of wetlands." (For the victims this might be translated, "no net retention of property rights") He was also largely responsible for the Clean Air Act, which will cost America about $50 billion a year (for starters), and he continually pushed for more international treaties to ban chlorofluorocarbons and address global warming. Don't be fooled by the urbane, pretty-boy facade. In spite of the Mozart duets Reilly sings with his wife, the First Fist is far more Papa Doc than Pappagallo.

It was Reilly himself who torpedoed the report of the congressionally commissioned National Acid Precipitation Assessment Program (NAPAP), which cost $600 million and took ten years to complete. Unhappily for Reilly and his Greenshirts, the NAPAP found acid rain a minor nuisance which could be easily remedied by truckloads of lime poured in affected lakes. Ignoring the report and the facts, Reilly portrayed acid rain as an environmental catastrophe. Then he smuggled it into the Clean Air Act of 1990, although he knew the billions mandated for coal cleaning would not significantly affect acid rain.

For those naive scientists who believe the facts count, Reilly has a ready muzzle. When renowned soil scientist and NAPAP staff member Dr. Edward Krug publicly pointed out the lack of facts to support the acid rain panic, EPA issued an official communique decrying Krug's "limited credibility" and accusing him of being "on the fringes of environmental science." Krug is now unable to get a job.

These antics offer only a sampler of Reilly's green shenanigans. We forebear to mention his ban on essential asbestos. Or his hyped-up campaign against dioxin and Agent Orange. Or his war against fire-retardant PCB, which has forced manufacturers to substitute highly inflammable mineral oil in transformers. Or the utterly silly hype about ozone hole-induced skin cancer. For the benefit of the untutored public Reilly and his green myrmidons purposely confound the mildest form of cancer, which is induced by ultra-violet light, with deadly melanoma skin cancer, which only appears on unexposed parts of the body. (How often have you been sunburned on your buttocks or the soles of your feet?)

Whenever we ponder EPA First Fist William Reilly, our mind uncontrollably wanders back to a German saying: *Das passt wie die Faust aufs Auge* – that fits like a fist in your eye. William Reilly is the green fist in America's eye.

JEREMY RIFKIN Born in Chicago, 1945.

Education: Wharton School of Finance, University of Pennsylvania, B.A., economics; Fletcher School of Law and Diplomacy, Tufts University, M.A., international affairs.

Organizational Connections: Foundation on Economic Trends; VISTA; People's Bicentennial Commission; People's Business Commission.

Question: How does one describe a political position at the far left of left? Answer: Jeremy Rifkin. Without training or credentials in science, Rifkin has become a very successful journalistic terrorist. He will sabotage any technology, as long as it appears on the cutting edge of research.

In 1967, Rifkin helped organize the first national rally against the Vietnam War. In the early '70s, he settled in Washington to continue his left-of-left activism. In 1971, he founded the People's

Bicentennial Commission as a sounding board for his socialism and to promote "social action."

After the Bicentennial, Rifkin founded the People's Business Commission, "dedicated to challenging the abuses of corporate power and to mobilizing public support for democratic alternatives to the present economic system" (read: promoting socialism). Of Rifkin's *Own Your Own Job* Ken Nash wrote approvingly in the June 15, 1977 *Library Journal*, "Rifkin's socialism is as American as apple pie, and he is perhaps our most talented popularizer of radical ideas."

The author of numerous books, Rifkin's latest hobby horse is genetic engineering. Given its potential for disasters, a conservative approach to such research may be desirable. Rifkin, however, descends to an anti-intellectual obscurantism that would stifle all scientific progress. There is simply no way that all the risks of life can be reduced to absolute zero.

Rifkin's activities are not limited to journalistic terrorism, but also include endless litigation against his victims. Rifkin is one of the "small is beautiful" folks as well. His paranoia and lack of scientific training have on occasion earned Rifkin the contempt even of the liberal scientific establishment. Commenting on Rifkin's book *Algeny*, Harvard biologist and evolution defender Stephen Jay Gould wrote "On the Origin of Specious Critics" in the January, 1985 *Discover*: "I regard *Algeny* as a cleverly constructed tract of anti-intellectual propaganda masquerading as scholarship."

JOHN DAVISON ROCKEFELLER III Born March 21, 1906, New York.

Died July 10, 1978.

Education: B.A., Princeton, 1929.

Organizational Connections: Rockefeller Foundation; The Population Council (founder); Agricultural Development Council; Rockefeller Brothers Fund; Rockefeller Family Fund; U.S. Commission on Population Growth and The American Future;

Planned Parenthood; Council on Foreign Relations; Institute for Pacific Relations.

Although now long deceased, John D. Rockefeller III deserves mention because of his activities in and funding of the depopulation movement. "Rockefeller supported basic research and training in the fields of agricultural economics and population studies, including the development of a safe, effective, and inexpensive contraceptive for use in the less developed world. Over time, these two activities became the control and interrelated elements of his approach to the problems of development and global interdependence. The work of both the Population Council and the Agricultural Development Council, as well as the efforts in scientific agriculture pioneered by the Rockefeller Foundation and leading to the so-called Green Revolution, was heavily influenced by...neo-Malthusian doctrines...These organizations sought to impress upon the U.S. government, Asian, and later African and Latin American governments, as well as international organizations, the importance of family planning programs and rational land use...

"Rockefeller occupied a unique position in American society because of his wealth and family name. He used both unstintingly to pursue a course of moderate reform aimed at eliminating the most overt abuses of the capitalist order and calling attention to the very great dangers which unchecked population growth posed to world civilization." [1]

It hardly needs to be added to this glowing propaganda tribute that the various Rockefeller foundations, and others subject to their influence, have been the major funding source of the Overpopulation Industry. The myth of overpopulation is a primary mainstay of the environmentalist worldview.

LAURENCE SPELMAN ROCKEFELLER Born May 26, 1910, New York.

Education: B.A., Princeton, 1932.

Organizational Connections: Rockefeller Brothers Fund; Citizens Advisory Committee on Environmental Quality; American

Conservation Association; Jackson Hole Preserve; Palisades Interstate Park Commission; Alfred P. Sloan Foundation; Greenacre Foundation; National Geographic Society; Memorial Sloan Kettering Cancer Center; New York State Council of Parks and Out-

---

1 Biographical Dictionary of Internationalists, Warren F. Kuehl, editor. Westport, Connecticut: Greenwood Press, 1983. p. 617 ff.

door Recreation; American Conservation Association (founder); National Recreation and Park Association; New York Zoological Society; Resources for the Future; Isaac Walton League; The American Forestry Association; Conservation Foundation; World Wildlife Fund; National Parks and Conservation Association; American Farmland Trust; Natural Resources Defense Council; World Resources Institute.

As overpopulation became the province of John D. III, Laurence's bailiwick is conservation. In spite of this apparent "division of labor," the Rockefeller brothers are not narrow. Recall the role of David's participation in the Third World Wilderness Congress at

Denver as described above.

When he began working in the family offices at Rockefeller Center, Laurence became involved in the conservation and park activities of his father, John D. Rockefeller, Jr. (It is outside the scope of this present book, but take it from us that the Insiders' involvement with "conservation" goes a long way back.) He has served on several New York State Park agencies and numerous federal government commissions and study groups, as well as initiating and financing some of his own. Through the Rockefeller foundations and his influence with other foundations, he has been responsible for funding a wide spectrum of environmental groups and causes.

In 1958, he founded the American Conservation Association, which columnist Warren Brookes calls the "mother ship of the conservation movement." Pure public spirited philanthropy, right?

Warren Brookes didn't think so. In a January 29, 1991 *Washington Times* article, Brookes charged that the environmental land grab has profitable as well as philanthropic purposes:

[This conservation elite, a] small group of mostly white, mostly Ivy League males, has learned how to work with and for two of America's wealthiest families, the Rockefellers and the Mellons, to put a growing share of the country off-limits to economic development, but much of it available for exclusive upscale enclaves.

The leading 'angel' in this green-lining network is Laurence Rockefeller, whose Rockefeller Brothers Fund is a key funding resource for a slew of environmental groups, including The Conservation Foundation (CF), and World Wildlife Fund (trustee), the American Conservation Association (ACA, chairman and director), the American Farmland Trust (AFI), the National Parks and Conservation Association (NPCA), the Natural Resources Defense Council (NRDC), and the World Research Institute.

Mr. Rockefeller has generously given a fortune in land to the nation...but as [columnist Alston] Chase points out, 'He also kept commercial interest in or new some of these places, and throughout his life has promoted the apparently contradictory goals of both resort development and preservation.'

Not surprisingly, that is precisely the model used by groups like The Nature Conservancy – creating exclusive preserves as a magnet for profitable upscale adjacent residential development that then is used to finance still more acquisition. One of Mr. Rockefeller's key protégés in this "Permanent Green Government" is William Reilly, now EPA administrator but believed to be heir-in-waiting as the next interior secretary.

Mr. Reilly has divided his career between top jobs financed by Mr. Rockefeller (CF and WWF) and bureaucratic assignments, beginning with the Council for Environmental Quality under President Nixon.

But Mr. Reilly's main interest is not in 'big environment' issues like acid rain or global warming, but with national land use planning. In 1972 Mr. Rockefeller named him executive director of the Task Force on Land Use and Urban Growth...

Out of this, Mr. Reilly became president of CF, the most exclusive and prestigious environmental think tank of all, which he later merged with WWF, whose chairman is Russell Train, a former EPA administrator...

When Reilly went to the EPA in 1989, Mr. Train took over CF, in addition to his WWF responsibilities. Mr. Train is also a trustee of NPCA, the AFT, the World Resources Institute...Reilly and Train colleagues are everywhere in the land 'conservation' game.

The Rockefellers, it seems, do very well doing good.

WILLIAM DOYLE RUCKELSHAUS Born July 24, 1932 in Indianapolis.

Education: Portsmouth Priory School, R.I.; B.A. Princeton, 1957; LL.B., Harvard, 1960.

Organizational Connections: EPA; Conservation Foundation; Urban Institute; National Wildflower Research Center; Weyerhaeuser; has been or is now on the boards of directors of Insituform of North America, Inc., Ranier Ban-corporation, Cummins Engine Co., Monsanto, Nordstrom, U.S. West, American Water Development, Control Resource Industries, Browning-Ferris Industries, Peabody International Corporation, Church and Dwight, Geothermal Kinetics, and Enesco; Georgetown Law Center Environmental Forum; Twentieth Century Fund; Pacific Science Center Foundation, Public Interest Advisory Committee, Harvard University Medical Project, Harvard J.F.K. School of Government; Council on Foreign Relations; Trilateral Commission.

Ruckelshaus is a star to watch, and bids fair to become the so-called "responsible spokesman for industry" in environmental matters. His family has ranked high in Indiana Republican politics for three generations. After two years at Princeton, Ruckelshaus was drafted into the army. He says his father, a member of his local draft board, was concerned over his lack of application at Princeton. It must have worked, because Ruckelshaus returned to Princeton and graduated in 1957 *cum laude*, then graduated from Harvard Law School in 1960.

He worked in the Indiana Attorney General's office and was already active then in environmental control activities. In 1966 he was elected to the Indiana House of Representatives and became the first freshman representative ever elected majority leader. Defeated by Birch Bayh in 1968 in the U.S. senate race, Ruckelshaus was taken into the Justice Department by John Mitchell. In 1970 he was named director of the new Environmental Protection Agency, and began actively pursuing municipalities and industry for water pollution.

In 1973, Ruckelshaus, then Deputy Attorney General, refused to carry out President Nixon's order to dismiss Archibald Cox, the first special Watergate prosecutor, in the "Saturday night massacre" of October 20, 1973. Overnight he became the saint of the liberal press. He also served a short stint as acting director of the FBI.

Ruckelshaus is a veteran of the "revolving door" between government regulators and regulated industries. After leaving the government, Ruckelshaus formed a Washington law firm with veteran lawyers from the EPA, insisting there was nothing illegal or unethical in representing clients in environ-mental matters. In 1975, he became senior vice president of Weyerhaeuser, one of the nation's largest wood products companies. Oddly enough, Weyerhaeuser afterwards became involved in several disputes with the EPA.

In March 1983, Reagan brought Ruckelshaus back for a second stint as head of the EPA, where he stayed into 1985. He is now chairman of the board and CEO of Browning-Ferris Industries, one of the largest waste disposal companies in the country.

Ruckelshaus comes as a package deal with his wife, Jill. Ms. Ruckelshaus was in the vanguard of frequent anti-Reagan reports from the U.S. Commission on Civil Rights, to which she was appointed by Carter. She also holds an M.A. in Education from Harvard and has been nicknamed the "Gloria Steinem of the Republican Party" for her support of feminism. Mr. Ruckelshaus has a good chance to appear as a very Green presidential candidate in the future.

JOHN CRITTENDEN SAWHILL Born in Cleveland, June 12, 1936.

Education: Gilman School, Baltimore; B.A., Woodrow Wilson School of Public and International Affairs, Princeton, 1958; Ph.D., NYU, 1963.

Organizational Connections: Colonial Eating Club, Princeton; Merrill, Lynch; NYU; Department of Energy; U.S. Synthetic Fuels Corporation; Aspen Institute for Humanistic Studies; boards of directors, Automatic Data Processing, Consolidated Edison, RCA and Philip Morris; Council on Foreign Relations; Trilateral Commission; now president of The Nature Conservancy.

Sawhill is yet another Establishment star in the Green galaxy. In 1960 he earned a Ph.D. in economics, finance, and statistics from NYU. While working there as an assistant professor he was also senior consulting economist for the House Committee on Banking and Currency. Sawhill returned to government in the Nixon Administration in 1973 as one of four associate directors of the Office of Management and Budget.

In December 1973, after John A. Love resigned from the new Federal Energy Office, Nixon appointed Sawhill deputy director under William E. Simon. In a burst of bureaucratic fervor, within two months Sawhill and Simon had increased the staff from 200 to more than 3,000. In 1974 Sawhill replaced Simon as FEO energy czar. As Nixon's star fell, Sawhill gained publicity by openly contradicting Nixon's assessment of the energy crisis.

The FEO was shortly changed to the Federal Energy Administration (FEA), and Sawhill rated the deregulation of natural gas prices his number-one legislative priority. Sawhill's confrontation of the administration continued with Gerald Ford, and in 1974 he was forced to resign.

From FEA Sawhill went to then deathly-ill New York University in 1975. In the red about $11 million when Sawhill arrived, he nonetheless brought it under control by 1977 and had landed huge endowment funds by the time he left in 1979.

In 1979 Sawhill returned to Jimmy Carter's Washington as deputy secretary in the Department of Energy. In 1980 he was appointed chairman of the U.S. Synthetic Fuels Corporation, and remained there until 1981. He is now the president of The Nature Conservancy.

JAMES GUSTAVE SPETH Born in Orangeburg, South Carolina, March 3, 1942.

Education: B.A., Yale, 1964; LL.B., 1969; B.Litt., Oxford, 1966; Rhodes Scholar, 1964-1966; law clerk to U.S. Supreme Court Justice Hugo Black, 1969-70.

Organizational Connections: Natural Resources Defense Council; Council on Environmental Quality; Georgetown University Law Center; World Resources Institute; Environmental Law Institute; Workplace Health Fund; Environmental and Energy Study Institute; Global Tomorrow Coalition; National Wildlife Federation; Council on Foreign Relations.

Touted as one of the "outsiders" brought into government by Jimmy Carter, Speth is anything but. There's no such thing as a Rhodes Scholar "outsider." Although Speth is perhaps not well-known to the public, he is nonetheless one of the most important environmental activists.

Speth co-founded the Natural Resources Defense Council. As a lawyer he has compared the environmental revolution to the civil rights revolution of the 1960s. "Inspired by the example of the NAACP's Legal Defense Fund, Speth and several other young attorneys founded the Natural Resources Defense Council, one of the first environmental law groups." (*Science*, May 30, 1980.)

Speth has done two stints on the Council on Environmental Quality, first as a member (1977-79), and then as chairman (1979-81). He is an outspoken anti-nuke. A May 30, 1980 Science article said that Speth believed "that the 1980s can be a time of major advances for the environmental movement – if the movement adopts the strategies necessary to build broad-based political coalitions, increases grass roots organizing l)y a hundredfold,' and curbs the political power of corporations through such measures as partial public financing of Senate and House elections."

Strategist Speth was then promoting the "conserver society, committed to doing more with less." He usually rims well in advance of the environmental pack. In 1980 Speth was already calling for "protecting prime farm land, scenic rural landscapes, and environmentally sensitive coastal resources (wetlands), slowing growth in energy consumption through conservation and renewable energy sources, leading a world-wide effort to protect the global commons from threats such as an excessive build-up of carbon dioxide in the atmosphere, the destruction of tropical rain forests, and desertification, and reduction of the risk of nuclear war." James (Gus) Speth is now the "coordinator" for environmental policy in the Clinton Administration. *(Science,* May 30, 1980.)

MAURICE STRONG Born 1929, Alberta, Canada.
Education: No formal education.
Organizational Connections: President, World Federation of United Nations Associations; co-chairman, World Economic Forum; member, Club of Rome; trustee, Aspen Institute; director, World Future Society; director of finance, Lindisfarne Association; founding endorser, Planetary Citizens; convener, Fourth World Wilderness Congress; trustee, Rockefeller Foundation, 1971-78; International Union for the Conservation of Nature and Natural Resources (IUCN); United Nations Environment Program (UNEP); First World Conference of the Environment (Stockholm, 1972); World Commission on the Environment ("Brundtland Commission"); United Nations Conference on the Environment and Development (UNCED) (June 1992, Rio de Janiero Earth Summit);

Business Council for Sustainable Development; Petro-Canada; World Economic Forum; Dome Petroleum.

We call him the Lizzie Borden of Environmentalism. Multimillionaire Canadian Maurice Strong has been active for 20 years in the International Union for the Conservation of Nature and Natural Resources (IUCN based in Geneva) and the United Nations Environment Program (UNEP). Supported by the Canadian government, he has directed or taken part in practically every major UN environmental initiative. He organized the First World Conference of the Environment (Stockholm, 1972) and the World Commission on the Environment ("Brundtland Commission"). Now Strong is heading up UNCED, the Earth Summit scheduled for Rio in June, 1992.

Most tantalizing of all, Strong's business background lies in oil and natural resource development. Who could better lead the Great Resource Grab to lock up the world's natural resources?

Exercising my gift for mammoth understatement, Strong's rise to power has been *meteoric*, and as unexplainable as that of Instant-General Dwight David Eisenhower. Born in Manitoba in 1929, Strong left home at age 14 and worked with the merchant marine in British Columbia and Hudson's Bay Co. fur traders in the Northwest Territory. In 1948, *at age nineteen*, he began corporate work as an *investment analyst* in Toronto – sort of like your yard boy joining the staff at the Manhattan Project. Soon he moved to Alberta where he became an executive officer with a number of mining and oil companies, including Dome Petroleum. In 1960, *at age 31*, he assumed the presidency of one of Canada's leading investment firms, Power Corporation of Canada. From the mid-'60s he started international work under Prime Minister Lester Pearson. In 1972 Strong became secretary-general of the UN conference on the Human Environment, the first Earth Summit at Stockholm. In 1973 he founded the UN Environment Program (UNEP) and served two years as executive director. P.M. Pierre Trudeau appointed him to establish and head Petro-Canada. Appointed to the UN Brundtland

Commission, in 1987 he helped write its report, *Our Common Future*.

To buttress the Earth Summit, Strong formed the *Business Council for Sustainable Development*, "a blue-ribbon group of 50 eminent business leaders from all regions of the world...to promote a clear understanding of and commitments to environmentally *sustainable development* within the private sector at the highest corporate level."

To the chairmanship Strong appointed Swiss industrialist Stephan Schmidheiny (yes, it is pronounced Schmitt-heinie). Other members include Peter Barenvik (Asea Brown Boveri), Kenneth T. Derr (Chevron Corp.), Maurice R. Greenberg [CFR;TC] (American International Group), Carl Hahn (Volkswagen), Paul O'Neill [TC] (Alcoa), Frank Popoff [CFR] (Dow Chemical), William Ruckelshaus [CFR;TC] (BFI), Lodewijk C. Van Wachem (Royal Dutch Shell), and Edgar Woolard (Du Pont).

Strong owns a large tract of land in Colorado which they call "the Baca." There Strong and his wife are establishing an international community of spiritualists, "complete with monasteries, devotees of the Vedic mother goddess, amulet-carrying Native American shamans, Zen Buddhists, and even Shirley MacLaine." Strong and his Danish wife Hanne believe in the coming of an apocalypse, a belief they share with former Canadian Prime Minister Pierre Trudeau, the Dali Lama, and *ga-ga* Shirley MacLaine. (Shirley knows the Baca is right for her: her astrologer told her so.) They are not only promoting a one-world government (substituting environmentalism for war), they are also supporting a one world religion to substitute for Christianity.

In May 1990, Daniel Wood interviewed Strong for West magazine. Strong presented the idea that the only way to save the planet from destruction is to see to it that the industrialized civilizations collapse. [*Honest, I am NOT making any of this up*]. Wood recounts the conversation:

I leave the Baca with Strong...He has a novel he'd like to do...It would be a cautionary tale about the future.

Each year, he explains...the novel's plot, the World Economic Forum convenes in Davos, Switzerland. Over a thousand CEOs, prime ministers, finance ministers, and leading academics gather...to attend meetings and set economic agendas for the year ahead..."What if a small group of these world leaders were to conclude that the principal risk to the earth comes from the actions of the rich countries? And if the world is to survive, those rich countries would have to sign an agreement reducing their impact on the environment. Will they do it?"...

The man who founded UNEP and who wrote parts of the Brundtland Report and who in 1992 will try to get the world's leaders, meeting in Brazil, to sign just such an agreement, savors the questions hanging in the air...

Strong resumes his story. "The group's conclusion is 'no.'" The rich countries won't do it. They won't change. So, in order to save the planet, the group decides: isn't the *only* hope for the planet that the industrialized civilizations collapse. Isn't it our responsibility to bring that about?

"This group of world leaders," he continues, "form a secret society to bring about an economic collapse...These aren't terrorists. They're *world leaders*. They have positioned themselves in the world's commodity and stock markets... [and have] engineered, using their access to stock exchanges and computers and gold supplies, a panic. Then, they prevent the world's stock markets from closing. They jam the gears. They hire mercenaries who hold the rest of the world leaders at Davos as hostages. The markets *can't close*. The rich countries..." And Strong makes a slight motion with his fingers as if he were flicking a cigarette butt out the window.

I sit there spellbound. This is not any storyteller talking. This is Maurice Strong. He knows these world leaders. He is, in fact, co-chairman of the Council of the World Economic Forum. He sits at the fulcrum of power. He is in a position to do it...

When the truth is finally told, Maurice and Hanne Strong fear the world will come to this...same conclusion: the global economy, sapped by credit and debt loads and environmental disasters, will simply come unstuck. And nothing – not even the inspiration of the Baca – can save humankind from itself.

Strong's megalomaniacal daydream speaks for itself. Material from UNCED Geneva headquarters smacks of a *cult of personality* being built around him. The modest soul even let PBS run a broadcast with the rat-gagging title, "Maurice Strong: A Man for All Reasons."

Strong is part of a terrifically dangerous group of elitists who actually believe they are Plato's "philosopher kings." They alone are fit to rule the world. After all, without their guiding light, nothing "can save humankind from itself."

RUSSELL ERROL TRAIN Born June 4, 1920 in Jamestown, Rhode Island.

Education: St. Albans, Washington, D.C.; B.A. Prince-ton, 1941; LL.B. Columbia University Law School, 1948.

Organizational Connections: Conservation Foundation; World Wildlife Fund; African Wildlife Leadership Foundation; International Union for The Conservation of Nature and Natural Resources (IUCN); Council on Environmental Quality; EPA; American Committee for International Wildlife Protection; National Parks and Conservation Association; American Farmland Trust; World Resources Institute; Council on Foreign Relations.

After World War II, Russell Train graduated from Columbia Law School, then went right to work for the government as a congressional tax lawyer. From there he moved to the Treasury Department, and in 1957 Eisenhower appointed him a judge in Tax Court.

As the story is now told, a 1956 African safari so stimulated Train's interest in conservation that in 1961 he founded the African Wildlife Leadership Foundation. In 1965 he resigned from Tax Court and changed vocations to become president of The Conservation Foundation. Four years later Train was appointed Undersecretary of the Interior. In January, 1970, he shifted to Nixon's Environmental Quality Council.

Under Train's presidency the Conservation Foundation began to concern itself with waste disposal, pesticides, and hunger. Earlier, in 1968, Lyndon Johnson had appointed him to the National Water Commission. President-elect Nixon appointed Train the head of a 20-member task force on resources and environment. To no one's surprise, the committee recommended the government spend more money on air and water pollution.

To appease environmentalists annoyed at the appointment of developer Wally Hickel as Secretary of the Interior, Nixon appointed Train Undersecretary. Train's first job was to head an intergovernmental task force to study the proposed Trans-Alaska pipeline. The strict construction regulations decreed by Train's task force helped delay pipeline construction long enough to destroy many independent oil companies.

In January, 1970, Nixon also appointed Train chairman of the new three-man Environmental Quality Council. Although Train was not appointed the first chief of EPA in 1970, he later succeeded William Ruckelshaus at that post. Train is currently chairman of the World Wildlife Fund and the Conservation Foundation.

And finally, there is George Herbert Walker Bush of Yale (CFR), Bill Clinton of Yale (CFR), and Albert Gore, Jr. of Harvard. Mr. Bush, in spite of his protestations, has backed every proposal of his EPA appointee, William Reilly, including the Rio '92 proposals.

Clinton accused Bush of only giving "lip service" to the environment, while asking the most strident environmentalist in the entire Senate to be his 1992 running mate.

Gore has endorsed every aspect of the Kennan, Gorbachev, Tolba and Strong "visions" for international environmentalism.

Our final eco-prophet to make the rank-and-file is Stephan Schmidheiny, a relatively unknown figure in the environmental movement, but extremely significant. The following article entitled, "Ecological Plea from Executives – International Group Urges Action at Rio" from the May 8, 1992 issue of the *New York Times* helps us put a finger on his importance:

> Geneva, 5/7 - Hoping to influence the outcome of next month's Earth Summit...a group of powerful international business leaders... called today for greater environmental awareness from governments & private businesses. The group said business executives had to start addressing environmental issues to survive.
>
> The group, organized by a maverick Swiss billionaire, Stephan Schmidheiny, issued a report today...

Pay special attention to that last bit about Schmidheiny "organizing" the Business Council for Sustainable Development. Even for the *New York Times*, folks who have been lying on cue, extravagantly, elaborately, and professionally for over one hundred years, this was a *very large* lie.

Green Dialectics

In the March 1992 issue of *Eco-Profiteer*, Franklin Sanders explained that the "Guardian of the Planet" and head of the Earth Summit (UNCED), Maurice Strong, had formed the Business Council for Sustainable Development (BCSD). In a classic pincers movement, while the Greenshirts in local eco-groups brought pressure for the Summit from below, this front group would promote Greenism *from above*.

Why on earth would corporations support the very environmental groups which criticize their own environmental record? Dialectics, or, as they say in the South, *"Pleeze don' thro' me in dat briar patch, Bre'r Fox!"* The Insiders' plan to *profit* from the environmental movement, which, in the not-very-memorable words of Senator Al Gore, will "become the primary organizing principle of the post-Cold War era." The environmental movement is about power, politics, and profits.

Giant corporations don't suffer from government environmental regulations, little companies do. Those annoying *entrepreneurs* bring new ideas to market, exploit new reserves of natural resources, and overturn the *status quo* of corporate profits, market share, and Insider control. Practical old John D. Rockefeller put it plainly: "Competition is a sin." From the Insider's viewpoint, the competition must be controlled, co-opted, or eliminated. All the catch phrases — environmentalism, socialism, communism, "sustainable development," government-business partnership – are simply code words for controlling the global economy through one-world fascism.

Business must be cartelized globally into a new *feudal stability.* That's the "sustainable" in "sustainable development." What the new overlords fear most is change — economic or political – which they don't control. Insiders have to *manage* the crisis, manipulate the forces. First and last, the environmental movement is about *control*: control of the world's economy, natural resources, and people.

Instant Schmidheiny

But back to Schmidheiny. How could he have "organized" the Business Council for Sustainable Development, when *Maurice Strong himself did that,* and *Strong appointed* Schmidheiny. We didn't make this up: This comes straight out of the Earth Summit News, July, 1991, No. 2, official publication of the United Nations Conference on Environment and Development (UNCED). Listen:

> The business council for Sustainable Development, a blue-ribbon group of 50 eminent business leaders from all regions of the world, held its first meeting in April in The Hague under the Chairmanship of Stephan Schmidheiny, the Swiss industrialist. In September [1990] Dr. Schmidheiny was appointed by Maurice Strong as his Principal Advisor

for Business and Industry [capitals in the original] with the primary task of promoting a clear understanding of and commitments to environmentally *sustainable development* within the private sector at the highest corporate level. He is also mandated to challenge business to examine its own performance in progressing towards this goal on a global basis.

In the past eight months Dr. Schmidheiny, who expanded his family's construction materials firm into a diversified company with a wide range of manufacturing activities, has devoted most of his time to the Business Council recruiting like-minded [CEOs] and board chairmen to serve with him, ... [and] at the same time he provides guidance to Maurice Strong on initiatives and activities undertaken by business during the preparatory process for the Earth Summit. (*Earth Summit News*, July 1991, page 7, turgid prose and emphasis in the original).

To a jaundiced ear this doesn't exactly make Schmidheiny sound like the "organizer" of the BCSD — more like Maurice Strong's stooge and gopher. But to hear the *New York Times* tell it, Schmidheiny was just lying in bed one night, his conscience tortured by all the world's environmental wickedness, when a light bulb clicked on in his billionaire brain: "Tomorrow morning, I'll run out and get together with the captains of industry and form a group of powerful international business leaders to promote environmental awareness, and we'll issue ecological pleas from executives." In pursuit of this Green Grail, he somehow hooked up with his own Millionaire Merlin, the "Wizard of the Baca," Maurice Strong. Next thing you know, Schmidheiny and his brother captains of industry are issuing pleas to George Bush to attend the Eco-Summit.

Would even the producer of a Grade B movie buy this silly plot? Would this scam even fool the Creature from the Black Lagoon, with his rubber rooster comb and swim fins? Apparently the *New York Times* thought it would fool its readers. Give me a break; this story has more holes than the ozone layer.

The Bashful Billionaire

When we first ran across Schmidheinys name in connection with the BCSD, it rang no bells and a quick research check didn't turn up anything. After his epoch-making "Ecological Plea," we started looking deeper, and turned up — nothing.

Or almost nothing. In the *International Who's Who* was an entry, but for Max, not Stephan, Schmidheiny: "Swiss engineer & industrialist, born 1908, married 1942, 3 sons; president & director of many companies in Switzerland and abroad, formerly National Councillor [equivalent of an American senator] and member Swiss Chamber of Commerce. Former Chairman Brown, Boveri." From 1969 through 1988, the same entry ran virtually unchanged, both in the Swiss *Who's Who* and the *International Who's Who*. Either the Schmidheinys had done nothing memorable for 20 years, or, like many other Insiders, they shy away from too much publicity.

Our research kept on coming up empty-handed, until we ran across the Dim & Bradstreet directory of foreign companies. Why not check through the list of Swiss companies.

Jackpot! Stephan Schmidheiny is listed as "Vorsitzen der" (president and chairman) of Anova AG (management consulting, sales SF5.5 billion, 50,000 employees), Eternit SA Succursale de Payern (1,500 employees, manufacture of concrete items), Landis & Gyr Holding AG (sales SF2.268 billion, 18,600 employees, open-end management investment), Leica International (yes, the cameras; sales 1.135 billion, 11,000 employees, management consulting), and Neuva Holdings (sales SF8 billion, 50,000 employees). He's a very busy billionaire.

But crowning the lot was ABB: ASEA Brown, Boveri, an electrical engineering and manufacturing conglomerate with sales last year of about $28 billion. Formed in 1987, ABB merged the Swedish electrical giant ASEA (owned by the powerful Swedish Wallenberg family) with the Swiss firm Brown Boveri. Schmidheiny is a director, along with Peter Wallenberg of Switzerland. Since Max

Schmidheiny was a Brown Boveri Director, and shared several other business addresses with Stephan, we concluded that Max must be Stephan's father.

ABB: Model for the Future?

An Insider case study all its own, ABB is perhaps the world's largest electrical engineering firm and manufacturer of electric power equipment. Contrary to the *Earth Summit News* report, ABB is largely the creation of president and CEO, Percy Barnevik, a 50-year-old goateed Swede.

Barnevik's philosophy for his multinational corporation may help to explain Herr Doktor Billionaire Schmidheinys close collaboration with His Greenness, Maurice Strong.

First, Barnevik is a strong believer in corporate decentralization, of a sort. ABB has 1,300 legal entities, with 5,000 profit centers in various countries. Barnevik has ruthlessly pared down the bureaucratic fat, using his "30-30-30-10" personnel approach: lay off 30%, transfer 30%, send 30% to separate marketing companies, and keep 10%. The strategy has paid off. ABB doubled operating profit from 1988 to 1990 — from $550 million to $1.1 billion.

Whoops – did we forget to mention that ABB has just a tiny interest in environmental politics? Of 1990 revenues, 10% came from power distribution, 12% from environmental control, 18% from power transmission, and 15% from power plants. Now would any of this 55% of revenues be affected by environmental regulations? Could this self-interest – *O perish the vile suspicion!* – be the basis for Herr Doktor Schmidheiny's Green Goodness?

But it's Barnevik's vision of the multinational corporation of the future that is really fascinating. "What we try to do in ABB is a microcosm of what Europe will eventually do as a whole." He says that "the future will belong to what he calls 'multi-domestic corporations' that combine national nimbleness with international vision and financial clout... 'You optimize globally, you call the shots globally, and *you have no national allegiances.*'" (Quoted in the *New York Times*, 3/2/92, emphasis added).

Significantly for the future, ABB's "lean and mean multi-national" structure is serving as the model for the re-organization of IBM into what IBM Chairman John F. Akers called a "commonwealth of businesses." Is the new ABB the future model for multinationals? Based on Barnevik's own words, these giant corporations will press their trans-national powers and contempt for national states to their outer limits.

Snookered Again by the NYT

The "Ecological Plea From Executives" was just another shabby *New York Times* hoax, like billing Fidel Castro as the "Robin Hood of the Caribbean." Now they're asking us to swallow the "spontaneous" greening of the captains of industry, and "Schmidheiny, the maverick Swiss billionaire environmentalist." It appears, rather, that Schmidheiny is just another spoiled rich kid playing at business and promoting one-world socialism to ease his own guilty conscience and maintain Insider power.

The media and the eco-establishment are also painting a picture of a supposedly *spontaneous* outburst of Corporate Green Consciousness. This, also, is Industrial Strength, Grade A *New York Times* Hogwash. The Corporate Greening is merely a classical pincers movement, the dialectic in action as the Insiders bring "pressure from above" (the greening of the "captains of industry") and pressure from below (the eco-maniacs in the streets).

Conclusion

After an examination of the major environmental groups, the people heading them, and the budgets they control, the power they exert, and the direction they provide, we agree with the assessment of Ken Weiner, Jimmy Carter's Deputy Director of the Council for Environmental Quality as cited above. "The Environmental movement is recognizing its issue is being taken away by the establishment. It has been said war is too important to be left to the generals. Some are wondering if environmental quality is too important to be left to the environmentalists."

With the Clinton appointments of Bruce Babbitt (CFR) to Secretary of Interior, Carol Browner, Gore's former assistant to head the EPA and Gus Speth (CFR) as "environmental coordinator" we see once more how the Establishment maintains its control while the unknowing radicals cheer the developments.

CHAPTER 7

NECESSITIE, THE TYRANT'S PLEA

In Milton's *Paradise Lost*, the first time Satan spies Adam and Eve in the Garden he muses that he is *forced* by circumstances to plot their fall from grace. Milton comments, "So spake the Fiend, and with necessitie, The Tyrant's plea, excus'd his devilish deeds."

Tyrants haven't changed much since Milton's day – or since Adam's. "Necessitie" is still their plea, and the eco-hype daily pumped out in the media is just one more example. The crisis, the emergency, the "necessitie" is needed to justify the "moral equivalent of war," and it's being created in advance of the war. The weapons are familiar from "goodness" crusades of the past: fear-mongering, exaggeration, suppression of dissent, emotionalism, an appeal to self- righteousness, and crude guilt manipulation.

Let me share a quotation with you from the Insiders' favorite pop-intellectual, Bill Moyers. This comes from the November 15, 1989, program of his PBS television series, "The Public Mind."

The basic text of our political system, *The Federalist Papers*, anticipated a government of reflection and choice. Forget it. Fifty years ago, Dale Carnegie wrote a new bible for American politics and called it *How to Win Friends and Influence People*. In it he said, "When dealing with people, we are dealing with creatures of emotions, creatures bristling with prejudice and motivated by pride and vanity." This famous evangelist of persuasion went on to say that the *art of human engineering*, as he called it, requires an ongoing appeal to the emotions. The opinion industry lives by this gospel that it's easier to motivate the heart than the mind, easier to stir up our feelings than our thoughts.

Vanity, love, anxiety, hope – these sell cake mix and toothpaste...and foreign policy, too." [emphasis added.]

Much as we may wish it otherwise, Mr. Moyers is absolutely correct. As we consistently repeat, for most people "perception becomes reality." And for the decade of the nineties, creating perceptions is not just an art form, but a way of life.

Here is one more significant quotation by Mr. Moyers from that same PBS television program: "Symbols and slogans. Slogans and symbols. The monologue of televisual values becomes the conversation of democracy."

As we settle into the nineties and beyond, our task is to sort out the reality and not be seduced by the "symbols," "slogans," and "the art of human engineering."

In the case of the environment, the media fear-mongering knows no limit. Here are just a few recent examples of how even the words are carefully chosen for maximum emotional effect: "Brink of Destruction is Here, Scientists Warn"; "Destruction of our planet's resources"; "Warnings of a nightmare world"; "No serious scientist questions the catastrophe theories"; "Changes in the atmosphere may be irreversible, with consequences second only to nuclear war"; "Breathing: Latest hazard to nation's health"; "Pesticides, toxic chemicals take to the airways"; "Acid rain destroys thousands of inland lakes"; "Earth's chemistry upset as rain forests vanish"; "Some of the smallest nations may be doomed"; "Thinner ozone layer paves way for more cases of skin cancer"; "The sky above: a fragile shield under attack"; "Pollution, 'a ticking time bomb.'" Even the sober *Wall Street Journal* (September 27, 1989.) headlined a book review of two recent eco-Jeremiads with "Kissing Nature Good-bye." Of course, editors write headlines to sell newspapers, but how many of you read this one: "CFCs 'not a threat to the ozone layer'" when 30 leading U.S. environmental scientists disputed the correlation between ozone depletion and the use of CFCs? Or this one: "Greenhouse effect a fraud, Senate told" when an environmental science professor refuted every claim that there is a global warming resulting from man-made emissions of "greenhouse gasses."

One side of the eco-discussion claims that disaster is just around the comer or has already arrived; the other, hardly ever heard or quoted, says there is no scientific basis for these catastrophe prophecies. Doesn't it seem that a fair-minded press, in the interests of ascertaining the truth in public discussions, might report BOTH sides of the story? Sure, and the check is in the mail, too.

In fact, refutations of environmental scare stories are often blacked out by the media. One case in point is the BBC documentary "The Greenhouse Conspiracy." Examining the four major points of global warming, the BBC team inter-viewed first the proponents of the theory, and then the opponents. Opposing scientists with international reputations proved conclusively that this hypothesis based on computer models was not only totally inaccurate but in fact manufactured out of whole cloth.

The media snapped at the opportunity to prevent the opposing view, right? Wrong. PBS turned down "The Green-house Conspiracy" as too controversial. None of the other major networks would air it, either. For a $35 donation you can order "The Greenhouse Conspiracy" from the Competitive Enterprise Institute, 233 Pennsylvania Avenue S.E., Suite 200, Washington, D.C. 20003.

Another refutation came from Icelandic filmmaker Magnus Gudmunson. "Survival in the High North" proves that the Greenpeace war on whaling and fishing in the North Atlantic will bring those economies into a severe strain. Gudmunson also proves that Greenpeace blatantly lied numerous times about data and the results of North Atlantic fishing. Although shown extensively in the Scandinavian counties, "Survival in the High North" has been consistently refused by U.S. networks and cable channels, including PBS.

In every case, the *evidence* is mounting, evidence which not only questions the major environmental disaster hypotheses – global warming, species extinction, resource depletion, acid rain, overpopulation – but totally refutes these scare stories. Utterly undeterred by this evidence, the print and broadcast media *continue* to censor the reputable scientific opponents and sign their litany of lurking environmental Armageddon's.

The threats to the environment, we are told, transcend all other interests: economic, racial, national, ideological, every other consideration pales before the great eco-threat. "Humanity must reintegrate itself into nature and ignore national, religious, and racial boundaries to cooperate in restoring the planet, says a declaration of international scientists and scholars" assembled by the United Nations Educational, Scientific, and Cultural Organization (UNESCO) in Vancouver in September 1989. Remember this when we discuss a bit later our predicted *legal basis* for a worldwide eco-tyranny.

In case you aren't convinced by headlines, there are emotional spurs, too: guilt manipulation, self-hatred, and misanthropy. "The destruction of our planet's resources touches every one of us," writes Tom Wicker in the *Seattle Post-Intelligencer*, (August 23, 1989.) "and each of us is in some way responsible."

Guy Dauncey, a British Green, writes that our "ruthless exploitation of nature," our "commitment to materialism and personal gain" and the West's "disproportionate consumption of the world's resources" have proven to be our undoing. The 20 percent of the world's population in the West are accused of consuming 80 percent of the world's resources.

For those not easily buffaloed by such crude guilt manipulation, the next question might be, "Well, so what?" Would everybody be more comfortable if we left the minerals in the ground, and hovered naked around peat fires like our ancestors? Apparently, the Greenies' answer is YES.

For others, a little guilt - just enough to take the edge off a sleepy conscience but not enough to make you really writhe - will not suffice. They want guilt deep enough for wallowing: "The quest for material wealth has brought humanity to the brink of destruction, a group of international scientists and scholars says," reports the *Canadian Press*. (August 25, 1989.) "We see man as the *destroyer and upsetter* of our whole world," said Digby McLaren, President of the Royal Society of Canada, at a conference sponsored by UNESCO [emphasis added]. It seems that every vegetable, animal, and protozoan has a right to exist on earth – except man.

There's more evidence of green media bias. In its Summer 1992 edition, *The National Anxiety Report* related that a Minneapolis-based PR firm, Pinnacle Worldwide, surveyed environmental reporters, who, by a margin of more than half, said they believe that public opinion plays a bigger role in environmental regulation than *good scientific or technical judgment.* The survey found almost half of the respondents felt that reporters and *editors are not becoming more skeptical about activists' claims.* It gets worse; fully two-thirds of those surveyed did not believe that environmental regulations are strong enough to properly protect the public, i.e., a raging bias in favor of more regulation.

At their plainest, environmentalists sometimes admit their willful dishonesty, indeed, even brag about it. In its October 1989 issue, *Discover* magazine quoted Stephen Schneider, a "pseudo-scientist" well-known for his hysterical predictions of global catastrophe, and this shows how much he values the truth:

We need to get some broad-based support, to capture the public's imagination. That, of course, entails getting loads of media coverage. So we have to offer up scary scenarios, make simplified, dramatic statements, and make little mention of any doubts we may have. This "double ethical bind" we frequently find ourselves in cannot be solved by any formula. Each of us has to decide what the right balance is between being effective and being honest.

Niccolo Machiavelli himself couldn't have said it better.

But folks may not be as gullible as the press believes. The *Polling Report* (June 19, 1989.) reports that "according to a new Gallup Poll, three-fourths of Americans now think of themselves as environmentalists and there are signs the environmental movement may have broadened its base during the last few years...Large majorities say they worry about pollution of rivers, lakes, and reservoirs (72%), contamination of soil and water by toxic wastes (69%), air pollution (63%), and ocean and beach pollution (60%). Majorities also express great concern about the loss of natural habitat for wildlife (58%)...and contamination of soil and water by radioactive wastes from nuclear facilities (54%)."

Sounds like the Greening of America, right? Then at least half of Americans must consider the environment as the greatest problem facing the country, right? Wrong.

"Asked to name the most important problems facing the nation, *4 percent* [emphasis added] now cite environmental issues; 34 percent, various economic problems; 27 percent, the drug crisis; and 10 percent, poverty and homelessness."

In other words, although three-fourths of the people polled consider themselves "environmentalists," only one American in 25 thinks that environmental issues are the most important problem facing the country. The environmental movement is a mile wide and an inch deep. In the 1988 election, virtually everybody wanted to be known as the environmental candidate, but by 1992 the politicians were either denouncing radical environmentalism or clarifying their former stance.

The amazing thing about those statistics, even if highly discounted, is how the American people could possibly be immune to the media's treatment of the subjects in question. Consider these facts. Not once has there appeared on a TV network or major cable system any program critical of the environmentalist pillars, i.e. ozone depletion, global warming, species extinction, resources depletion or population explosion. Not once has any of the countless studies by responsible scientists refuting these theories even received featured treatment in *Time, Newsweek, U.S. News,* or the front page of the major daily.

Not once in all the hoopla surrounding Earth Day 20 were any of the faulty, preposterous, or outright falsehoods of 1970's celebration examined as to their accuracy, twenty years after the pronouncement.

As a result of this media distortion and flim-flam, not once in over 20 years, right up to and including this very day, has a committee of Congress been convened to examine the facts and sort out the distortion. This, in spite of the fact that billions and billions and billions of taxpayers' dollars are being spent in the process.

From Their Own Mouths

It isn't necessary to rely on our word to prove the case for media bias. On October 2, 1991, an article appeared in the *New York Times* (page B1) which laid out exactly how environmentalism had permeated the Hollywood scene. It also offered a welcome opportunity to skewer the green pharisees on their own spit.

An Ecology Gala
(with bird chirps) in Hollywood

Los Angeles, October 1 - The invitations said, "In the spirit of the event, we urge you to carpool." But there wasn't a carpool in sight Monday night as the film and TV stars, studio chiefs, executives, writers, and agents climbed out of stretch limousines, Mercedes's, BMWs, and other gas guzzlers for the biggest celebration ever of Hollywood's commitment to its favorite cause, the environment.

Nearly 700 of the town's elite, including such performers as Robert Redford, who delivered the keynote speech, Barbara Streisand, Sting, Ted Danson, and Jane Fonda, streamed into a glitzy movie set bedecked in recycled paper at Sony (formerly Columbia) studios in Culver City to eat organically grown chicken and farm- raised salmon and pay tribute to some TV shows, movies, and music videos that have effectively used environmental themes. The recorded sounds of birds chirped in the background]...which stirred criticism, private and even public, from some environmental groups.

"Given the crisis we're facing in the environment, given the fact that grassroots organizations are struggling to keep their doors open and just meet a payroll, this gala evening just seems a little too self-absorbed," said Robert Hattoy, the Sierra Club's regional director, who wasn't invited...

The show – replete with music and envelope-opening that resembled the Academy Awards – marked the Environmental Media Association's (EMA) first annual awards program and raised $500,000. The group was set up in 1989 by the pregnant wives of three moguls: Lyn Lear, whose husband is Norman Lear, the producer; Cindy Horn, wife of Alan Horn, co-founder and managing partner of Castle Rock Entertainment, and Susie Field, whose husband, Ted Field, is chairman of Interscope, a group that produces movies, TV shows, and records.

"We realized we didn't know what was safe to eat, whether the air we were breathing was hurting our fetuses and what the water might be doing to the children we might have," said Mrs. Horn [*who didn't mention what abortion was doing to 1.5 million other fetuses this year*]. "Thanks to our husbands, who have access to some of the most influential media people, we decided to put together EMA"

The result has been an organization that, because of its show business ties, seeks to have popular television programs...include in their scripts such environmental messages as the need for recycling and cleaner air...

A number of the stars and executives who showed up at the gala seemed defensive about their way of life.

Mr. Lear, for example, a prominent and outspoken liberal, deplored the "Hollywood-bashing part of the press that tests the sincerity of everyone in this room." Earlier, Mr. Lear acknowledged in an interview, "We're like every other human being. You do what you can. It's very damned hard re-orienting your life. I haven't bought a new car in three years. I asked how can I be an environmentalist and not buy a fuel-efficient car. I'm sorry, I wasn't ready to do it. I bought a Mercedes. It's the same human dichotomy everywhere."

Mr. Danson, a well-known Hollywood environmentalist, said his car was his "Achilles' tendon [sic]." As he walked into the studio, waving and smiling at photographers, he said, "I tried to find a car that went 30 miles a gallon. I'm not Mr. Clean. That's an area I need to work on." And then he told a questioner, "You can't afford the luxury of being too cynical."

Asked about the disparity between the consumption and lavish style here and the need for environmental sacrifices, Tina Brown, *Vanity Fair's* editor, said: "Obviously, there is some of that. Whatever the dichotomy, like it or not, the realities of life are these people in the entertainment industry are the most powerful forces in communicating a message. If they can get into a hit TV show, it sends a message into the psyches of millions of kids. That's a tremendously valid thing."

You can imagine how this left us feeling. When Mr. Sanders read it, he almost slipped a cog:

There I was, starting a fire in the living room stove, wrestling with the same old human dichotomy – should I buy a '75 Volkswagen, or a '76? Will we make it to the end of the month, or starve? – and as I was crumpling up the *New York Times* to start the fire so my family could avoid the old human dichotomy of freezing to death, my eyeballs lit on this article.

Yup, I could really empathize with old outspoken liberal Norman Lear, just a-wrasslin' with those same human dichotomies I was a-wrasslin' with and tryin' to do better. Just like homefolks. We have the same problems around here: If a passenger pigeon flew through the front door, we wouldn't know whether to eat it raw, cook it, or call the Sierra Club. Most of us Tennessee environmental activists have the same dichotomies, except those who had them surgically removed when they were kids.

I could empathize with well-known Hollywood environmentalist Ted Danson, too, even if he doesn't know his Achilles heel from his Achilles tendon, or his – err, his head from his elbow, and can't walk and chew bubblegum at the same time. I'm not Mr. Clean, either. No sirreee! Last time I bought a new car back in 1970, I tried to find one that went 30 miles an *hour*, let alone 30 miles *a gallon*. Probably nuclear physics and anatomy are areas he needs to work on as well - not to mention basic English.

Ahh, well, you do what you can. Enough of this wrestling with human dichotomies. Susan, hand me my fishing pole! I'm headed down to the reactor pond to catch us a mess of nuclear snail darters. Nothing like deep-fried nuclear snail darters to warm you up from the inside out on a cold winter's night – except maybe a baked spotted owl.

Mr. Sanders finally came around when we threw a bucket of cold water on him and promised he wouldn't have to read the *New York Times* for the next seven days.

Conclusion

Nobody goes to war, not even the "moral equivalent of war," when there isn't one. So the drums must beat to the throb of the presses, and the propaganda weapons must be forged on the anvil of "60 Minutes," "Good Morning, America," "Donahue," TV sitcoms and dramas, and the nightly news. When they are finished, they will have forged "Necessitie, the Tyrant's plea."

Footnote:

Now and then a few articles critical of the environmentalist fear-mongers creep into the press. Below is a short list you may find valuable.

* "Acid Rain: the $140 Billion Fraud?," Warren T. Brookes, *Consumer Alert Comments*, November 1990.

* "The Apocalypse Boosters: Raining in Their Hearts," Ronald Bailey, *National Review*, December 3, 1990.

* "The Benefits of Global Warming?," Warren T. Brookes, *New Dimensions*, July 1990.

* "Fact and Fancy on Greenhouse Earth," *Wall Street Journal*, August 30, 1988.

* "Global Warming Forecasts May Be Built on Hot Air," Carolyn Lochhead, *Insight*, April 16, 1990.

* "The Global Warming Panic," Warren T. Brookes, *Forbes*, December 25, 1989.

* "Government is Eroding Our Liberty," Walter Williams, Memphis *Commercial Appeal*, August 16, 1991.

* "Greenhouse Gas," Peter Huber, *Forbes*, October 30, 1989.

* "The Hot Air Inflating the Greenhouse Effect," *Business Week*, June 17, 1991.

* "The Ozone Hole that Didn't Eat the World," Ronald Bailey, *Forbes*, October 30, 1989.

* "Pseudo-Scientific Hot Air," Andrew R. Solow, *New York Times*, December 28, 1988.

While we have scoured the news media for articles of the type listed above, it is not overstatement to point out how few and far between they are in relation to the pro-eco-blitz. For every article or news item calling any of the major Greening agenda to question or task, there are hundreds, if not thousands, promoting same. Television is even worse. I can't think of one program aired on any network which refutes global warming, population explosion, ozone holes, etc., etc. Yet, in their annual 1991-92 catalog of available PBS Videos, The Public Broadcasting Service lists 10 pages of programs, averaging 6 videos per page; each on some unquestioned aspect of what they title Environment/Ecology.

Notoriously and necessarily, wars depend on a steady supply of ready youth. Along with the media, the American educational establishment is rising to the environmental challenge. In the next chapter we'll look at what some teachers call "brainwashing for a good cause."

CHAPTER 8

BRAINWASHING
THE CHILDREN

Give me four years to teach the children and the seed I have sown will never be uprooted.

- V.I. Lenin

For two months in the summer of 1990, a friend of mine played host to a German teenager. My friend, who had studied at a German university in the early 1970s, made this report:

I remember how far Left most German university students were, but especially those studying to be teachers. It took no genius to see that turning these people loose on the German education system would severely radicalize the children.

I was expecting our guest to be fairly well brainwashed, even though he came from a conservative family, by German standards – at least they voted Christian Democrat. Still, he had been indoctrinated in such a way that he showed enormous blind spots that refused to yield even to overwhelming facts.

He recognized the left-of-left bias of most of his teachers, but when it came to the environment, he was almost hopeless. In his hometown, residents are required to sort their garbage for recycling. This was necessary, he told me, especially with paper because our extravagant use of paper meant so-and-so many trees had to be cut down and lost forever.

Here was a case where I thought I had him. I explained to him that there is no virtue whatever in recycling paper, since recycled paper is neither cheaper nor better than first-run, and needs more bleaching than first-run. I pointed out that it was paper companies, among other users, who *plant* over 6,000,000 trees every day in America, and that America has over 20 percent more trees today than 20 years ago.

None of this did any good. He remained unconvinced, because his conviction was at a level of conditioning that reason could not reach. I've noticed that Europe is usually 1-1/2 to 3 years ahead of us on things like this, and I shudder to think how American students are now being brainwashed about environmental issues.

My friend had good reason to "shudder."

Get Them Young

The object of brainwashing is to inculcate an attitude or mindset which, through frequent and unchallenged repetition, becomes a fixed and unquestioned set of beliefs. Brainwashing works best when done by an authority figure in a controlled environment where the indoctrination cannot be questioned or subjected to reasonable scrutiny – like, for example, in grade school. Beliefs cultivated in children become in later life their most unconscious and unchallenged beliefs, and the hardest to change.

Whether Nazi, Stalinist, or Greenie, the long-term goal of brainwashing children is to overcome the opposition by capturing the minds of the next generation. Indoctrination insulates minds, dosing them out in advance to facts and reason. In fact, successful propaganda will cause the victim to deny plain reality whenever it conflicts with indoctrination.

These lessons have not been lost on the environmentalists. Since the facts are not on their side, they prefer propaganda – the earlier, the better. As you would expect, most major environmental groups have children's programs. Many even publish their own children's magazines, but environmental scare stories are often published as truth in many other juvenile magazines, from *Boy's Life to My Weekly Reader*.

In March 1990, a new children's environmental magazine was launched. Called P3 (because Earth is the third planet from the sun), it includes articles about the planet, its environmental problems and how children aged 7-10 can learn to "safeguard" the environment.

Randi Hacker, editor-in-chief and co-publisher says, "We have to teach them a responsible environmental ethic, and we have to start it out while they're young, while they still have all their raw feelings about the earth." The first issue tells children to write politicians to help save elephants and to walk or ride their bicycles instead of riding in an automobile.

"Every action everyone takes makes a difference," says Jackie Kaufman, P3's co-publisher and editor.

Green "Education"

Eco-brainwashing is already a fact in American schools. *The New York Times* for November 21, 1989, reported:

> Educators and environmentalists say that schools across the country are reporting an increase in classroom demand for environmental education...Government officials and other spokesmen, sometimes dressed like magicians or superheroes, go to schools with messages of garbage awareness. *Several teachers describe the campaign as brainwashing for a good cause...*By and large the environmental groups are active and moving into education. [Emphasis added]

> Teachers also walk a delicate path between inspiring students and scaring them...Asked about the need for cleaning up the environment, Elizabeth Smith, a fifth-grader, began, "We have to, or soon our whole life span is going to go," and ended with a sputtering noise and a slicing motion of her hand.

Not all parents are fooled. As the *Wall Street Journal* (June 26, 1990) reported, "Some parents argue that the approach taken by many schools is too simplistic. Younger students aren't shown the drawbacks of strict environmental laws, such as the effect on products' costs or resulting job losses, and are led to become self-righteous advocates of causes they don't fully understand."

Too young to discern phony arguments and cooked facts, children can't spot the brainwashing. But then, they're not supposed to. *Complexity* is death to brainwashing. As that accomplished "educator" Herr Adolf Hitler noted:

All propaganda must be so popular and on such an intellectual level, that even the most stupid of those towards whom it is directed will understand it. Therefore, the intellectual level of the propaganda must be lower the larger the number of people who are to be influenced by it.

Out of the Mouths of Children

Not even all the children are fooled. From an Australian newspaper comes this poignant letter:

As a 16-year-old senior student, I read with sadness and anger a letter in your newspaper written by...geography students...

I feel extremely sad when I read such letters because I know that the majority of my fellow students really do believe that this planet is doomed. And why do they believe it? Because they have been brainwashed. This is why I become angry.

The education system is such (at least in Victoria) that we, as students, only receive one side of the debate on the environment. Not once can I remember ever being presented with the industry sector's viewpoint on this debate.

Even more damaging, however, are [radical environmentalists]. These people are not only damaging, they are dangerous.

They preach images of a world dying before our very eyes in the next 50 years. Because these people are given publicity, they succeed in striking fear into a lot of people's hearts — especially children's.

It is a sad and sorry world in which we live if the children of today believe the world will not survive to see them as the future leaders. A sad world indeed.

Pint-Sized Eco-Comrades

Terrorized by exaggerated or outright false environmental horror stories, children are radicalized at an early age. In New Brighton, Minnesota, sixth-graders reacted to their environmental indoctrination by demanding that the school cafeteria switch to re-usable lunch trays. The school board refused and the children (sixth graders, remember) staged a cafeteria sit-in resulting in a number of suspensions. They appeared at the next school board meeting to persuade the board to do away with disposable trays and buy $145,000 worth of new cafeteria equipment.

In Brandywine, Maryland, three 12-year-olds observed the waters of Tam Wall's Branch had turned muddy. Tracking upstream they found well-drillers dumping slurry into the branch. When the workers refused to stop, the children circulated petitions and prepared to picket. They got their fathers to call county authorities. The county called the owner, who stopped the dumping.

At Ipswich Middle School in Massachusetts a group called Students Against Vandalizing the Earth (SAVE, get it?) complained because their cafeteria trash inventory turned up hundreds of non-recyclable juice containers. They gathered more than 8,000 petition signatures to urge the Massachusetts legislature to subject the containers to the states container deposit law.

In Saginaw, Michigan, high school science students dis-covered "unsafe" levels of coliform bacteria in the Saginaw River. After they published a 24-page tabloid and campaigned door-to-door, the city council put an $85 million bond issue on the ballot to build separate storm water and sewage systems.

To Wisconsin go the dubious laurels of leading the nation in environmental indoctrination. A 1985 Wisconsin law requires public schools from kindergarten through the twelfth grade to integrate ecology into the curriculum. A 1989 law established an Environmental Education Board with $200,000 in grant money to develop environmental education projects. Thousands of schools around the country incorporate Green teaching into every subject from English to Health to Science. In Connecticut, one study even enlists high school students to collect and forward rain samples to test for "acid rain." Environmental "instruction" is also required in Arizona, and late in 1990, the Washington State Board of Education added it to the list of compulsory areas of study.

Nor are the changes agents in the Education Industry slow to pick up the cudgels. By 1977, the Tennessee Education Association's (TEA) Representative Assembly (the governing body) had already passed this resolution:

> The Tennessee Education Association believes that environmental education for the public school systems of Tennessee should be given high priority by the appropriate state agencies of Tennessee. The association also believes that the development of adequate programs in conservation and preservation of resources in Tennessee should include more specific directions in environmental education for the public schools of Tennessee. The Association believes that conservation of energy, development and management of sources of fuel, maintenance of air and water quality, and the development of adequate land use policies to manage soil, forests, and wildlife will be significantly improved by the responsible participation of an informed citizenry.

> The TEA seeks support in fine with the following principles:

> (1) An awareness, understanding, and concern for the environment with its associated problems, and
> (2) The knowledge, skill, motivation, and commitment to work toward solutions to these current and projected problems.

Students who were first exposed to environmental propaganda during the Earth Day 1970 have now grown up to become teachers themselves. These have an activist bent that reaches far beyond watching movies about Bonzo, Great Elk of the North. They want pint-sized activists. Salt Lake City elementary school teacher Barbara A. Lewis talks of developing "an army of kids who are problem-solvers." (*Wall Street Journal*, April 30, 1992, p. Al.) This "nationally-recognized pioneer in environmental education" has written a book, *The Kid's Guide to Social Action*, which has been sold to about 13,000 other teachers. *The Kid's Guide* teaches children how to telephone, write letters, poll the public, organize voter-registration drives, and change laws.

This enthusiasm for creating a corps of kid spies, burning with hot zeal for a cause they don't even understand, reminds us of a passage in George Orwell's 1984. In that dismal view of the police state of the future, the hero, Winston Smith, has been arrested for "thought crime." In the holding cell he sees his brainwashed neighbor, Parsons. "Who denounced you?' said Winston.

"'It was my little daughter,' said Parsons with a sort of doleful pride. 'She listened at the keyhole. Heard what I was saying [in my sleep], and nipped off to the patrols the very next day. Pretty smart for a nipper of seven, eh? I don't bear her any grudge for it. In fact I'm proud of her. It shows I brought her up in the right spirit, anyway.'"

Corporate Brainwashers

In the very same spirit, not only private environmental organizations provide environmental education to schools. Corporations, eager to cash in on the "environmental partnership" among business, government, and non-governmental organizations, also provide their own programs. While the National Audubon Society produces an ecology program which 500,000 elementary students will see this year, Dow Chemical ponied up $95,000 for a pilot program for 7th graders in Michigan. Dow Chemical, AT&T, Exxon, and 3M are developing an environmental training program for about 200 middle-school teachers.

Is it only an accident that all are also members of the National Wildlife Federation's Corporate Conservation Council as well as Maurice Strong's Business Council for Sustainable Development? Or are these green corporate do-gooders simply cashing in on the environmental movement?

Whatever Happened to Bugs Bunny?

Not to be outdone by their fellows in the classrooms, TV moguls are preparing and producing mind-altering messages of their own for the nation's youngsters. Cliff Kincaid reported on one such effort in *Media Monitor* for September 10, 1990:

> A plan by cable broadcaster Ted Turner to air a cartoon show for children this fall called "Captain Planet" is facing opposition from the nuclear power industry and some conservative Christians who think it promotes witchcraft. But Barbara Pyle, V.P. for environmental policy at TBS and executive producer of the show, sees nothing controversial about it. She said, "We've combined environmental issues into action adventure cartoons with comedy."

> According to published reports, Pyle participated in a May conference on environmentalism sponsored by a publication called the *Utne Reader*. She told the gathering that she "met a lot of resistance and was considered to be a real fringe lunatic for many, many years." She also said that, "I feel that I'm here on this planet to work in television, to be the little subversive person in television.

> I've chosen television as my form of activism. I felt that [if] I was to infiltrate anything, I'd do best to infiltrate television. I do have an ax to grind," Pyle said.

> Pyle admitted she made those statements. But she claimed that the right-wing press picked up those statements to discredit environmentalism. She said her statements meant that "television can be used for good. Our goal is to use television to inform people about these issues."

> The show, scheduled to debut this fall in 180 markets, features five superheroes who battle environmental destruction by getting magic rings from "Gaia," described as 'the spirit of the earth.' Together they summon "Captain Planet," who is "earth's greatest champion" and battles the villains. Noted celebrities are behind the voices of the

characters, including Ed Asner as the villain Hoggish Greedly, LeVar Burton as superhero Kwame, and Whoopi Goldberg as Gaia.

Another villain seems to represent American business. He goes by the name Looten Plunder, and is said to be suave and urbane but plunders the planet for profit.

Pyle also suggested it was a coincidence that the show uses a character, Gaia, that is associated with the Wicca religion and witchcraft. Barbara Pyle said that's "news to me." To her, Gaia only represented "love and respect for nature." She said she picked the character of Gaia and that it is supposed to represent a "mother figure" common in many ancient religions – but not Wicca – that represents the love of nature.

Now the debate is over. "Captain Planet" has been on the air for over two years and airs in most markets on Saturday morning. Check out your own TV schedule and tune in or maybe all you will have to do is look over your child's shoulder. Every episode is loaded with a green propaganda so twisted and virulent that even Herr Goebbels would turn away in disgust. It's impossible to describe every nuance and spin, but in this case we don't have to. You can see for yourself.

Not only are the education establishments and TV promoting environmental programs – now the YMCA has created the "Earth Corps." As the *Seattle Post Intelligencer* reported on October 20, 1990:

"We're out to save the planet," said Darrion Erlinger, 15, of Garfield High School. "Somebody has to."

"Said Garfield student Erin Kimura, 14: "We don't want our kids to grow up only seeing flowers in pictures, or having to wear gas masks to go outside."

Erlinger and Kimura were among 250 Earth Corps members who attended workshops on environmental education yesterday at the National Oceanic and Atmospheric Administration [in Seattle]....

Hal Alabastor, NOAA spokesman, said yesterday's workshops launched NOAA's commitment to support the local Earth Corps — the first program of its kind in the country. Developed in Seattle a year ago by Metrocenter YMCA as a way to involve youth in environmental issues,

Earth Corps has since grown from 270 to 2,000 high school students....

Nan Little [director of the YMCA's international programs] said she wants the program to expand not only nationally but internationally. New York, Chicago, Atlanta, and Milwaukee are among the city's planning Earth Corps programs, while people from Brazil, Sri Lanka, the Soviet Union and even Ireland have expressed interest.

Whether on TV, in the classroom, or in youth groups, all betray the same underlying false presuppositions: HUGE, globe-threatening problems menace the environment, and man *can* and *must* do something about them. Goebbels would turn Green with envy.

None of the brainwashers (and certainly none of the brainwashed) ever stop to think how small man is compared to the whole globe. In the words of the late world-renowned climatologist Dr. Iben Browning, "[Climatic] changes are so enormous, so incredibly enormous, that I don't see how anyone could have the egotism to think that he has any influence over it."

The Greenies don't want anyone, least of all your children, to understand environmental changes in perspective or to debate the facts. They just want the schools with your tax dollars to inculcate your children and sow their seeds of Green. If you doubt how successful this program has been, just take the time to stroll into your nearest grade school and ask the principal how things are going on the environmental awareness curricula. You won't believe

CHAPTER 9

THE PEOPLE HATERS

Error may not be eternal, but certain errors are awfully persistent. The one issue almost every environmentalist champions is "overpopulation." It furnishes the glue which holds together the pantheon of environmentalist causes. In the typical words of Paul Ehrlich, "Chief among the underlying causes of our planet's unease is the overgrowth of the human population and its impacts on both ecosystems and human communities. Those impacts are the threads linking all the seemingly unrelated problems...and others besides." (Ehrlich, *The Population Explosion*, New York: Simon and Schuster, 1990. Page 11.)

This same red thread of error perseveres from Aristotle to the French Revolution, Malthus, Charles Darwin, Margaret Sanger, Aldous Huxley, and Paul Ehrlich: the world faces imminent starvation and economic catastrophe as a result of over-population, the major cause of poverty.

Pseudo-Politics: The Revolutionary Model

During the French Revolution, when the arrogance of man proclaimed "All is new in France," a singularly "new" idea appeared: depopulation. Soon after the revolution began, radical Jacobins began to hound the middle class, the *bourgeoisie*, whom they viewed as their inevitable enemies. "The natural consequence of this policy carried out against the mercantile *bourgeoisie* by the attacks on the manufacturing towns of France was of course to create vast unemployment," wrote Nesta Webster in her book *World Revolution*.

Because the Revolution also destroyed the upper classes, the great "luxury" trades were decimated – joiners, potters, tailors, weavers, gilders, bookbinders, embroiderers, and domestic servants were thrown out of work. Vast hordes of unemployed crowded the street. The loss of "luxury" industries and manufacturers dislocated related and dependent industries. Since the entire economy is interdependent, no great class can be eliminated without idling other classes. "Socialists," Webster continued, "are fond of describing luxury workers as parasites; obviously then if one destroys the animal on which the parasite lives *one must destroy the parasite, too. (The Population Explosion*, p. 43) [emphasis added.]

Adding to the unemployment problem was the revolutionary calendar. The Revolution eliminated the numerous religious and state holidays and instituted a ten-day week with only one half-day holiday. Three-and-a-half working days were added to every two weeks, three working months to every year. The lengthened work week meant that fewer and fewer workers were needed for an already reduced work load.

"But toward the end of 1793 it became evident that there was no possibility of absorbing the residuum created...It was then that the *Comité de Salut Public* [Committee of Public Safety], anticipating the Malthusian theory, embarked on its fearful project – the system of depopulation." There were two factions in this project. One wanted to reduce the 25 million population of France by one-third; another wanted to reduce it to one-third - "but a reduction to eight millions, that is to say to one-third, was the figure generally agreed on by the leaders."

Bacchus Babeuf, himself a conspirator against established order and generally in accord with the terrorism of Robespierre, wrote:

"In the eyes of Maximilien Robespierre and his council, depopulation was indispensable because the calculation had been made that the French population was in excess of the resources of the soil and of the requirements of *useful industry*...to be able to live at ease; that hands were too numerous for the execution of all works *of essential utility* – and this is the horrible conclusion, that since the superabundant population could only amount to so much... a portion of *sans-culottes* [revolutionaries] must be sacrificed; that this rubbish could be cleared up to a certain quantity, and that means must be found for doing it." [Emphasis in the original.]

The system of the Terror was thus the answer to the problem of unemployment...If the hecatombs carried out all over France never reached the huge proportions planned by the leaders, it was not for want of what they described as "energy in the art of revolution."...Compared to the results they had hoped to achieve, the mortality was insignificant; compared to the accounts given us by "the conspiracy of history" it was terrific... According to Prudhomme the total number of victims drowned, guillotined, or shot all over France amounted to 300,000, and of this number the nobles sacrificed were an almost negligible quantity, only about 3,000 in all. (*The Population Explosion*, pp. 45, 46.)

Pseudo-Science: The Malthusian Model

English churchman and economist Thomas Robert Malthus (1766-1834) laid the pseudo-scientific groundwork for the modem people-phobia. Malthus's father Daniel was a close friend of Jean Jacques Rousseau, French philosopher and originator of the anti-civilization, "noble savage" theory undergirding much of modern environmentalism: "Go back into the woods and become men!"

In 1798, Malthus published the first version of his *Essay on Population* in which he advanced three theories: first, that population growth had outstripped food production; second, that better living conditions stimulate higher birth rates; and third, that the British population increase was due to a rising birth rate.

All three theories have been proven utterly false. Population growth at that time (1798) had not outstripped food production, and *has not to the present day*. Nor do better living conditions stimulate higher birth rates beyond a certain point. In fact, as living conditions improve, the birth rate usually declines (the so-called "demographic transition"). Not only does this demolish Malthus' contention that population increased geometrically while food production increased arithmetically, but, as we shall see, population growth tends to go *negative* as leisure time increases.

Finally, the British population increase was not due to a rising birth rate (it was actually dropping at the time), but rather to a death rate reduced by the revolution in health care.

Eugenics and Racism

Malthus' theories not only stimulated Charles Darwin's theory of evolution, they also gave rise to the eugenics movement, the study of human hereditary improvement by genetic control. Inherently racist, eugenics attracted more and more followers into the 20th century. Along with "the white man's burden," eugenics enshrined itself into the Anglo-American Establishment and the popular mind as the only "sensible and scientific" course. So weak was the opposition that eugenics was even incorporated, with tragic results, into numerous American state laws providing for the sterilization of "undesirables" and "mental defectives."

The eugenics movement reached its open climax with the Nazis in the Third Reich. After the Nazis' defeat, eugenics should have disappeared as a discredited and unscientific philosophy. However, it merely went underground, camouflaging itself with the *guise* of anti-racism, a cynical lip service to freedom and racial equality. While even today depopulationists remain very sensitive to charges of racism and to the exposure of their eugenic history, their deeds still reveal the same racist trends.

The "white man's burden" with all its racial arrogance may be clearly seen in Lionel Curtis' 1916 work, *The Problem of the Commonwealth*. Curtis was a quintessential member of the British Establishment, one of the most important members of the Round Table and the CFR's British counterpart, The Royal Institute for International Affairs. He wrote, "In [the British Commonwealth] the function of government is reserved to the European minority, for the unanswerable reason that for the present this portion of its citizens is alone capable of the task – civilized states are obliged to assume control of backward communities to protect [sic] them from exploitation by private adventurers from Europe...The task of preparing for freedom the races which cannot as yet govern themselves is the supreme duty of those who can."

Radical feminist and depopulationist Margaret Sanger (1879-1966), founder of Planned Parenthood, transplanted the people-phobia to America from Britain. In London, Sanger's mentor and lover, Havelock Ellis, was the disciple of Francis Galton, Charles Darwin's cousin and the first systematizer and popularizer of eugenics. Sanger's other radical socialist friends, H.G. Wells and George Bernard Shaw, founders of the elitist Fabian Society, were already committed eugenicists, and Sanger fell right into line.

> She was thoroughly convinced that the "inferior races' were in fact "human weeds" and a "menace to civilization.".... She yearned for the end of the Christian "reign of benevolence" that the Eugenic Socialists promised, when the "choking human undergrowth" of "morons and imbeciles" would be "segregated" and "sterilized." Her goal was "to create a race of thoroughbreds" by encouraging "more children from the fit, and less from the unfit." (George Grant, *Grand Illusions: The Legacy of Planned Parenthood.* Brentwood, Tennessee: Wolgemuth and Hyatt, 1988, p. 91.)

Once back in America, Margaret was not above publishing an article by Ernst Rudin, Hitler's director of genetic sterilization and a founder of the Nazi Society for Racial Hygiene: "Eugenic Sterilization: An Urgent Need." In 1932 Margaret outlined her ideas in her "'Plan for Peace,' calling for coercive sterilization, mandatory segregation, and rehabilitative concentration camps for all 'dysgenic stocks.'" (*Grand Illusions*, p. 92.)

The same racism runs through the activities of the depopulationists today, who reserve their special ire and attention for those teeming, spawning brown, yellow, and black millions in the developing nations. They replace the old military colonialism with a new type based on "science." After all, *it is easier to exercise influence than to exert control.* Busy as an infertile worker bee, Margaret's first international efforts were launched in 1952 in India, the very volcano of breeding humanity.

Politics, Not Poverty

How widespread is acceptance of the over-population myth? In 1973, the head of the special Republican Task Force on Population and Earth Resources (who also happened to be the U.S. Ambassador to the United Nations) wrote:

"Population growth and how to restrain it are public concerns that command the attention of national and inter-national leaders....It is quite clear that one of the major challenges of the 1970s...will be to curb the world's fertility."

That man, incidentally, was George Bush. (*The Population Explosion*, p. 195.)

But is population really the culprit behind poverty? More often politics, not population, causes famine. No sophisticated research is needed to discover that the former Soviet Union, once the bread basket of Europe and a grain exporter, must now import grain from the United States, where the government actually pays farmers to idle their fields because caves, silos, warehouses, and storehouses are already overflowing.

Since ancient times the record is clear: increased population is an indicator of prosperity, not poverty. (See the Durants' magnificent history*, Story of Civilization*, Vols. I, II, III.) Yet, like their French Revolutionary forebears, today's prophets of overpopulation presuppose there are too many people for the earth's available resources. Like Malthus, they confuse mathematics with demographics.

Let's define our terms. By "overpopulation" the Greenies usually mean that population exceeds the amount of arable land necessary to sustain life. But if that's a problem, then why is the most densely populated country on Earth, the Netherlands, *a net exporter of foodstuffs*? India and China, two of the hungriest lands in the world, are among the least densely populated countries on the basis of "people per square mile of arable land."

Just how much room is there? "Farmers use less than half of the earth's arable land and only a minute part of the water available for irrigation." (Jacqueline Kasun, *The War Against Population*, San Francisco: Ignatius Press, 1988, p. 34.)

What about *desertification*? Isn't arable land being eaten up by overgrazing Africans? Aren't greedy developers swallowing up prime farm land? Nope. "There was 9 percent more total arable land in 1960 than in 1950 in 87 countries for which data were available and which constituted 73 percent of the world's total land area. And United Nations data show a 6 percent rise in the world's arable, permanent cropland from around 1963 to 1977." (Julian Simon, quoted in Kasun, *op. cit.*, p. 37.)

In mid-1989 the world population was estimated at 5,234,000,000. If you put them all into the state of Arkansas (and our federal government would probably try, given enough school buses), each person would have 277.36 square feet, or an area 16 feet, eight inches square! Most people in America don't have bedrooms that big.

What about resources? Aren't we running out of minerals and oil? Even the alarmist eco-prophet Dr. Barry Commoner admits that is no threat: "That argument [for a no-growth, steady-state society] is based on the misconception that the earth is a closed system with finite resources. It's just not true. Yes, mineral resources are finite; but with enough energy available they can be recycled and re-used indefinitely. And the energy needed is available." (*Mother Earth News*, March/April 1990.)

But recycling is not yet necessary.

With regard to fertilizer, [Oxford demographer Colin] Clark has pointed out that the world supply of the basic ingredients, potash and sulfates, is adequate for severed centimes, while the third major ingredient, nitrogen, is freely available in the atmosphere, though requiring energy for extraction. Since the world's coal supply is adequate for some 2,000 years, this should pose no great problem.

There is very little probability of running out of anything essential to the industrial process at any time in the foreseeable future. (Kasun, *op. cit.*, p. 36, 39.)

The Myth of Mass Starvation

But aren't people *starving to death* all over the world? Not at all. Only about 2 percent of the world's population suffers from serious hunger, and in the past 30 years Lesser Developed Countries (LDC) life expectancies have risen by more than a third while LDC death rates for one-to-four- year-olds have dropped nearly half. Again quoting Kasun:

In the first place, world food production has increased considerably faster than population in recent decades. The increase in per capita food output between 1950 and 1977 amounted to either 28 percent or 37 percent, depending on whether UN or U.S. Department of Agriculture figures are used...More recent UN and U.S. Department of Agriculture data show that world food output has continued to match or outstrip population growth in the years since 1977. Some of the most dramatic increases have occurred in the poorest countries, those designated for "triage" by the apostles of doom. For example, rice and wheat production in India in 1983 was almost 3.5 times as great as in 1950, considerably more than twice the percentage increase in the population of India in the same period. (Kasun, *op. cit.*, p. 33.)

Doesn't population growth inevitably mean poverty? No. Every new mouth also comes with a pair of hands: more consumers, but more producers as well. Population density is actually a spur to the wise use of resources. Who would argue that vast, empty Australia is as intensively land-managed as densely-populated Holland? In the past decades, the West is seeing a cleaner environment for much the same reason: in free market economies, the scarcer a commodity, the more carefully it will be conserved. As eco-debunker Dr. Petr Beckmann has noted, "It is no longer true that the air is polluted in America." (*Moneychanger*, April 1990.)

How much population can the earth carry? Demographer Colin Clark of Oxford reckons that an American-type diet could be provided for 35.1 billion people (seven times the present population). On a Japanese diet, the earth could feed *22 times* the present population. (Kasun, *op. cit.*, p. 35.)

Roger Revelle, former director of the Harvard Center for Population Studies, estimated that world agricultural resources are capable of providing an adequate diet (2,500 kilocalories per day), as well as fiber, rubber, tobacco, and beverages, for 40 billion people, or eight times the present number. This, he thought, would require the use of less than one-fourth – compared with one-ninth today – of the earth's ice-free land area. (Kasun, *op. cit.,* p. 35.)

The most recent example of tying population growth to starvation can be found in Somalia. As the media showed hours of heart-wrenching film of starving children nothing was ever reported about the fact that this beleaguered country had only three years earlier been a net exporter of food stuffs. The implied reason for all the agony was "population."

The Myth of Reliable Statistics

Remember that gloomy estimates of smothering population growth are just that: estimates, educated guesses. These estimates are based on extrapolations of (1) guesses about population size in ancient times, and (2) assumptions of a steady rate of growth.

Clearly no hard population data exists for ancient times. Yet we find both Aldous Huxley (*Brave New World Revisited*, 1958, p. 7.) and Paul Ehrlich setting world population at 250 million in A.D. 1. Never loathe to hazard a guess, the eco-seer Ehrlich goes a step further: he estimates human population at 5 million at the end of the last Ice Age, 8000 B.C.! (*The Population Explosion*, p. 52.)

With guess work, all entries are equal. Baron Montesquieu (1689-1755) was a French philosopher and political scientist much admired by the American Founding Fathers. In his *Spirit of the Law* (1748) he estimated, building on the work of ancient historians Appian and Diodorus Siculus, that in Caesar's day Gaul alone had a population of *two hundred million*. (Claude Fleury, *The Manners of the Ancient Israelites*, 1681; English translation by A. Clarke, London: W. Baynes, 1805; pp. 51-60.) If that is the case, then modern population levels could represent severe *reductions* from ancient levels.

But even modern population statistics are estimates at best. After 200 years of decennial head-counting, over 30 percent of those polled refused to answer the 1990 United States census. Even Paul Ehrlich, the high priest of depopulation, admits that population estimates in Kenya, for example, vary by 40 percent. When local Heads thought the census was for taxation, they said there were about 30 [sic] people in their area. When told the census was to determine if they met the 35,000 population eligibility for a new hospital, the Heads agreed, yes, there were at least 35,000 people there. (Ehrlich, *The Population Explosion*, p. 300, Footnote 18.)

The population bomb recently fizzled in Nigeria, too. In May the World Health Organization issued yet another warning about the danger of population growth, worrying that the number of people on the globe is 'likely to double from 5.4 billion today to 10 billion by 2050, before leveling off around 11.5 billion after the year 2150." But the most recent census in Nigeria, allegedly the world's tenth most populous country, calls into question the accuracy of today's population alarmists. The Population Reference Bureau estimated Nigeria's mid-1991 population at 122.5 million. The December 1990 edition of the UN Population Fund journal reported the 1990 count at 117 million. In June, 1989 the Planned Parenthood Federation of Nigeria said the 1989 population was "about 112 million and could reach 165 million by 2000 and 200 million by 2015." In their 1990 puffball jeremiad, *The Population Explosion*, population alarmists

Paul and Anne Ehrlich claimed "Nigeria's population, 115 million in 1989, is projected to reach 160 million in 2000...and over 530 million in 2050..." Similar numbers emerged from calculators at the Population Crisis Committee, The Population Council, Zero Population Growth, the World Bank, the UN, and the Agency for International Development.

Then, on March 20th, Nigeria released its November 1991 census total: 88.5 million! Those Nigerians are pretty swift. Maybe they move around so fast the people-haters counted 'em twice? (*Wall Street Journal*, May 12, 1992.)

Or consider Nicaragua. The 1987 *World Almanac* estimates Nicaragua's 1985 population at 2,232,000. The 1988 *World Almanac* reckons 1986 population at 3,342,000, a modest 49.7 percent increase and a mighty testimonial to the fertility of socialism. Apparently the fertility spasm didn't last long, since the 1990 *World Almanac* estimates mid-1989 population at 3,500,000, with an average annual rate of increase of 3.5 percent. Variations such as these render all population "estimates" suspect.

The Myth of Steady Growth

The assumption of a steady, geometric rate of population growth is also shaky. Plagues periodically ravage the globe. Beginning in 1345, for hundreds of years the Black Death ravaged Europe and in some areas claimed as much as 90 percent of the population (In *The Population Explosion* pseudo-scientist Ehrlich admits a 25 percent loss, p. 54). These and other well-attested plagues can only mean that population has never been on a steady growth curve.

One can only guess how AIDS, with a 100 percent mortality rate and 20 million cases projected for 2000 A.D., will affect that growth rate. In an interview shortly before his death, internationally renowned climatologist Dr. Iben Browning noted that about every 400 years some plague roughly *halves* human population worldwide. He estimates that by 2040 *half* the world's population will have died from AIDS.

Indeed, the modem depopulationists assume that the growth rate is increasing in the face of the facts to the contrary. Fertility rates in Asia, Latin America, and especially Africa, now appear to be slowing. Moreover, the so-called "demographic transition" has occurred in every developed nation: as living conditions improve, birth rates decline sharply, in some cases to negative levels. Even Paul Ehrlich admits that the populations in Denmark, Austria, Italy, Germany, and Hungary are actually *shrinking*.

The "demographic transition" hits hardest when society develops a leisure class. Self-imposed birth control by the upper class has repeatedly occurred, causing historian Will Durant to speculate that this phenomenon contributed to the decline of both Athens and Rome.

"Fertility in the United States has been steadily declining for two centuries. And it has been below replacement level since 1972. In Western Europe, the figures are even more frightening: the Netherlands saw its fertility rate plunge 53% in just 20 years. The French rate has dropped 32% in just 11 years. Only Finland has been able to avoid the suicidal bent of the rest of the continent, prompting France's [former] Prime Minister Jacques Chirac to exclaim, 'Europe is vanishing...soon our countries will be empty.' In the Third World regions of Asia, Africa, and Latin America, fertility rates are now declining almost as rapidly. As a result, the worldwide birth rate is now falling faster than the mortality rate for the first time in recorded history. And the trend appears to be accelerating." (Grant, *op. cit.*, p. 35.)

The *Seattle Times/Post Intelligencer* of March 31, 1991, reports that "a new specter is haunting Europe: youth deficits." Demographers are warning that by the year 2000, twenty-four countries in Europe, Asia, North America and Australia will see a relative drop in their 15 to 24 population group, "a segment of the population critical for labor-force replenishment and social stability." The results will be labor shortages, graying populations trying to finance pension and medical expenses through a shrinking labor-force base, new immigration pressures, and declining economic growth.

"Even the CIA is concerned. 'Youth deficits are unique in modem history,' the agency noted."

In Japan, especially, concern about population replacement has led the government to call for "more children." The undeniable, unavoidable bottom fine for anyone willing to examine the facts is:

There is no population explosion.

The Depopulation Establishment

The Cassandras of overpopulation have built a powerful lobbying industry: Zero Population Growth, National Abortion Rights Action League, The Population Council, Population Crisis Committee, Population Institute, the United Nations Fund for Population Activities, and of course, the Big Mamma – or Big Un-mamma – of them all, Planned Parenthood Federation.

Where does the money come from? In the early 1920s funding was provided in the U.S. by the Rockefeller, Ford, Carnegie, and other family foundations. (Grant, *op. cit.*, p. 90.) Foundations and corporations still provide huge amounts for depopulation groups, but most of the millions flow from the U.S. Treasury and the United Nations.

How big are the bucks? In 1989 Planned Parenthood, with branches, offices, and tentacles all over the known world, had a budget of *$299,000,000*! The Population Council, which funds research worldwide, showed a balance sheet in 1989 with assets of $89,924,283, which included $38,774,521 in the John D. Rockefeller III Memorial Fund alone. Yet the numbers here are small potatoes to what is currently being proposed by governments and international agencies, all in the name of "population control."

The Tactics of Terror

If by now you're wondering how the population control myth could gain such a vast following, consider this example of what was being served up to our kids over 15 years ago:

> It was a traveling exhibit for schoolchildren. Titled "Population: The Problem Is Us," it toured the country at government expense in the mid-1970s. It consisted of a set of illustrated panels with an accompanying script that stated:
>
> "[T]here are too many people in the world. We are running out of space. We are running out of energy. We are running out of food. And although too few people seem to realize it, we are running out of time."
>
> It warned that, "driven by starvation, people have been known to eat dogs, cats, bird droppings, and even their own children," and it featured a picture of a dead rat on a dinner plate as an example of future "food sources." Overpopulation, it threatened, would lead not only to starvation and cannibalism, but to civil violence and nuclear war.
>
> The exhibit was created at the Smithsonian Institution, the national museum of the U.S. government, using federal funds... (Kasun, *op. cit.,* p. 21.)

Eating rats? Bird droppings? Our own children? No wonder the environmentalists are so worried about overpopulation. Today, overpopulation propaganda is so pervasive, so unchallenged, that even to question it is equal to admitting membership in the Flat Earth Society.

Examining the hierarchy of the people-phobes, no one stands higher than the high priest Paul Ehrlich. This mainstay of the talk show circuit and "Tonight Show" regular takes everything to its illogical extreme – and beyond. Ehrlich eliminates the need for a *reductio ad absurdum* of their arguments; he is the *reductio ad absurdum.*

With typical environmentalist gall, this "expert" is *not* a demographer at all, but a specialist in – *butterflies*. In 1968, when Ehrlich published his first hysterical bombast, *The Population Bomb*, the peak in the U.S. birth rate had already been passed for *ten years*. By the time he published his third edition in 1978, the U.S. birth rate had dropped through the replacement rate (reached zero population growth and gone negative) five years before.

But facts, no matter how they may contradict his thesis, don't bother Paul Ehrlich one bit. *The Population Bomb* opens with this whopper: "The battle to feed humanity is over. In the 1970s and 1980s hundreds of millions of people will starve to death in spite of any crash programs embarked upon now." Nonetheless, 22 years later, humanity, now 5.3 billion strong, keeps on munching away. Ehrlich is undeterred. From the lofty heights of the ivory depopulation tower he continues to ignore the facts and predict overhanging, momentary disaster in his latest crop of horror stories, The Population Explosion.

All the myths and tactics of the depopulation establishment meet and in Ehrlich. Over and over he warns that "civilization [or life itself] as we know it is about to cease." Is he a bar, or just completely ignorant of the facts?

Ehrlich picks his statistics with a masterful deceit, wringing maximum hysteria out of every twisted fact. In *The Population Bomb*, he projects that at then-current rates of population doubling, in 900 – yes, nine hundred – years there would be sixty million billion (i.e., a quadrillion) people on earth, (p. 4.) Now this is a man with an eye to the future!

Four pages later we find out why he concentrates on doubling rather than *growth rates*: the growth rates are minuscule. We back-figured the yearly rates of increase, and they won't exactly turn your hair gray: U.S.A., 1 percent; Austria, 0.4 percent; Denmark, 0.8 percent; Norway, 0.9 percent; UK, 0.5 percent; Poland, 0.9 percent;

Russia, 1 percent; Italy, 0.8 percent; Spain, 1 percent; Japan, 1.12 percent.

Twenty years later, Ehrlich tells us (p. 210.) that at a 3.3 percent growth rate the doubling time for Kenya is "a little over 20 years," when in fact – we are picky – it is 23 *years*. Similar generous rounding outrages mathematics throughout the book. He tells us (p. 208.) that India's food situation was deteriorating in 1965, while in fact from 1950 to 1983, India's food production increased 3.5 times, *twice* the population increase in the same period. (Kasun, *op. cit.*, p. 35.)

Doktor Ehrlich's major expertise (assuming he really does know something about butterflies) is the *politics of envy*. He incites class hatred with remarks like the following: "The rich played a major role in putting the poor in their present dilemma." The rich, of course, include those greedy millions in America who are snorting up all the earth's resources. The U.S. is the "most niggardly" in foreign aid – again twisting statistics – because we give only 0.2 percent of our GNP, a mere $10 billion, and only $197.9 million to "population assistance." (pp. 218-219.) He continues:

Rich kids are a much greater threat to our future than poor kids, especially when the rich kids are raised to think the highest human calling is to make more money and spend it on gadgets. Our society must evolve to the point where it would be disgraceful for one's daughter to marry a real estate developer who has turned a piece of Arizona desert into a subdivision with an artificial lake, helping to increase southwestern water deficits... (p. 231.)

On Ehrlich's list of Depopulationist Good Works are eating more vegetables and less beef, wearing sweaters and keeping your thermostat down, taking a Sunday bike ride, using doth diapers, etc. (p. 228.)

We emphasize that people who care so much for children that they want to have more than two can accomplish that through adoption or being foster parents – unless what they really care about is their own egos rather than what will happen to their children's world, (p. 229.)

Come on, folks! How can you just sit there eating while there maybe somebody, somewhere, starving to death? The purpose of all this is to make you *feel guilty*. *People with guilty consciences can be controlled – people who respect themselves, know their own innocence and responsibilities, and make their own value judgments, can't.*

The Payoff

Like most of his fellow eco-maniacs, Doktor Ehrlich's favorite solution is coercion. All of his substantive solutions require the use of government force, regardless of his lip service to the contrary. While lamenting (briefly) the well- documented coercion in the infamous Red Chinese population program, (*Population Explosion*, pp. 205-210.) which includes forced sterilizations and the arrest of late- term pregnant women for forced abortions, he can't resist admitting that, well, at least it works.

Ehrlich may have mellowed some since his *Population Bomb* days when he wrote, "We should have sent doctors to aid in the [Indian] program [of forced sterilization] by setting up centers for training paramedical personnel to do vasectomies. Coercion? Perhaps, but coercion in a good cause." (p. 151.)

Today he still cries, "We must have planning!" If our own government won't or can't plan properly, then surely a world government can. Too strong? That's not what he really means? What else could he mean when he says:

Worldwide cooperation will be required to address effectively the consumption and technology elements of the human environmental impact...Successful international regulation has historically been achieved by bringing it in through the back door – by creating agencies to regulate in areas where national government had no jurisdiction, such as the Law of the Sea...

Unwillingness to surrender national sovereignty has always been the main stumbling block to establishing a world government...A World Court also exists, but it too has no power to enforce its decisions...In time, a tradition of observing World Court decisions and international regulatory sanctions could be built into a true government system worldwide.... (pp. 223-224.)

Ehrlich drones on and on about a "fair" distribution of resources and the need for a "transformation" of society. Although we are presently being overwhelmed with evidence that socialism has been a complete failure for the past 70 years, Ehrlich still wants socialism. And like all socialists, he isn't above coercion to get what he wants: "Needless to say, doing [the alternative] would require a transformation of society. The cost would include giving up many things that we now consider to be essential freedoms." (Ibid., p. 181.)

Finally, this prevaricating people-hater is not satisfied with zero population growth. He has upped the ante since 1968: "population *shrinkage* below today's size eventually will be necessary." (p. 238.) Some of you will have to go. The question everyone must ask is, "Who decides?" Obviously, Herr Doktor Ehrlich and his colleagues think that job should be left to them.

Why?

This dismal and discouraging exercise could have been expanded far beyond Ehrlich's ravings. We could have reported the thousands of abortions performed daily by Planned Parenthood, the Orwellian pseudo-science of The Population Council, the nightmare of forced sterilizations and abortions in India and China, or the depopulation manifestoes that issue daily from thousands of self-appointed mother-monitors around the world.

There is not only a political and pseudo-scientific model for the depopulation myth, but also a dark spiritual model. Their moralistic posturing is as tinny as it is ridiculous. The population control they envision is not the unselfishness they tout, but rather the ultimate selfishness. The people- haters purchase smug comfort, convenience, and illusory safety at the price of the fives of the despised never-to-be-born. It is covert human sacrifice.

This gratuitous hatred of humanity is deeply rooted in the environmentalist idea that man is the most despised of all creatures and must not multiply and subdue the earth. In the human faces around them the depopulationists perceive no love, no worth, no dignity, no interest, and no common ground. Rather, every countenance reveals an annoyance, a nuisance, a threat, a hated competitor, what the Nazis contemptuously termed a *nutzloser Fresser* – a useless eater. Man is not the crown of creation, but a "cancer." The sad truth is, the depopulationists hate man because they hate themselves; they hate themselves because they hate the God who made them.

CHAPTER 10

MORE ECO-MYTHS
EXAMINED

In the last chapter we saw that the myth of overpopulation is the basis for most of the scare stories promoted by environmentalists. Presently there are also three other major Green terror stories: global warming, the hole in the ozone layer, and acid rain. Hang on while we de-bunk some bunk.

Global Warning: This Way to the Egress

By now almost everyone has heard about the "Greenhouse Effect": The earth's atmosphere is almost transparent to ultraviolet radiation, but almost opaque to infrared (heat) coming back from the earth. Carbon dioxide and certain other gasses in the atmosphere absorb and re-radiate most of the infrared back toward the earth. This is similar (but not identical) to the effect of a glass window pane in a greenhouse.

As usual, the Greenies have found a monstrous footing upon the tiniest and most ambiguous facts. The entire global warming terror story has been built on an observed increase in the so-called greenhouse gases and this simple natural phenomenon, the greenhouse effect. According to their theory, global temperatures will rise so high that hotter, drier weather will curtail food production, polar ice-caps will melt, coastal lands will be inundated, and we will all pant to death on the beach at Topeka, Kansas.

On the alarmists' side are a small minority of meteorologists who insist the earth is getting warmer, the greenhouse effect is closing in, and global warming is an imminent catastrophe. On the other side, doubting and disbelieving, are the majority of meteorologists – and the facts.

There are signs that the reputable scientific community is distancing itself from the Greenhouse journalistic terrorists. At the annual congress of the Australian and New Zealand Association for the Advancement of Science in February 1990, a number of speakers pointed out the danger of alarmist tactics and scenarios. Here are some of the problems with global warming theories:

** Most are based on computer model simulations. Their predictions are no better than the data fed into them – garbage in, garbage out. Since all of the complex factors of climate (from sunspots to seismic activity) and their inter-play are not yet fully known or understood, these computer simulations are inevitably limited at best, useless at worst. In fact, using long-past data, the computer models fail miserably to predict actual results.

** The earth's climate has undergone huge variations in the past, long before the industrial age. How can man-made factors be separated out from natural factors or trends? Normal cyclical changes, such as the hot, dry weather the El Niño current brings up the California coast, cause short term panics.

** Natural factors (volcanoes, natural methane sources, seasonal variations, etc.) are orders of magnitude greater than man-made factors, and include negative feedback loops which tend to maintain temperature stability.

** The heat-exchange effects of the earth's ocean surfaces are not completely understood, but have a crucial effect on climate in complex interaction with heat, water vapor, and clouds in the atmosphere. Natural cycles tend to be self-regulating. If global temperatures rise, then ocean evaporation rises as well, cooling off the atmosphere.

** Volcanoes inject into the air huge amounts of dust which can cause further cooling. Volcanic activity seems to be on the upswing while sun cooling due in the next century may significantly cool the earth.

** Some studies show that polar ice caps are growing, not shrinking.

** Human activity could not possibly count for more than half the increase in carbon dioxide. Where is the rest coming from?

** The National Oceanic and Atmospheric Agency has concluded that rising sea levels would mean a wetter world which would increase food production, enhance forest growth, and enlarge water supplies.

Global temperature has been constant for the last 150 years. In fact, according to renowned climatologist Dr. Iben Browning, we may be entering a spell of slightly cooler weather. Put up your helmet, Chicken Little – we've been had again.

Here's the real danger of global warming. Disaster warnings are printed on the front page because fear sells newspapers, but the retractions and rebuttals are buried between the sow-belly quotes and the classifieds. In spite of the evidence that they are untrustworthy, half-baked computer models are still being used on the basis that some prediction is better than none at all – even if its probability of accuracy is less than 30 percent. Shaky doomsday forecasts based on unreliable, incomplete computer models are becoming the basis for multi-billion dollar national policies.

In legislatures around the world, the Greenhouse Hot Gas Effect has preceded the Greenhouse Effect. Numerous treaties have already been signed to combat the so-called Greenhouse Effect. Most of these aim at slowing the growth of carbon dioxide emissions. All will cost billions of dollars and millions of jobs – needlessly. In fact, these treaties are based on theories and computer models as airy as the Emperor's new clothes. Government policy is being driven by emotional waves and storms generated in the media by irresponsible pseudo-scientists, rather than by sound scientific advice.

The result is ridiculous. "Assuming...that something can realistically be done about the man-made sources, there remain volcanoes, termites, ruminating animals, and other natural sources. Ruminators belch methane, and termites carry a bacterium in their guts which decomposes 90 percent of their food into carbon dioxide. The grand total from the termites alone comes to some 50 billion tons of carbon dioxide, or 10 times the present worldwide production by fossil fuel burning. This may be hard to believe, but it's hard to argue with the facts." (*Science,* 5 November '82: "Termites – a potentially large source of carbon dioxide and other gases")

"It is a problem that awaits resolute action by the not-yet-established CATF (Citizens Against Termite Flatulence)." (Dr. Petr Beckmann in *Access to Energy,* August '88.)

Finally, on the subject of global temperature changes, allow me to quote from a bona fide eco-authority, whose speech before the Swarthmore College student body April 19, 1970, was reprinted in the paperback book *Earth Day –The Beginning.* Rushed into print in May 1970, following the first Earth Day celebration, this Bantam Book paperback was distributed to millions as "A Guide For Survival." With an Introduction by Earth Day National Coordinator Denis Hayes, it compelled some 50 contributors all of whom were giving speeches or writing papers for the fateful Day. Far and away the most lengthy essay and the most prominently featured, was the Swarthmore speech of Kenneth E.F. Watt. Dr. Watt is, according to the book, "an ecologist and professor of zoology at the University of California, Davis. Hear him now as he warns his undergraduate listening audience to the dangers awaiting them should the air pollution continue":

If present trends continue, the world will be about four degrees colder for the global mean temperature in 1990, but eleven degrees colder in the year 2000. This is about twice what it would take to put us into an ice age. The most reasonable explanation one can make of all the available evidence right up to the moment is that the cause is the constantly increasing mass of smog-produced clouds all over the world.

"Warming" or "cooling," it really doesn't matter as long as you can create a crisis and people have short memories.

"The Ozone Hole That Didn't Eat the World"

"'It's terrifying,' one overwrought government scientist told the *New York Times* recently. 'If these ozone holes keep growing like this, they'll eventually eat the world.'" (*Forbes*, October 30, 1989, p. 224.)

In the few minutes left to us before the ozone hole eats the world, it is helpful to remember some ozone frauds of the past thirty years. Chlorofluorocarbons (CFCs) are only the latest victim of ozone-gassing. We have been told the ozone layer could be destroyed by:

** Testing of the Supersonic Transport (SST), banned in 1971 because of supposed effects of exhausting water vapor, nitrogen oxide, or chlorine;

** Nuclear devices exploding in the atmosphere and spreading nitrogen oxide;

** Increased nitrogen oxide production by nitrogen fertilizers, animal wastes, combustion-produced nitrogen oxide, expanded growth of legumes (bacteria in their root nodules fix nitrogen), infection of non-leguminous plants with nitrogen-fixing bacteria, or by green mulching;

** Release of chlorocarbons and chlorofluorocarbons;

** Use of bromine-containing compounds as soil fumigants;

** Re-entry of the space shuttle producing nitrogen oxide;

** Release of carbon dioxide and CFCs, cooling the stratosphere and shifting the concentration of ozone. This would cause it to thicken, rather than thin. (Environmentalists won't talk about this one anymore, because it means that the so-called Greenhouse Effect would cancel out the Ozone Depletion threat!)

Hysterical environmentalists are now screaming that the ozone layer is being destroyed by the release of CFCs, which allegedly produce free chlorine when they are broken down by sunlight in the upper reaches of the atmosphere. The chlorine, in turn, attacks the ozone, thinning out the ozone layer at the South Pole until it results in a gigantic hole. Or at least that's the theory advanced in 1974 by F. Sherwood Rowland and M. Molina, two chemists from the University of California. Conveniently enough, in 1985 British researcher Robert Watson "discovered" a hole in the ozone layer over Hailey Bay, Antarctica.

The only problem was that the hole, a seasonal phenomenon caused by the circulation patterns of southern winds and increased sunlight with changing seasons, had already been discovered by the dean of ozone researchers, Dr. Gordon Dobson, *in* 1956. Mention this little-known piece of scientific trivia to the Ozone Holers, and they will turn Green (on the outside, red on the inside) and admit that's true, but insist that the levels now are below the levels in Dobson's time.

Ozone Holers also won't bother to tell you that the Antarctic volcano Mt. Erebus, which has been erupting since 1982, contributes about 1,000 tons of chlorine gases into the atmosphere *each day*, or about half the volume supposedly produced by CFCs. In fact, volcanoes spew 36 million tons of chlorine gases into the atmosphere every year, versus a puny 750,000 tons for CFCs.

The "problem" of the ozone hole keeps presenting new challenges to the fear mongers. By the summer of 1992 and just in time for the Rio Conference, the darn "hole" ups and disappears. But undaunted, the conferees in Brazil, while admitting that the "hole" had temporarily closed, warned that "next time" it will come back with a vengeance.

This sort of hogwash may be a lot of things, but science it is not. The closest thing I can find which duplicates this type of reasoning is the screenplay in a Class B western movie. Yet, billions of your tax dollars and whole industries are being dismantled and created because of "ozone depletion."

Acid Rain: Propaganda Gone Sour

According to the environmentalists, burning fossil fuel causes acid rain. Nitrogen and sulfurous oxides become nitric and sulfuric acids which ruin the forests when they are washed out of the atmosphere as acid rain. The problem with the Greenies' theory is, it's not that simple. Some lakes go acid, while others go alkaline, with no discernible cause.

Where large areas of forest damage had been ascribed to acid rain in West Germany, researchers found that in most cases the damage was caused by a microbe that had nothing to do with acid rain. Environmentalists also like to claim to the unsuspecting that the rain is as acidic as battery acid. This bit of nonsense is carried to its extreme in such Saturday morning cartoon shows as "Captain Planet." Episode after episode give the children viewing the program a vision of "acid rain" that decomposes human flesh and disfigures the body quite like battery acid. Like I said above, if you doubt the validity of these charges, tune in for yourself.

In 1980, the U.S. Congress commissioned the ten-year, $600 million National Acid Precipitation Assessment Project (NAPAP). Released in 1990, that report was aimed at acid rain, but confirms that only two percent of U.S. lakes are actually acidic, and that nearly 70 percent of those were acidic in pre-industrial times.

According to Dr. Petr Beckmann of *Access to Energy*, "lakes that did turn acid [sic] failed to take any notice of coal burning at all. Coal burning has only recently exceeded the levels of the 1950s or so, but in the 1950s the acidity of the lakes was perfectly constant." (*Moneychanger*, April 1990.)

Unfortunately for the Greenies, the NAPAP shows that the major reason for acidification of waterways is *reforestation*! The Adirondack lakes are apparently *returning* to their normal acidity.

Worst of all, it is clear-cutting of forests and slash-and-bum clearing *that best reduces acidity*! What's a Greenie to do? In the face of these facts, it's fairly hard to justify the $140 million dollar acid rain program Congress voted to throw at the "problem."

Unquestionably, there is massive pollution here – the pollution of the plain scientific truth by distortions, data- twisting, half-truths, and outright lies. The polluters are the power-hungry, ambitious, pseudo-scientists, and journalistic terrorists of the environmental movement.

Chapter 11

A Field Guide
To Greendom
(Eco-Organizations)

Through clever and constant application of propaganda, people can be made to see paradise as hell, and also the other way round, to consider the most wretched sort of life as paradise.

- *Mein Kampf* (1925), Adolf Hitler

As Herr Hitler noted, the success of propaganda depends on the continuity of its application – but an unbroken flood of propaganda on a single topic requires wide streams of money, gigantic organization, and a compliant media. The Greening has it all! The environmental movement (and the Insiders behind it) could teach Herr Hitler a thing or two. The number of eco-organizations, the consistency of their shared themes and activities, the size of their memberships, and the sums expended are as vast and breath-taking as the Grand Canyon. A cursory examination of 31 of the more important eco-groups reveals a claimed membership of more than 8,750,000 people and combined annual budgets in excess of $820 million.

Funding for environmental groups also reveals volumes about their supporters. While these groups earn some income from publishing, consulting, and membership fees, the huge, choke-a-mule bankrolls come from foundations, endowments, corporate grants, United Nations agency grants, and of course, that old standby financier of mischief, U.S. government grants.

Why would seemingly respectable foundations finance revolutionary movements? Why would corporations like ARCO, Dow, Ford, General Electric, Union Carbide, Alcoa, AT&T, Browning-Ferris Industries, Chrysler, Conoco, DuPont, Exxon, IBM, Merck, Shell Oil, Unocal, American Cyanamid, 3M, Monsanto, ITT, Phillips Petroleum, and Weyerhaeuser finance their most outspoken and vicious critics? The simple answer is also the one that most refuse to acknowledge – *they profit by it.*

Common Environmental Themes

Like raindrops around a speck of dust, even the most preposterous ideas coalesce around some grain of truth. For environmentalism, that grain of truth is man's obligation to manage earth's resources wisely, even though the Greenies pervert this duty beyond all recognition. Below is a selection of recurring environmentalist themes. Oft repeated "code words" are in quotes. Most of these are "watermelon" themes: green on the outside, but red clean through. They contain the *essence* but avoid the *form* of the S-word: socialism.

The "soldiers" of the environmental movement – unsuspecting single-issue advocates – are often naively unaware that its seemingly *disconnected* aspects ultimately mesh together. Members are attracted through slick advertising promoting the "conservation" theme. Once they join a group, month-by-month the membership magazine indoctrinates them with more radical environmentalism and "fellow traveler" ideas.

And certain ideas inevitably do travel together. The overpopulation myth, for example, is seldom mentioned in isolation; it comes connected to food policy, global warming, dwindling resources, or threatened wilderness. Examining these themes reveals their cohesion and interconnection. Bear in mind that while we have taken all these themes directly from published statements and self-descriptions of the groups fisted, probably none of the groups listed here supports *every one* of these ideas. What follows is a look at the "application of propaganda" as these groups practice it.

Land Use Control

"Wise management of earth's resources" is the running dog for the stringent government land use control that environmentalists favor. Under this heading of conservation come "protect the rain forests/stop tropical deforestation," "desertification," "preserving for future generations," "toxic substance control," "wildlands or wetlands preservation," "wilderness" area preservation, and the "responsible" use of energy resources and non-fuel mineral deposits.

In general, these include opposition to any land development, or an insistence that development be strictly controlled by government. In other words, they want the "abolition of property in land and application of all rents of land to public purposes, abolition of all right of inheritance, the bringing into cultivation of waste lands, and the improvement of the soil generally in accordance with a common plan." (Planks 1,3, and 7 of the Communist Manifesto.)

Politics

Politically, environmental groups identify almost totally with a *left-of-left* agenda. Most groups enthusiastically support the "peace" movement, nuclear disarmament, and arms control of any kind, including the banning of handguns. Paying lip service to such high-minded rhetoric as "democracy," "pluralism," "grass roots," "local control," and "decentralization," the truth is quite the opposite: conform or else! The only peculiarity of this system is that Green intolerance has a local, rather than a distant, enforcer. Regardless of size, every group embraces the theme, "think globally and act locally."

Eco-groups also "seek solidarity" with the advocates of "just distribution of wealth," "elimination of sexism/racism," and "non-violent activism" (Earth First!, Greenpeace, Green Action Network). Nearly without exception Greenies believe there is a world overpopulation problem which must be controlled, *with force if necessary.* Under the cover of "population control" lies the ultimate power: *the power to determine who lives, and who dies.*

One step removed but fully in keeping with this elitism comes the theme "wise management of resources." Wise elites from government and Non-Governmental Organizations (NGOs), in "partnership," will plan for the rest of us.

And within the councils of "the wise," we poor boobs are just so many BTUs of "renewable resource." In the Green world of the future, humans are to be managed like crops, woodlots, or cattle. This makes the Greenies' discussion of "food policy" all the more frightening.

Economics

Like Ivory soap, environmental economics is 99-and- 44/100 percent pure – hysteria and socialism. Self-proclaimed or media-made "experts" demand "alternate energy sources" and "energy conservation," while they insist (with straight faces) that only eight percent of America's electricity use is "really needed." In fighting pollution, eco-economics promotes what columnist Tony Snow calls the "You may die" hypothesis: every risk, no matter how statistically remote, must be blotted out, never mind the cost. One newcomer idea with *enormous* financial and investment potential is "restoration" – users/owners must restore land to its pristine wilderness condition.

Green economics heavily emphasizes government "planning" and a "just distribution of wealth" (Communist Manifesto, Planks 1, 2, 3, 4, 5, 7, 8.) Undergirding all is the assumption that government has the right to determine the best use of your property - all of your property. (Manifesto Plank 1.)

Lately, Green "economists" are pushing for a "Green GNP," i.e., a GNP which includes "environmental costs" such as pollution, depletion of resources, etc. Since these costs can only be estimated and are thus wholly speculative, the Green GNP promises a nightmare of political wrangling as Green advocacy groups slap the media and legislatures with their own estimates of the "true" cost of things. The goal of the Green GNP is to justify taxes and other controls on economic activities the Greens dislike, such as you driving your personal automobile. Theirs would be exempt, of course, because their car is owned by a "tax-exempt foundation."

Green Theology

A pseudo-theology must take shape to sell these ideas. It is called a "biocentric worldview," which means that a roach has the same right to exist as a *man*. From this flows the need to "protect wildlife," which, left alone in the woods or sea, apparently can't do that for themselves. Starting with whales, elephants, and dolphins, this theology is working its way down the biological ladder to snail darters and desert turtles. Only domestic mice, rats, snakes, and spiders still remain outside the scope of their bio-centric sympathy. If past is prologue, however, we will soon see proposals outlawing rat poisons and insect sprays.

The "biocentric ethic" and its cousins are also known as the "environmental ethic," "biocentric worldview," or even the "land ethic." The casual reader will *under*estimate how consistent and serious environmentalists are when they talk about "deep ecology," "interconnection of all life," and the "interrelationship of nature and man." Pressed to the point they will generally concede, sometimes aggressively, that they mean man is *almost* as good as the animals. Man has no "preordained right to totally modify, develop, and otherwise exploit the entire planet for our own use and whim." (Dave Foreman) "An ant is as much a part of God, as a polar bear, or a koala, or you and me...I think they're all spiritually equal." (Australian Richard Jones)

Normal folks can scarcely believe how far dedicated Greenies take this theology of misanthropy. Shortly before Earth Day 1990, National Park Service biologist David M. Graber showed his fervor in the *Los Angeles Times*: "Human happiness, and certainly human fecundity, are not as important as a wild and healthy planet. I know social scientists who remind me that people are part of nature, but it isn't true. Somewhere along the line – at about a billion years ago, maybe half that – we quit the contract and became a cancer. We have become a plague on ourselves and upon the Earth. It is cosmically unlikely that the developed world will choose to end its orgy of fossil fuel consumption, and the Third World its suicidal consumption of landscape. Until such time as *homo sapiens* should decide to rejoin nature, some of us can only hope for the right virus to come along." I suggest it is at this point that the AIDS-infected homosexual community opts out of the Greening.

Another religious-philosophical hobbyhorse is "preserving genetic diversity" and "species conservation" under its many other names. This seems very odd, since most environmentalists are evolutionists. Why struggle so hard against the evolutionary inevitability of extinction? In the words of their philosophical forebear, Ralph Waldo Emerson, "A foolish consistency is the hobgoblin of little minds. With consistency a great soul has simply nothing to do."

Environmentalist theology also stresses a "future focus" and "sustainability." This means that we will conserve the world for our children, so that they can conserve it for their children, so that they can conserve it for their children, etc. etc., world without end, Amen. Nobody will ever use anything except the fewer and fewer children envisioned by depopulation advocates.

Globalism and Environmental Colonialism

Environmentalists view the Lesser Developed Countries (LDCs) of the Third World as their special laboratory for sociological experimentation. Citing "Third World resource management needs," they usually demand "appropriate technology for the Third World." Greens concern themselves with the impact of the LDC debt crisis on local "resource management programs." There is also plentiful talk about the "partnership" among multi-lateral development agencies (UN, World Bank, etc.), government, and NGOs.

Most of all, the environmentalists can't forgive the LDCs for producing babies. Greens are constantly whining about the Third World "overpopulation" problem, and they are loaded with coercive suggestions for solutions to the "problem."

Just as body lice can carry typhus and fleas bubonic plague, enviro-organizations are also enthusiastic carriers of globalism. Ecocant repeatedly includes "transboundary pollution problems," *global* environmental regulation, and the insistence that environmentalism is a cosmic cause above all other interests. Greens also tout international control of fisheries and ocean resources, not to mention international environmental controls which will include a force of eco-cops or an eco-swat team and a world court. At the April 1990 Trilateral Washington Plenary, former Canadian Environment Minister Lucien Bouchard said, "[W]e may require an international authority granted the power to impose measures on sovereign states." Go back and reread the Flora Lewis piece about the "breathtaking" Soviet proposal, it's all there.

Many Voices, One Chorus

Now that we have examined a few of the "themes" of eco-mania, let's turn to the organizations themselves. Led by a remarkably small number of folks at the top, these organizations continue to propagate certain ideas with faultless consistency, creating, maintaining, and expanding a monumental pressure group.

Abetted by a sympathetic press corps, Green propaganda has been immensely successful *vis-a-vis* the unsuspecting public, overwhelming the seldom-heard facts. As we have seen, the elitist controllers of the organizations have a hidden agenda; the lowly ecogroup members are simply the soldiers needed to accomplish that agenda. Here are some of the means:

* *Green education* not only indoctrinates the membership, but also focuses public debate on environmental issues. Children and students are attracted and trained through radio and TV programs, outings, projects, and even summer "student internships," which also identify and train future Greenie leaders.

* *Green research* offers environmental groups a means to support and reward environmentalist "scholars." Research also provides a steady stream of statistics and studies to agitate in public debate - studies legitimized and credentialed (not just in spite of, but *because* of their bias) by the environmental movement itself. Fellowships not only pay researchers, they also create credentials for environmentalist "scholars," and, through foreign exchanges, help to foster international contacts and networks.

* *Green prizes*, like research and publishing, allow the environmental movement to reward and legitimize its own. Prizes stir up the faithful, promote those professionals "destined" for greatness, legitimize the recipients, and confer prestige and credibility. Planned Parenthood, for example, bestows the Maggie Award for "media excellence." You can be sure it won't be awarded to *Pro-Life Review*. Nevertheless this one-sided prize will be mentioned in the media and on resumes as "the PRESTIGIOUS Maggie Award."

* *Green networking* provides funding and people to other eco-groups locally, nationally, and internationally. With full self-consciousness, they also coordinate activities and information with other groups in a worldwide network which prevents duplication of efforts and enhances use of resources.

* *Green litigation*, or "legal defense" as it is called, openly admits patterning its tactics on the civil rights movement. Litigation (judicial or administrative) throws a two-fold punch at its target. Land developers, for example, find (1) it may halt development altogether, and (2) it costs the developer/defendant unrecoverable thousands in legal fees, even if he wins. Legal attacks are usable over a wide range of circumstances: logging, mining, land use, wilderness designation, utility construction, and species preservation.

* *Green lobbying* is where the rubber hits the road. Most of the organizations examined in this article are headquartered in Washington, D.C., with additional offices, in some cases, in all of the state capitals, or major cities. "Assisting policymakers" means *setting* environmental, conservation, land use, and other government policies. It is a major means of capturing the future. Greenies testify before state and federal legislatures as "experts," consult (give "technical assistance") for government agencies, and lobby outright. Here the benefit of self-certification becomes apparent, since the environmental movement can present to legislatures scores of "experts" on any subject, all credentialed by the movement itself.

Besides on-the-spot lobbying, environmental organizations also mobilize their members and the public to set the agenda for public debate and to pressure legislators on specific issues.

* *Green direct action* includes private conservancy transactions, buying land directly for nature preserves. Often the NGO later turns this land over to state or federal governments, sometimes with the environmental organization retaining management.

Debt-for-nature swaps as described above are another active measure. Thanks to 100 percent tax write-offs in U.S. law, environmental groups can buy (or receive as gifts) blocks of Third World debt at pennies on the dollar. This debt can then be swapped to the debtor nation in return for designating areas as nature preserves or parks. Again, the environmental group is often appointed the manager of the preserve. These preserves do not extend hundreds or even thousands but millions of acres.

As the environmental movement becomes increasingly radicalized, expect to see more direct action "non-violent" measures to "protect" species or the environment. This includes tree-spiking to prevent logging (tears up equipment and endangers loggers and sawyers), blockades, publicity stunts, sit-ins, and even the outer limits of violence such as terrorist bombings. (In May 1990, two Earth First!ers whose car blew up in Los Angeles tried to blame the explosion on the FBI.)

Huge Numbers, Bulging Budgets

By the way, being Green can pay, and handsomely. In 1988, the top 30 eco-organizations in the United States had budgets that totaled over $1.1 billion.

Leaders of the eco-movement rake in the filthy lucre just as readily as their greedy enemies: Jay Hair (National Wildlife Federation) is paid $200,000 a year; Fred Krupp (Environmental Defense Fund), $125,000; Peter Berle (National Audubon Society), $120,000; George Frampton, Jr. (Wilderness Society), $120,000; John Adams (Natural Re-sources Defense Council), $117,000, and Robert Cutler (Defenders of Wildlife), $100,000. These figures do not include benefit packages. They're not doing bad "doing good."

Keep in mind one frightening fact: expenditures opposed to the Greening *do not* reach even two percent of this total. And that includes monies spent on special referenda, such as California's Big Green Initiatives.

By the time you read this, that number will have multiplied. New organizations and foundations are springing up almost daily. An example of a recent creation is The Surfrider Foundation. Ostensibly, the group was founded because of pollution on the California beaches which "endangers" surfers. As reported on "ABC Nightly News" September 9, 1991, Surfriders' lawyers were able to press a lawsuit against two pulp mills in Northern California resulting in a $100 million judgment to "clean up the beaches." Needless to say, Peter Jennings's spin made Surfrider appear to be nothing more than conscientious kids working on a good cause. Right – and the Wolf was only trying to get Little Red Riding Hood's Grannie to buy aluminum siding.

CHAPTER 12

AN END RUN:
THE LEGAL BASIS

We've seen that both governments and radical environmentalists want power over vast areas of the earth; but, what legal basis can they use? After all, in the West (and most of the rest of the world), victims won't give up their property and their rights without a whimper.

The answer lies in treaty law. Article VI of the U.S. Constitution reads, "This constitution, and the Laws of the United States which shall be made in Pursuance thereof; and all Treaties made, or which shall be made, under the Authority of the United States, shall be the supreme Law of the Land..."

Although one could rightly argue that no treaty can abrogate the rights guaranteed by the Constitution, nevertheless the Insiders' past approach, both here and abroad, has been to introduce *under treaties*, laws which would never be approved by national legislatures. Thus we can look for international treaties, especially United Nations treaties, to be advanced as the cutting edge of the legal attack on private property rights in building the ecological super-state.

It's a classic end run – around the Constitution.

The Politicians Turn "Green"

Already we noted that the "threat to the environment" has been billed by policy planner's – and thus the media – as a disaster so potent that it transcends all national and ideological interests. It is a "*global* problem above politics," we are repeatedly told. But, at the July 1989 Group of Seven economic summit in Paris, we witnessed the "greening of the politicians." The economic summit became the "eco-summit."

As the *Fresno Bee* asked and reported in an August 20, 1989 article:

What is curious, however, is why - during the past 12 months – environmental politics has gone from virtual international obscurity to center stage...One possibility, of course, is that environmental consciousness has finally trickled up into the high political reaches. Margaret Thatcher's conversion to environmentalism is by now almost legend...One might also say (cynically, perhaps) that the success of environmental parties in the recent elections to the EEC Parliament put fear into the hearts of Western Europe's leaders...

[T]he pressures on European leaders to respond are very strong, and most seem to recognize that the world is entering a period of great change and fluidity in international politics. This is where environmental issues come in. Protection of the environment is, almost literally, a "motherhood" issue (as in "motherhood and apple pie")...

This then is the gist of how the agenda is pushed forward:

While one might quibble over the costs of protecting the environment, almost no one is overtly in favor of destroying it...*Hence, the environment provides an almost perfect arena for East-West cooperation.* [Emphasis added.]

Nor was the Bush Administration slow to pick up the environmental bone. "The world's deteriorating environment has become a top economic policy concern of the United States and other industrial nations..." William A. Nitze, a top environmental policy official at the State Department, said, "This is now an issue of consequence that has risen to the top of the international agenda." (*New York Times*, May 15, 1989.) In all likelihood, by the time you read this, the Environmental Protection Agency will have been elevated to Cabinet status, as Bill Clinton has made an unequivocal statement to make it happen. The only debate as of January 1993, is just how sweeping the powers of the office will be and whether Congress will be able to exert some micro-management over the new department.

The UN is Ready

But how will the Constitution actually be abrogated? The answer, or one of them, appeared in the *New York Times* on November 9, 1989:

Warning that global warming could cause devastating floods and food shortages in wide areas, Prime Minister Margaret Thatcher of Britain called on the United Nations today to complete by 1992 a treaty that would require action toward stabilizing the world's climate. Mrs. Thatcher told the United Nations General Assembly that the treaty should be supplemented by specific, binding agreements regulating the production of gasses that trap heat in the atmosphere...Mrs. Thatcher said the restrictions would have to be *obligatory and their application carefully monitored.* [Emphasis added.]

This year's United Nations General Assembly is expected to approve a resolution next month setting up a negotiating body to draft a climate-stabilization treaty for approval by the second World Environment Conference, which is to meet in Brazil in 1992.

As noted above, the 1992 Brazil meeting was to be the Eco-Biggie for international codification of the worldwide Green agenda and the treaty called for in 1989 was one of the major "legalities" to emerge from Rio '92. Knowingly or not, Thatcher was reflecting the exact same strategy for UN mandates first outlined by George Kennan in his April 1970 article in *Foreign Affairs*.

A ready institutional framework already exists at the UN in the form of a horde of agencies and treaties. One prototype is the 1972 United Nations Educational, Scientific, and Cultural Organization (UNESCO) "Convention concerning the protection of the world cultural and natural heritage," or World Heritage Treaty.

The Treaty set up a World Heritage Committee within UNESCO, allocated funding, and established procedures for listing cultural and national "heritage" sites worldwide. And doesn't this pique your interest: the convention calls for cooperation with "international and national governmental and *non-governmental organizations* (NGOs)." [Emphasis added.] The structure is very similar to that called for in the American Heritage Trust Act – not accidentally, since it is the UNESCO World Heritage Treaty that prescribes such national Heritage trusts.

Under the World Heritage Organization, signatory nations have listed official "heritage" areas around the globe. In New Zealand almost half the South Island is slated for World Heritage listing. In Australia the result of World Heritage listing has been to run farmers, loggers, and ranchers off land they have used for generations. Looking at what has actually taken place, and what has been planned in Australia, it appears that UNESCO may eventually assume governmental *sovereignty* over the area, i.e., that the assignment of "Heritage" status could be construed as a *cession of national sovereignty* over the areas in question.

How close does this come to home?

About four years ago I took an automobile trip up the Olympic Peninsula of northwestern Washington. Since I had lived there for seven years as a young boy, I was anxious to show my youngest children (Lauren, then age 8, and Josh, age 5), "Where Daddy lived when he was your age."

Off we went with great weather and some of the most beautiful country on the face of the earth as targets for the excursion. Arriving at Lake Crescent in the Olympic National Forest, we were disappointed because there was no room at the Inn. I really didn't expect there would be, but went hoping for a last-minute cancellation.

I was a little miffed, as I explained to everyone within earshot, what a shame it was to have only one overnight facility on a fifteen-mile-long lake. And that, in the name of "protecting the environment," we were fast approaching the point where anyone who didn't want to backpack or hug a tree would ultimately be locked out of the area. In the process of grousing my way out the door, I picked up the brochure for the Lake Crescent Lodge – which incorporated information on another National Park facility in the Olympic Mountains, Hurricane Ridge Lodge.

Casually leafing through the four-color foldout, I dam near choked. There, prominently displayed on the front and back of the brochure, was an emblem about the size of a nickel. Within the center of the emblem was a surrealistic rendition of mountains and trees and very small lettering reading, "Olympic National Park." And in clearly readable type, arching the top and bottom of the outside ring, it stated, "United Nations World Heritage Site."

Can you believe it? I go searching for my roots, and end up with a shock tantamount to a root canal. Looking back on it, I feel sorry for my young companions. While doing their level best to cool my rage, they also had to endure my indignant babblings for several hours. It's bad enough to write about these things when it's Amazon basins or Third World hinterlands, but when it hits you right between the eyes in your own backyard, it stops being an intellectual pursuit and quickly becomes an emotional battleground.

Olympic National Park is only one of the World Heritage sites in the U.S. As of December 1987, 17 U.S. national parks and historic sites were fisted, including the Everglades, Great Smokey Mountains, Mammoth Cave, Yellowstone, Grand Canyon, Yosemite, and, most appalling, the Statue of Liberty and Independence Hall.

But as I pointed out earlier, the World Heritage Organization isn't the only existing UN environmental agency or treaty. In 1982 the UN created the UN Commission on Environment and Development, chaired by none other than the Globe '90 star speaker, Norwegian socialist Gro Harlem Brundtland. The Commission published a report, "Our Common Future," which is the typical "humanity-is-running-out-of-resources-and-ruining-the-globe" fare. As my collaborator Franklin Sanders has argued in his newsletter, "The Brundtland Report is nothing less than a scheme for a socialist world order, managed world economy, and massive redistribution of the world's wealth." If you believe he is overstating the situation, just write the UN and get your own copy of "Our Common Future." It isn't even subtle.

Then there is also the United Nations Environmental Program (UNEP), whose executive director is the previously-cited Egyptian, Mostafa Tolba. Tolba oversees a worldwide staff of 600 with an annual budget of $50 million and growing. The *Atlanta Journal* of July 14, 1989, gushes, "He played a pivotal role in negotiating the world's first international agreement to protect the ozone layer. He persuaded 100 nations to agree to stop dumping toxic wastes in the Third World. Now he is laying groundwork for a treaty to stave off potentially disastrous climate changes." And, if that were not enough, there is the United Nations Tropical Forest Action Plan – and the UN-sponsored Intergovernmental Panel on Climate Change (IPCC).

Already-existing UN environmental treaties include the 1985 Helsinki Protocol to the UN Convention on Long- Range Transboundary Air Pollution, the 1988 Sofia Protocol to the UN Convention on Long-Range Transboundary Air Pollution, and the 1989 Montreal Protocol on Substances That Deplete the Ozone Layer.

As reported in the *New York Times* of October 27, 1989, the next step is a treaty to limit carbon dioxide (CO_2) emissions:

The Bush Administration is facing increasing pressure from other nations, Congress, and environmental groups to take more aggressive action on the problem of global warming...On one side is the EPA, which favors bolder steps by the U.S., including stabilizing the CO2 emissions known [sic] to cause global warning...

The State Department official responsible for coordinating government policy on global warming, William Nitze, said this week that because of growing international pressure, the United States will probably have to accept a goal of stabilizing CO_2 emissions... White

House officials favor a worldwide agreement that would initially acknowledge the problem of global warming and later work out specific steps to deal with it.

This particular UN "world conference" was also part of the schedule for Brazil in 1992 under the auspices of Tolba's UNEP. Arguing that poverty itself promotes environmental degradation by encouraging deforestation or overgrazing, the so-called Third World members are pressing the industrialized countries to make *debt relief* and higher prices for their exports part of the final package. (*New York Times*, January 3, 1990.) [Emphasis added. Notice the "debt to environment" link is ever-present.]

At Rio '92 the entire theme of the conference was to bash the U.S. for being stingy on the question of Third World transfer payments in the name of "lessening the impact" of environmental necessities.

Eco-Courts and Eco-Cops

Apropos Margaret Thatcher's "Proposal" for "*binding* agreements" and "*obligatory* restrictions" with "*carefully monitored application*," binding agreements are bound down and monitored in *courts*. But what court exists to take cognizance of these existing and projected treaties?

Re-enter Mrs. Gro Harlem Brundtland of Norway. Brundtland is now in the forefront of a worldwide campaign to establish a World Court for settling "international environmental conflicts."

To hammer the nails down a bit tighter, you should know that right after Secretary of State Baker and Soviet Foreign Minister Shevardnadze met in Jackson Hole, Wyoming in the summer of 1989, I caught a small news item on the agenda for their discussions.

While the mass media predictably focused on the so-called "arms limitations" discussions, one completely ignored item said that they had also held talks about the role of the World Court.

"Arms control talks" – that's so Dan Rather can entertain the masses; "World Court developments" – that's for the Insiders.

I called Senator Steve Symms' office about this and asked his assistant, Andy Jaswick, to contact the State Department and find out what Baker and Shevardnadze discussed about the World Court. Andy called me back the next day and told me that the material on the World Court discussion was "not available."

I suggested he take it a step further, and encourage Senator Helms (the ranking Republican on the Senate Foreign Relations Committee) to make the same request. Back came the same response.

In the glow of *glasnost* and the "End of the Cold War," why should this one subject be so confidential? Let me tell you what I think. Very soon the U.S., the "new" Russia, and the EC will make some sort of joint declaration, expressing their eagerness to strengthen the pillars of "international law." To prove their sincerity, the multi-lateral groups will agree to subordinate their "narrow national interests" to the World Court – thus demonstrating their joint leadership in "making the world safe for democracy," "the environment," and the New World Order.

If all of this has a familiar ring, it should, for as far back as the post-World War I period and the debates surrounding U.S. participation in the League of Nations, the Insiders, led by then-chairman of the Establishment Elihu Root, nixed the League and championed the World Court.

Watch for the drumbeats to increase on the whole subject of international law. The debate surrounding the adjudication of the Noriega case and future drug wars was just the overture. The real orchestration is yet to come.

When these schemes bear their rotten fruit, American citizens will wake up to realize that many of their Constitutional protections have been transferred to an international body. In the process, we will all become "citizens of the world."

But what's a court without cops? The People's Republic of Massachusetts has already led the way with its own "special strike force to prosecute polluters." (*Atlanta Journal,* July 10, 1989, p. A7.) Will the "war on drugs" furnish the model for a future "war on polluters" with a special federal government Pollution Enforcement Agency (PEA)? The bill passed by the Massachusetts House on March 28, 1990, would indicate that. It includes among its many provisions an office of international environmental affairs, an office of pollution prevention, and an "office of enforcement."

Proposed pollution controls for Los Angeles are so picayune, so draconian, that we have to ponder what sort of petty but terrifying tyranny might be established in the name of "saving the environment." The *Atlanta Journal* (July 10, 1989.) reports that the "South Coast Air Quality Management District has developed a sweeping three-stage plan to bring the region's air up to federal standards by 2007." Stage One, to be implemented by 1994, calls for pollution reduction gear on outboard and inboard motor boats, requiring the use of radial rather than bias ply tires, ethanol emission controls for bakeries, more efficient exhaust hoods in restaurants, limitations on vehicle registrations, elimination of deodorants using certain propellants, higher parking lot fees, forced installation of perchloroethylene recovery devices at dry cleaners, staggering of work hours, a ban on gasoline lawn mowers, and – no, I am not making this up – banning barbecues that use starter fluid.

While all this might sound ridiculous, it is very serious when combined with the surveillance capability of modem technology. The fiery December 1988 *Moneychanger* reported that:

> United Nations agencies, multilateral aid agencies, and private non-governmental environmental organizations (NGOs) have already put together a massive worldwide *surveillance* database. This was unveiled at the Fourth World Wilderness Congress in September 1988 as the

'World Wilderness Inventory," prepared by the Sierra Club at the behest of the Fourth World Wilderness Congress. According to official literature "only areas of at least 400 square kilometers (1 million acres) were inventoried, because the constraints of this particular study did not allow identification of smaller wilderness areas, *though they, too, are of interest.*" [Emphasis added.]

It isn't just our unjustified paranoia that makes this vast information gathering project stink of dictatorial ambitions. The architect of this Wilderness Inventory, Sierra Club researcher J. Michael McCloskey, was quoted in the same *Moneychanger* piece: "'It is from this inventory that reservations of major new protected areas can be made. This land will no longer be anonymous back country and bush which is nibbled away with impunity.'"

Editor and co-author Franklin Sanders asks, "Impunity? Impunity means *unpunished*. Who is planning the punishing here, and what is the crime? Is it a crime to use your own property as you see fit? This statement well displays the frightening totalitarian implications of satellite/computer technology surveillance such as this GRID (Global Resources Information Database) system. It also reveals an unhealthy coercive bent in Mr. McCloskey." As I reported in the March 1990 *Insider Report*, Mr. McCloskey isn't the only one looking to provide a method for "environmental crimes." Professor Robert Woetzel bragged that he had a "done deal" for a new World Court system which will transcend national laws. (More about that in a moment.)

The already snowballing problem of maintaining personal privacy in an age of massive commercial and governmental databases becomes even more threatening when one considers that present satellite technology allows the identification and viewing of areas as small as *ten square feet!* It is bad enough to have a bureaucratic Peeping Tom peering over your shoulder at every credit application you fill out. But what if the bureaucrat, like Mr. McCloskey, possesses an "unhealthy coercive bent"?

One of those bureaucrats is Carlo Ripa de Meana, the European Community's Commissioner for the Environment. At an April 1991, scientific meeting on climate change in Turin, Ripa announced plans for a force of environmental inspectors for the EC.

Ripa lamented the "lack of judicial means for the international community to protect the environment." What's the Eco-Commissar's solution? Force, and lots of it.

Through Ripa at the UN Conference on Environment and Development, the EC proposed a "permanent international tribunal" on the environment. Just as the Geneva convention regulates treatment of prisoners of war, this tribunal would decide how environmental rules applied in war. "To enforce its decisions, he wants the tribunal to command a corps of 'Green Helmets,' similar to the 'Blue Helmets' of UN peacekeeping troops."

Not everyone is willing to go along with Ripa's totalitarian bent.

The proposal for a UN corps of Green Helmets has received mixed reactions. Developing countries are likely to view it as "environmental imperialism," said some experts at the conference in Turin..."I don't mind the green helmet, but I haven't got a black shirt to go with it," said one British scientist in Turin, referring to the uniform worn by Italy's fascists in the 1930s. Ripa was dismissive: "There are always silly people who make comments like this. I don't care what they say." (*New Scientist*, April 27, 1991, p.16.)

A comic nightmare vision of the future looms before us: the guests are assembled in the back yard, relaxing with cool drinks. It's a sultry summer afternoon. The host comes out of the patio door with a plate full of raw hamburgers. He reaches the barbecue grill, puts down the burgers, pulls out his starter fluid, douses the charcoal, and fights it.

Thousands of miles out in space, a red fight blinks in the Environmental Strike Force Satellite of the PEA (Pollution Enforcement Agency). Alarms sound in the local PEA office and the

Eco-cops jump on their non-polluting ten-speed bicycles, turn on their flashing lights and sirens, and pedal over to Mr. Suburban's back yard. With machine guns and fire hoses at the ready, they break down the backyard gate, douse the offending fire, and haul our host off to an Environmental Re-education Camp for 30 years of planting crocuses.

Impossible, you say? Well, in the comic scenario outlined above – probably. But, not so in a *realpolitik* sense. In the Fall 1991 issue of *Foreign Affairs* there appeared a feature article by former CIA Director Stansfield Turner entitled "Intelligence for a New World Order." In this piece Turner states, "Washington can easily construct a system that will detect any significant activity on the surface of the earth, day or night, under clouds or jungle cover, and with such frequency as to make deliberate evasion difficult...such a system would cost $5 billion to purchase and $1 billion per year to operate." The bottom line to Turner's piece is, "We must, then, redefine 'national security' by assigning economic strength greater prominence." Included, of course, is the moral equivalent of war: "threats to the environment."

Let me add a parenthetical comment. Since the founding of the Council of Foreign Relations in 1921 and its quarterly *Foreign Affairs* the next year (1922), every major "proposal" for international policy first appeared within the pages of *Foreign Affairs*, long before it became reality. The George F. Kennan 1970 environmental policy blueprint, as cited above, is a classic example.

A Stronger World Court

As I hinted above, I fully expect to see a treaty proposed which will, in effect, elevate the role of the World Court and put the U.S. along with its former adversary in bed together as world cops. Further evidence of this dynamic is coming thick and fast.

In a letter to the *New York Times*, Eric Cox, Executive Director of the Campaign for United Nations Reform, said:

Since the United States is conducting an alleged war on drugs, why doesn't the Bush Administration support the creation of an international criminal court to deal with those who violate international conventions against traffic in narcotics?...

Since the United States claims to support international law, why doesn't the Bush Administration demonstrate such backing by favoring an international criminal court to allow the reach of world law to gain jurisdiction exactly where it is needed – directly over individuals who commit internationally recognized crimes...

In this same vein, an incredible article appeared in the *Santa Barbara News* on April 9, 1989. It shows how far the planning has already gone to eliminate our constitutional protections and grant frightening new powers to an international tribunal. The article is based on an extensive interview with Robert Woetzel, whom the reporter describes as "an Oxford-trained scholar, a lecturer at UCLA, and director of the University of Santa Barbara's International Studies Program."

The article describes Woetzel's efforts thus: "For 25 years he has taken the lead in bringing to life an idealistic pet project that finally appears to be a *done deal*: The establishment of an international criminal court." [Emphasis added.]

I am going to quote almost all of this article, for if it is indeed a "done deal," then you need to know what sort of "major decisions are being prepared" in the name of *glasnost, perestroika*, and the New World Order.

Robert Woetzel calls it "the golden rule of the 21st century." A simple idea, really.

"Individuals always have been and always will be expendable if they do wrong," he says. "The basic concept, which I think every holy book from the Bible to the Koran preaches, is that we have to be accountable – under God, if you wish, but certainly under the consensus of nations.

"There is already a World Court at The Hague, but that forum is designed only to resolve disputes pitting nation against nation. The final judgments in the World Court often are made by those with national, and thus partisan, interests. Many countries – including the United States - have objected, rightly or wrongly, to such one-on-one scrutiny.

"There's a kind of collective guilt if you lose, and that's totally unacceptable to some sovereign nation states," Woetzel said of the World Court. "The states don't want to be taken to court."

An international criminal court, on the other hand, would be less sectarian, he believes. It would be set up, he says, as an impartial, "depoliticized" body, composed of an international panel of judges selected for their lack of "extreme" national partisanship, thus allowing, in concept, a more objective system of justice. Cases would be directed against groups, corporations, and individuals, including individuals within governments who have carried out criminal acts of international proportions.

"The basic concept is that world peace must be based on justice," Woetzel said during the recent interview from his home/office on Tunnel Road, perched high in the foothills above the Mission. "Justice is larger than just the law. There must be a relationship of responsibility to rights."

Based on the Nuremberg principles applied against Nazi war criminals, the international criminal court would prosecute persons or other responsible entities for crimes that, Woetzel says, are generally viewed as an affront to every civilized person, crimes that know no geographic boundaries. People could be tried *in absentia*, and the death penalty can be meted out in some cases.

What kinds of offenses would be prosecutable?

"International drug trafficking, terrorism, hijacking, hostage-taking," Woetzel replies. But that's not all. Ecological crimes like the illegal dumping of ocean wastes, and economic crimes like inside stock manipulation that might threaten the stability of various nations also are included on the roster of offenses.

"We make sure," he says, 'that individuals, groups, corporations, states, and governments can be held accountable for their actions.

"We have drafted something we call the code of offenses against the peace and security of mankind, which is like a development - from Cain and Abel to our modem times - of a global code of justice, which all parties recognize, and which is based on consensus among peoples, nations, and states.

"It's very important for us to assert that accountability. We've tried other approaches. The United States tried to pressure Noriega (in Panama); it tried to pressure Mexico, and to pressure the Turks and the Colombians on the question of drug traffic. It didn't work."

Woetzel has won congressional support for his project, in addition to an endorsement from about 80 percent of member countries at the United Nations. Ironically, the United States is so far among the minority of UN members that has withheld its full endorsement. The American Government might feel a bit threatened by the notion of its officials being brought to justice by such a broad-based court, Woetzel says. But the government appears to be reluctantly heading toward future support, he added.

"In terms of the U.S. record, we have nothing to fear except fear itself,' he says. The idea is to let the chips fall where they may. Any government has a few rotten apples in the barrel, and there are not any rotten apples (in the United States) who have ever been condemned."

Despite the legalistic and diplomatic hurdles it still must surmount, the international criminal court is heading toward the bricks-and-mortar phase. Woetzel is embarked upon a $50 million fund-raising project to finance the court system – most of it through private donations. To avoid the threat of political patronage, governments are prohibited from making monetary donations.

But at the same time, it is governments that, by endorsing and participating in the international court, will give it legal and moral legitimacy.

Woetzel said the court will be headquartered, by 1993, in Tobago, a small island in the West Indies. 'Regional centers' are to be established in Berlin, Malta, Beijing, and southern India. The plan even includes a prison for criminals convicted by the court. They could end up being housed under lock and key at St. Helena in the South Atlantic. This is a highly appropriate locale; Napoleon spent his time in exile there.

"It's interesting if you think how small the world has become," Woetzel said, "and how effective you can be. Out of that little office where I work, overlooking the tranquil Pacific, from a hillside above the Old Mission, I'm in touch daily with the leaders of governments in the world. And out of there, I maneuver and cajole and pressure and what not, to get a greater world order."

Professor Woetzel died during the spring of 1992, before he could witness his proposals at the Rio Summit. But if he had a "done deal" – and recent events would bear him out – then his death does little to deter the effort and reality of an international "criminal court."

In George Orwell's nightmare novel of the totalitarian world of the future, *1984*, Winston Smith is arrested and tortured by Inner Party man O'Brien. In the midst of his "re-education" O'Brien calmly explains:

Power is not a means; it is an end. One does not establish a dictatorship in order to safeguard a revolution; one makes the revolution in order to establish the dictatorship. The object of persecution is persecution. The object of torture is torture. The object of power is power. Now do you begin to understand me?

CHAPTER 13

THE EARTH SUMMIT

The Great Event To Save The Planet, Rio's mighty Eco-Spasm, has now come and gone. It's time to shovel away the composting detritus left by the carnival crowd and judge what really happened. Somewhat intellectually fastidious and therefore nauseated, we feel much as did Rio Earth Summit janitor Manuel De Soto, who remarked while sweeping up litter near a meeting on waste management, "These Greenies have nice speeches, but in practice they're pigs."

We, however, were not disappointed. We were expecting the Insiders to act just like Adolph Hitler. He told the world precisely what he intended to do in *Mein Kampf*, then everyone acted *surprised* when he actually did it. The Insiders did the same. Should we be surprised?

We prefer to ignore the Green propaganda pronouncing the Summit a failure, and prefer to evaluate the Earth Summit by how many of its *stated goals* it actually accomplished.

In chapter one we discussed *Beyond Interdependence* where veteran one-worlder James MacNeill lays out the Earth Summit Agenda. We said it included:

(1) adopting an "Earth Charter" setting out new principles for government relations and an agenda for the 21st century;

(2) adopting an "agenda for action 'Agenda 21'" – "Most importantly, the agenda will designate the national and international agencies that will bear responsibility for the first phase of implementation, *tentatively set for the last seven years of this century*";

(3) possible signing of new treaties, on global warming, deforestation, and bio-diversity;

(4) forming new international institutions of control.

How much of this agenda did the Earth summit complete? First, Number (3) called for signing new treaties on global warming, deforestation, and bio-diversity. The global warming and bio-diversity treaties were signed, although George Bush, under political pressure from home, bowed out on bio-diversity. "Declarations" were adopted "by consensus" on forest principles (deforestation, No. 3), Agenda 21 (No. 2), and a "Declaration on Environment and Development" (Earth Charter, No. 1). Also proposed but not yet formally established is the Sustainable Development Commission (No. 4).

Second in the "Goals Accomplished" category is an international environmental superagency to take global control of environmental concerns. In his 1970 "Proposal," George Kennan presented this superagency as the *sine qua non* of international environmental protection. Crucial here is Kennan's demand that the agency incorporate a globalist bureaucracy staffed by "true international servants, bound by no national or political mandate."

Behold, out of the Earth Summit's travail has been born not just wind, but the new agency, the Sustainable Development Commission (SDC). This new watchdog will monitor compliance with commitments made at the Earth Summit.

The Earth Summit was also an occasion for pursy old globalists to dust off the decrepit United Nations and push for expanding its powers. The words in the *New York Times* practically glowed red hot on the page. The "UN remains the only international framework that exists for approaching global challenges..." Naturally the SDC will be a United Nations responsibility.

It Was a Big Party

Before we proceed to the treaty specifics, ponder the scope and scale of the Earth Summit. It was the biggest conference of governments ever held: 178 countries attended. More significantly, the Earth Summit more firmly established Non-Governmental Organizations (NGOs) as the volunteer elitist dictators of the future. As we have said before, the future Green government will be a "partnership" of business, government, and NGOs – in a word, fascism. For all the New World Order's talk about democracy, a mighty host of one-worlders were busy subverting it in Rio. Why should NGOs rule the rest of us, since they are nothing more than self-appointed/anointed experts? Welcome to a government of pressure groups, and not of law.

Thirty-five thousand made the pilgrimage to Rio. Thirteen thousand private Greenies representing nearly 1,000 NGOs from 160 countries showed up along with 8,000 journalists. (There was a separate-but-equal Eco-Spasm for NGOs across town.)

And lo!, what a group of Green gonzos they were. The Spiritualist Division for the New Green World Religion were all there, beads, bandannas, and talismans at the ready. Dizzies from around the world were attracted by the green lights at Rio. The 6/7/92 *Commercial Appeal* asked:

> What do Jane Fonda, Placido Domingo, the Beach Boys, Jerry Brown, the Dalai Lama and Pele have in common? They're all on hand or expected at the Earth Summit...

> Early on, a top attention-getter was Tibet's Dalai Lama. He prayed at the opening of the summit and applauded a song by the moderator – John Denver. He then headed across town where he was introduced by New Age guru Shirley MacLaine [who else?]. Among the most eagerly awaited arrivals has been [Jane] Fonda, who is to come with husband Ted Turner.

Busy behind the scenes was Hanne Strong, wife of Maurice the "Guardian of the Planet" and "Wizard of the Baca." You remember Hanne? She founded a so-called religious retreat at the Baca in Colorado for sundry spiritualists, shamans, and shams from all over the globe. While the planetary bigwigs met across town, she was

organizing prayers for the success of the conference – led by the
Great Thumb god, no doubt.

One Good Surprise

The myth of overpopulation is the keystone of the Green religion.
One piece of good news from Rio was the surprising coalition
opposing birth control which emerged. It linked up the Vatican,
conservative Islamic nations, and "feminists who argued that male-
dominated governments should not interfere with women's lives."
Truly, it's an odd alliance that links the Vatican and femi-nazis.

Bush Ambushed

Out of place and out of sorts was the Green president, George
Bush. He became the Green Grinch of the Summit by refusing to
sign the bio-diversity compact and allegedly gutting the global
warming treaty. The conference put Bush in big trouble politically.
First, he had to appease the Greenies by showing up at Rio. Second,
he had to assuage those disgruntled souls beginning to suspect the
Greening will cost somebody his job – and better Bush's than theirs.

The Accords

For some reason lost in the misty wrinkles of time, United
Nations treaties are (annoyingly) not called treaties, but conventions
or accords. We suspect this is where bureaucrats use language to
prevent communication. Those documents signed at Rio include two
treaties ("conventions," which become new international law) and
three "accords." The accords are billed as non-binding agreements,
but as we shall momentarily see, that's meaningless camouflage.

The Global Warming Convention

Walking his tightrope, Bush bragged that the global warming
treaty did not commit to *specific* emissions reductions. Nevertheless
it commits to reductions *in principle*. William K. Stevens of the *New
York Times* described it as a "long-term framework that can become
a forceful instrument for controlling heat-trapping gasses."

After signing, Bush challenged other industrial nations to join the U.S. by January 1, 1993, in laying out detailed plans for controlling emissions. He said he intended the proposal to accelerate the treaty's practical effects. These specific emissions timetables are exactly what Bush bragged so mightly he had *avoided* in his canny dickering over the treaty! Alas, the "treaty thing" is getting out of hand.

There is only one problem with a global warming treaty: there is no such problem. There is no clear scientific evidence of global warming. On the contrary we've had one of the coldest Junes on record. (After the eruption of the volcano Krakatoa in 1886, the world had three years of sub-normally cold weather. The 1990 Mt. Pinatubo's eruption was the largest since Krakatoa. Meteorologists are now saying the cold weather will extend into 1995!) Worse, any emissions limitations will inevitably reduce economic development and industrial production. What other way is there to reduce CO_2 emissions, which are primarily the product of fuel usage, the primary ingredient in all economic production?

The global warming convention is a legally binding treaty which the U.S. signed. It has become an *enforceable* part of international law. The treaty requires every signatory to devise an "action plan" for reducing pollution and to report regularly on meeting the plan's goals. It recommends curbing emissions of CO_2, methane, and other so-called greenhouse gasses.

All parties must create and update national programs to mitigate climate change. Obviously they can only accomplish this by controlling human-generated emissions of greenhouse gases. Industrialized countries must limit their emissions of greenhouse gases, protect forests and other systems that absorb greenhouse gasses, and *demonstrate they are taking steps* toward meeting these objectives.

Within six months of when the treaty takes effect and periodically afterwards, all parties must report on what they have done "with the aim of returning individually or jointly to their 1990 levels" of emissions. The treaty also mandates periodic review of progress and scientific knowledge about climate change.

Industrialized countries must also help finance and provide technology to developing countries to meet treaty commitments. At first this will be funneled through the Global Environmental Facility, a new international aid program, still firmly in control of the World Bank. We'll have more to say about the implications of this treaty later.

The Bio-Diversity Convention

For two objections Bush refused to sign the bio-diversity treaty. First, he claimed it surrenders control of the World Bank environmental funds to an undefined number of treaty signing nations. We wouldn't want control of anything to slip out of the World Bank's warm, wet hands, now would we? Second, Bush said the treaty undercuts American patent laws, business practices, and biological research.

The bio-diversity convention is a legally binding treaty. It requires national inventories of plants and wildlife, national plans to protect endangered species, and sharing research, profits, and technology with nations where the genetic resources originate. (Do you understand? *Individuals* develop genetic resources, but *governments* get the benefits. Most UN treaties work this way.)

Three other accords were "adopted by consensus," whatever in the world that means. We suspect it means that they will become international law without the bothersome technicality of ratification by the signatory nations.

The Declaration on
Environment and Development

This is a supposedly non-binding statement, but "non-binding" means nothing. The principles which the document establishes become the presuppositions of all subsequent negotiations and transactions upon the affected topics. The declaration establishes 27 broad principles for guiding environmental policy. Protecting the environment as part of economic development, safeguarding eco-systems of other countries, and giving priority to the needs of developing countries are all emphasized.

Agenda 21

Agenda 21 is a detailed – *800 pages no less* – action plan outlining steps for achieving sustainable development in every environmental sector. Of course, it provides that the North (that's us) must pay for it. It is a non-binding blueprint to clean up the global environment and to encourage environmentally sound development. Agenda 21 was adopted [Passive voice – nobody knows who's responsible] by consensus *after* the developing countries dropped their demand for specific aid commitments from the industrialized countries to pay for the plan. Don't worry – they'll be back, with their hands out.

Statement on Forest Principles

Yet another non-binding declaration, this one recommends that countries assess, individually and with other countries, how economic development affects their forests. The U.S. was already doling out the dough for global forest aid. Although Bush wouldn't sign it, he committed another $120 million to international forest programs, on top of the $150 million the U.S. was already spending.

New Environmental Aid

Making the world safe for salamanders is going to cost plenty. For at least the last 20 years, socialists of every stripe, from Willi Brandt to Gro Bruntland, have been trying to foist world relations into a scheme of their own Marxist devising: rich Northern hemisphere versus poor Southern hemisphere. In short, the South has its hand out. This is nothing less than new clothes on the same tawdry for international wealth redistribution. The modest goal is to "eradicate poverty" in the whole world – talk about a black hole! Bush resisted picking up the whole tab, but only because it's an election year. The bleeding hearts want the North to commit to giving away 0.7% of GNP annually in aid to the South. Currently, total aid averages 0.45% of GNP in the industrialized nations.

The elitist do-gooders pillory the U.S. for refusing to meet the 0.7% goal. However, in absolute (not percentage) terms the U.S. out gives the rest of the world by mega-ducats. In 1990, the U.S. shelled out $11,924 *billion* in foreign aid, along with another $5 *billion* in credits (a total of $16,229 billion). In 1988, total world aid was $56 billion, of which 86% came from the OECD countries. That includes the U.S., which in 1988 blew $10,141 billion, or 18.1% of the total OECD foreign aid. The $10.141 billion wasn't the whole story on U.S. foreign aid, since it doesn't include credits and military aid. Japan was the next closest patsy, with a contribution of about $9 billion. France gave almost $7 billion, West Germany about $4.7 billion, Italy $3,183, the United Kingdom $2,645, Canada $2,342, the Netherlands $2,231, the Saudis $2.1, and Australia one billion. Sanctimonious socialist Sweden, which postures self-righteously about its generosity to the starving nations, handed out a munificent $1.5 billion, about a tenth of the total U.S. contribution. So much for the critics of U.S. charity. (Former congressman Ron Paul says Congress will dump $22 billion into direct foreign aid next year. Indirect aid he estimates at *more than $100 billion*, almost twice the total OECD total.)

At Rio, the European Community said it will offer $3-5 billion in new environmental aid over the next five years. Bush proclaimed, "We...stand ready to increase U.S. international environmental aid by 66% above the 1990 levels, on top of the more than $2.5 billion that we provide through the world's development banks for Agenda 21 projects."

Japan will increase environmental aid to developing countries from $2.3 billion spent in 1989-1991 to $7 billion over the next five years. This increases the Japanese contribution from $800 million a year to $1.4 billion. Germany says it will send overseas more than $6.3 billion a year to developing nations.

The U.S. and others are considering creating a new fund for the World Bank's International Development Agency next year as a source of *free* environmental loans to the world's poorest nations. The $1.3 billion *Global Environmental Facility* was established three years ago at the World Bank to finance Third World environmental projects. That comes up for renewal next year, and the participating nations are expected to double or triple it.

The Bigwigs Brag

What did the Eco-Summit bigwigs brag about in the closing session on June 14th? Brazil's president Fernando Collor de Mello is anything but mellow lately, since he had been plagued by pre-summit revelations of corruption released by his own family. Collor said the Summit "Consecrated [sic] a concept that human development and protection of the earth's environment are inextricably intertwined." (Just think: "Our Summit, which art in Rio, hallowed be thy name...") Big news. Strong, MacNeill, and Company have already been parroting that line for years.

Of course, UN Secretary General Boutros Boutros-Ghali played a great role in Rio. Boutros-Ghali, mindful of neurotic sensibilities of his Green constituency, doused the audience with this dose of guilt manipulation: "Today we have agreed [sic] to hold to present levels the pollution we are guilty of. One day we will have to do better – clean up the planet." First, of course, let us start by cleaning out the Americans' wallets.

The Bottom Line

To conclude rashly from Bush's minimalist global warming treaty and his refusal to sign the bio-diversity treaty that the Eco-Spasm was a failure would totally miss the point. As we noted in the beginning of this article, the Summit, successfully completed the foreordained agenda. *The point was to shift environmentalism to spot number one on the world's agenda, replacing even war itself.*

The well-orchestrated comic opera in Rio will be bally- hooed as the "start of a new era." Legal terrorist and eco-elitist Gus Speth of World Resources Institute intoned, "The U.S. has totally missed the point that the axis of world affairs has shifted from East-West to North South. Issues of equity [read wealth re-distribution] and environment will dominate post-cold-war politics." Nor should we forget Senator Albert Gore, crawling up from the Green primeval slime with this worthy dictum: "Environmental protection is the single organizing principle of the planet now."

The lack of emission reduction timetables in the global warming treaty is wholly inconsequential, as is Bush's failure to sign up for bio-diversity. These *tactical* details subtract nothing whatsoever from the *strategic* victory: the principles of radical environmentalism have been enshrined into international law. *When* they take effect is immaterial; *that* they take effect is crucial. The international environmentalist agenda has been imposed on national economic sovereignty *in principle*, and enshrined in international law.

Several commentators understood this very well. In the *New York Times* Paid Lewis wrote, "It is the *start* of a process that could eventually change the way the world approaches economic growth..." (Emphasis added)

Gregg Easterbrook explained it best in *Newsweek* (6/16/92):

Missed in the rush to express on-camera despair [about the failure of the Earth Summit] is this: the *treaty incorporates into international law the notion that nations must consider the global environmental consequences of internal economic decisions.* This "has the potential of forcing governments to change domestic policies to a greater degree than any international agreement I can think of," says Jessica Tuchman Mathews, vice president of World Resources Institute. Legal precedents often start small but grow to instruments of great power...In ecology, governments and economists have long resisted the notion that nature has a standing independent of national law. Now George Bush, John Major, Helmut Kohl, and the other capitalist leaders will sanctify that idea, creating a new logic of "green rights" they will find increasingly difficult to oppose. (Emphasis added.)

Conclusion

Because we cherish individual freedom and economic liberty as our own lives, the Green fascism of the Rio Earth Summit alarms us. The lunatics have seized the asylum. Worse yet, they have seized the halls of government. The Green Revolution is another elitist attempt to eradicate the precious liberties which the Western World has been 2000 years building. Green pharisaism wants to create a world super-state which minutely controls every human life according to some elitist's notion of what is good for us.

We nevertheless hope that around the world, beginning in the United States, many are now penetrating the Green mist around environmentalism's Holy Grail. The right questions, questions of reason and common sense, are being thrown at the Green cultists. How will we pay for this? Is this even worth doing? Environmentalism's only response is a perfervid *religious insistence* on its own righteousness, no matter what it costs, no matter how many it condemns to poverty. While it is certainly possible that men can combine sensible environmental stewardship with economic development, it can't be done the Green Way. Rio's road is the road to economic catastrophe.

Yet the Greens' success at Rio is neither decisive nor permanent. Before any of these treaty takes effect, they must be ratified by a minimum number of signatories, usually fifty. There's many a slip 'twixt *signing* a treaty and *ratifying* it. Ask Woodrow Wilson. For those of us who have been watching the Greenies prepare the Eco-Spasm, its completion is an anticlimax, not the beginning of a New World Order. The Green tide can be turned.

The Greenies tell us we have to fight poverty in the Third World. The best way to fight poverty — in the Third World or in America – is not to become part of it. Someday sense will return.

A Scorecard:
The Earth Summit Treaties

Two Treaties:

Bio-diversity Convention

A legally binding treaty which requires national inventories of plants and wildlife, national plans to protect endangered species, and sharing research, profits, and technology with nations where the genetic resources originate. (Bush refused to sign charging the Convention infringes patent rights and contains open-ended financing commitments.)

Global Warming Convention

This legally binding treaty (the U.S. signed) requires every signatory to devise an "action plan" for reducing pollution and to report regularly on progress toward the plan's goals. It recommends curbing emissions of CO_2, methane, and other greenhouse gasses alleged, but not proven, to cause global warming. It sets no firm timetables, however, for emission reduction. Within six months of taking effect and periodically afterwards, all parties must report on what they have done "with the aim of returning individually or jointly to their 1990 levels" of emissions. Industrialized countries must finance and provide technology to developing countries, initially through the Global Environmental Facility of the World Bank.

Three Accords Adopted by Consensus:

Declaration on Environment and Development

Anon-binding statement of 27 broad principles for guiding environmental policy, it merges environmentalism with economic development, emphasizes safeguarding eco-systems of other countries, and gives priority to the needs of developing countries.

Agenda 21

Agenda 21 outlines a detailed action plan with steps for achieving "sustainable development" in every environmental sector. It forces the industrialized countries ("the North") to pay for it. This non-binding 800 page blueprint outlines steps to clean up the global environment and encourage environmentally sound development. Agenda 21 was adopted by consensus after developing countries dropped their demand for specific aid commitment from the North.

Statement on Forest Principles

A non-binding document that recommends nations assess the result of economic development on their forests, individually and with other countries

CHAPTER 14

LEGAL TERRORISM

The first requisite of an effective Superfund [cleanup] program is
a clenched fist. - Eco-czar William Reilly, 1989

In the fall of 1990, CBS began a new weekly show, "E.A.R.T.H. Force." The pre-show PR gushed, "A diverse group of top-notch professionals has been specially selected to fight against threats to the world's ecological balance... Together, they work to save the world's environment from its worst enemy – man." The previews showed these crusaders, geared up in quasi-military uniforms, rushing around the world shutting off pipeline valves, halting environmental crises, and hunting down "profit-greedy polluters."

Reminiscent of "The Man from U.N.C.L.E." and its promotion of the United Nations, this production vividly revealed how much of the environmentalists' cant our television moguls have swallowed – and how eager they were to inflict that propaganda on us. The couch potatoes were being sold the idea that some sort of ecological "swat team" must deal with the otherwise uncontrollable ecological crisis, and that polluters (the very personification of evil) deserve whatever they get – especially if they are "beyond" the reach of the law. (Never mind that the innocent get what the drug dealers deserve, too.)

Mercifully, "E.A.R.T.H. Force" was cancelled a few weeks into the fall 1990 TV season. It seems Mr. and Mrs. America didn't appreciate the thought. But the publishers at CBS sure gave it their all.

What you may not at first appreciate is how this attitude reflects the breakdown of the "presumption of innocence," "due process," and the widespread radicalization of our legal system. More importantly it reveals the propaganda for a strategy of *legal terrorism* designed to accomplish radical changes in American law and society.

A Lesson from Previous Terrorists

Today's green terrorists are applying the lessons learned during the French Revolution's Reign of Terror and the "legalities" of Stalin's show trials. This strategy is necessary because, until recently, there has been little popular or legislative support for the revolutionary changes envisioned by the environmentalists' program.

While the public is willing to pay lip service to environmental concern, numerous referenda and other actions demonstrate clearly that the vast majority of Americans don't want *to suffer* because of it. When the environmental bull gores their personal ox, threatens *their job, their* comforts, and *their* disposable diapers, opinions change overnight.

Facing a reluctant, fickle, and environmentally shallow populace, the eco-radicals have found the solution: sidestep the already existing law. Tax-exempt "advocacy groups" and government agencies supply the shock troops for the legal blitzkrieg, all cheered on by the fawning media.

The Natural Resources Defense Council, co-founded by Rhodes Scholar and Clinton "environmental coordinator," Gus Speth, is a case in point. *Science* magazine reported on it in May of 1980:

> Inspired by the example of the NAACFs Legal Defense Fund, Speth and several other young attorneys founded the NKDC, one of the first "environmental law groups.".... [Russell] Train [in the NRDC] had a key role in helping to bring on, in the 1970s, an *"environmental revolution"* that Speth has compared to the civil rights revolution of the 1960s. Some 20 new environmental laws, including the clean air and clean water laws, were enacted during the decade to *mandate* a complex web of

federal and state regulation that is proving difficult to put in place and implement. [Emphasis added.]

In the 1988/89 annual report of the Sierra Club Legal Defense Fund, Michael Fischer, Executive Director of the Sierra Club, wrote, "Litigation is a powerful tool. Not only does it result in direct environmental victories, but the *threat* of suits greatly increases our lobbying clout, especially at the state and local level." [Emphasis added.]

Destroying Justice

As Robert Bork points out in *The Tempting of America*, the process of destroying justice in the name of "the law" started well before the turn of this century. And it was totally premeditated. The activists, knowing that their radically statist programs couldn't be installed through legislatures, were forced into an end run around the Constitution and the people through the Judicial and Executive branches.

The revolution was to occur at four levels: (1) packing the courts; (2) passing remedial legislation; (3) enacting administrative law, and finally, (4) issuing "regulations" which have the full force of government authority.

The agencies – and "legalities" – spawned by this process now employ tens of thousands of bureaucrats, spend billions of dollars annually, and terrorize compliance in every aspect of our national life. The revolutionary agenda is accomplished *indirectly* by running around the legislatures and courts. Congress delegates authority to independent agencies with no specific powers, only a general "mandate" for enforcement. The Environmental Protection Agency is only the latest example of a legacy most exemplified by the fearsome power of the IRS.

In varying measure, these agencies are cop, judge, and jury. They all possess legislative powers, executive powers, and judicial enforcement powers – which means they can define law, impose fines, civil penalties, injunctions, and in some cases, even criminal sanctions. Legal proceedings have been removed from a "judicial" to an "administrative" setting.

We are no longer protected by a presumption of innocence. These entities operate on a presumption of guilt. Administrative law replaces constitutional and common law rights. The accused, with limited resources, faces legal extortion from an unpitying prosecutor with unlimited resources, and the law becomes whatever the bureaucrats say it is through their congressional "mandate."

Completing the Legal Revolution

But activist judges and fanatical bureaucrats cannot complete the legal revolution alone. Enter the radical legal beagles, the running dogs of radical revolution, and the "advocacy groups." In a technique pioneered in part by Ralph Nader, the well-heeled, media-trumpeted, private-but-"public interest" advocacy groups push a willing judiciary and bureaucracy further down the Green Road of Revolution.

Under a vastly enlarged definition of "standing" (who has the right to sue), they enter the courts to institutionalize their ideas of what the congressional mandate should mean. Thus they become law-givers, and the shift of legislative authority has rolled full circle, from legislature to bureaucracy through an activist judiciary to *private groups*. Now we have government by an unelected elite according to their own radical program.

Legal Terrorism

The stage is now set for the application of *environmental legal terrorism*. Remember as you read that Lenin, one of history's most effective terrorists, said that the only point of terror is terror. Therefore, *expect* your sense of logic and justice to be outraged. The point of environmental legal terrorism is *not to clean up* the environment, but to *clean out* the opposition and bludgeon the population into obedience to Green goals.

Punishment Before the Fact

Weapon number one in the terrorists' arsenal is the shift in the law from *reactive to proactive*. From antiquity, the law has become engaged only after a factual, objective offense. Undergirded by the socialist notion that ALL risks, no matter how slight, must be eliminated from human existence, reactive law has been replaced with proactive law which swings into action *before* any act has been committed. If there is a suspicion you *might* commit a crime, the bureaucrat – who changes the law itself according to his subjective whim – acts to *prevent* you.

Thus saccharine, which *might* cause bladder cancer in any rats persistent enough to drink three bathtubs full of diet cola every day, must be banished. CFCs, which might possibly, under *some* unreliable computer models, have *some* effect on the ozone layer, must be banned. Or alar. Or PCBs. Or name your "poison."

Pre-Trial Seizure

If you can be held guilty for something you haven't yet done, it's obvious that you can be punished before the fact as well. In the 1986 Anti-Drug Abuse Act, Congress decided to hold *bystanders* criminally liable for the acts of others! Prosecutors were authorized to seize "any property" which they allege (only *allege*, not *prove*) is the proceeds of crime or money laundering. Not only does the victim lose his property without trial or recourse, he is also stripped of his ability to hire a lawyer to defend himself. Now the victim is really ready for sacrifice.

Tailoring New Offenses: "RACKETEERS"

The prototype law for parleying small crimes into great ones, creating new offenses, and pre-trial forfeiture is the 1984 Racketeering Influenced Corrupt Organizations Act (RICO). Imitated in almost all state codes, RICO creates a new crime of "racketeering" (a "pattern" of activity requiring two acts). This was sold as a way to pound only the Mafiosi, but it has hardly been limited to gangsters.

The provisions of this Frankenstein's monster have been enforced against everyone from estranged spouses to abortion protesters. Ninety percent of the time it is now used by private parties suing legitimate businesses and individuals. The financial threat on the civil side is pure terror: triple whatever damages a jury awards. Combine this with the threat of pre-trial confiscation and the public embarrassment of being labeled a "racketeer" and even the stoutest heart quails.

The greens are already applying RICO. In June 1990, a federal jury convicted two New York City men and six waste-hauling companies of racketeering in a case involving illegal dumping of medical waste and asbestos. Under RICO forfeiture provisions, the eight accused "agreed" to pay a total of $22 million.

Radicalizing the Law

Objective law affords prior notice so that people can *avoid* criminal acts. But when the law becomes subjective, when legislatures refuse to define offenses but issue only generalized mandates to bureaucracies ("clean up the air" – "protect the environment," "a pattern of activity"), then the very definition of the law becomes unknowable, liable to change with the bureaucrats' subjective perceptions.

Ex Post Facto Law

Green legal terrorists love *ex post facto* law: yesterday's lawful act is made today's environmental crime – *after the fact*. One leading principle of environmental law enforcement is that to commit an offense, *it is not necessary that the perpetrator knew or could know there was a danger. Neither is it necessary that the crime was a crime when committed.* Environmental laws do away with the tiresome necessity for due process of law.

The accused becomes responsible for independent or unforeseeable causes. Even where the user should have known the risks, or was informed of the risks, the manufacturer, middleman, insurer, and in some cases even the lenders are held responsible for his misdeeds.

It is not even necessary that the manufacturer or middleman *knew* there was a risk. That DDT was discarded years ago by means acceptable and according to hazards known at the time is no defense to a later charge *after* other supposed dangers become known. Manufacturers are being held liable for not possessing knowledge *that did not exist at the time.* Relying on past state-of-the-art technology is *NOT* a defense.

Extending Liability: The Lightning Bolt Theory

The lightning bolt theory of law looks for some scapegoat. Since knowledge or intent doesn't matter, it's enough that you were in the area at the time the "crime" was committed: *somebody* must pay, and that means whoever can be reached now. Liability is fixed *without intent or responsibility*, after the fact.

Probably the most correct solution would be to apportion out any cleanup costs (if a cleanup is even necessary) with some sort of general tax, but this is a *politically undesirable* solution. Therefore a scapegoat must be found to pay, and the goat least able to dodge politically, i.e., industry and business, wins the prize. Of course, this violates both logic and due process: the victim had no means to limit his liability or avoid the crime.

How serious is this clenched fist? Hungarian Immigrant John Pozsgai found out when he cleared out a dry stream on his own property and moved a mass of rusting junk. Mr. Pozsgai, it seems, escaped the red comrades in Hungary only to be captured by the green comrades here. For cleaning off his own lot he was convicted of 40 felony counts of knowingly filling in five acres of federally-protected wetlands. He went to prison. Does the mighty Eco-Czar Reilly even know or care about John Pozsgai?

Also from the syndicated column of Walter Williams (Memphis *Commercial Appeal*, August 16, 1991.) comes another real life nightmare.

Dennis and Nile Gerbaz, two elderly gentlemen living near Carbondale, Colorado, were ordered by the Environmental Protection Agency to report to federal court and pay a fine of $45 million. Their neighbor had performed some work which diverted the Roaring Fork River and caused it to flood about 10 acres of the Gerbaz land. The EPA denied the brothers a permit to remove the obstruction and rebuild their levee. The Gerbazes thought they had the right to protect their land without a permit and restored the river to its original channel. The EPA claimed that when the river flooded the Gerbazes's land it created a "wetland," and you can't destroy wetlands without a permit, even if it's your own land.

A Risk-Free Existence

Behind this madness lies one key socialist presumption: eliminating all risk from human existence. Fearful manufacturers can no longer assume a fixed level of competence within society. Thus, producers are made liable for everything, consumers for nothing, and American society has been radically changed from a commonwealth of self-responsible, self-reliant souls to an asylum for incompetent, irresponsible, dangerous morons who expect someone to protect them from their own imprudent stupidity.

Manufacturers are being held liable for whatever way consumers use their products, even if the use involves assuming inherent risk or an obviously foolish application. That's why your new hammer has a label warning you not to comb your hair with it, or your chain saw label warns you that chain saws should not be used to clean your teeth. The result is the infantilization of the average man.

In what must be the *ne plus ultra* of extending legal liability, the case of *Horton vs. American Tobacco Co.* went to trial in January 1988 in Lexington, Mississippi. The family of Nathan H. Horton, who died of lung cancer in 1987, charged the company with "marketing a defective and unreasonably dangerous product," i.e., tobacco. In April 1990, the Hortons' attorneys issued information packets that alleged that tobacco companies were targeting blacks and other minorities (Albanians? Swazilanders? Byelorussians?), which resulted in a mistrial and change of venue.

Terrorism on Five Major Fronts

Environmentalists have pushed and are still pushing an extension of liability on five major fronts: (1) piercing the corporate veil; (2) subsequent owners; (3) insurers; (4) industry groups and manufacturers, and (5) lenders.

Piercing the Corporate Veil

Corporation's – fictional legal persons with a legal existence distinct from their owners and managers – exist to limit their owners' liability. Corporate stockholders aren't responsible at law for corporate debts or actions. This is the so-called "corporate veil."

However, the protection of the "corporate veil" is being ripped away by environmental cases, with horrifying results for owners, managers as well as directors. Commercial Metals of Springfield, Missouri and its manager were indicted on felony charges of violating hazardous waste disposal laws...A former Browning-Ferris Industries official was found guilty in Ohio on eight criminal violations of state hazardous waste laws...Three men and eight firms were indicted for operating an illegal landfill on Staten Island. The owner of a Louisville, Kentucky demolition company was found guilty of violating the Superfund Law and the Clean Air Act.

And the liabilities just keep on coming. Parent companies and individuals may be held liable for a subsidiary's actions: Kayser Roth was held liable for $846 million. Rockwell shareholders sued 14 current and former directors and officers charging they led the firm to violate disposal laws.

Subsequent Owners

Liability for environmental misdeeds is by no means limited to those who actually committed the crime. Subsequent owners are equally liable, even if they acquired the property after the fact and sold it before discovery of the problem. Consider: Powers Chemco, innocent purchaser of land polluted by the prior owner, was ordered by a New York Appeals Court to pay the cost of the toxic waste cleanup.

In 1954 Allied Signal bought a closed-down chromium processing plant in Jersey City as part of a larger deal. Although Allied sold the plant just a few months later, the state now holds it responsible for cleaning up the plant's chromium slag.

Atlantic States Legal Foundation, an environmental legal advocacy group, is asking for legal fees – plus $12.6 million in civil penalties – from Tyson Foods for polluting waters at a Blountsville, Alabama processing facility which was in violation when Tyson purchased it in 1986. Tyson acted quickly to solve the problem, but the 11th U.S. Court of Appeals overturned a lower court's dismissal based on Tyson's correction of the problem in 1988, after the suit was filed.

Big asbestos claims pushed Kohlberg Kravis Roberts & Co.'s $2.4 billion leveraged buy-out of Jim Walter Corp. into bankruptcy court. KKR had known that a Jim Walter unit, Celotex Corp., once made asbestos products, but figured that because Celotex was a separate subsidiary, claims could be confined to it. Anyway, Celotex was sold *three months* after the Jim Walter buy-out was completed. KKR and Hillsborough Holdings Corp., the KKR company that took Jim Walter private, are being sued by 80,000 asbestos "victims," with claims of over $3 billion. Hillsborough ran for cover in bankruptcy court in December 1989. (*Wall Street Journal*, April 2, 1990, p. A2.)

Is it any wonder that the poison pill of hidden pollution liability has become a major factor in acquisitions and takeovers?

Insurers

In June 1990, the Wisconsin Supreme Court ruled that a landfill operator's insurance policies cover damages resulting from pollution occurring over many years. Under the so-called "pollution exclusion" insurers have argued that policyholders aren't covered for damages from pollution released gradually. Policyholders have countered that they are due coverage as long as they didn't intentionally cause or expect the pollution.

One hundred twenty property owners living near a landfill site sued the company and its insurer for $9.6 million compensation for property damage. In a 6-1 decision the Wisconsin court held that since the "pollution exclusion" was ambiguous, it had to be resolved in favor of the policyholder. Dissenting Judge Donald Steinmetz said the court's decision means that an insurance policy "now becomes a deep pocket to pay for business mistakes." (*Wall Street Journal*, June 22, 1990.) You bet.

Industry Groups and Manufacturers

Both industry groups and manufacturers have been held collectively liable for pollution beyond their control. New York City has asked $50 million in damages from six lead pigment paint manufacturers to clean up and monitor lead paint in city-owned buildings.

Take the case of PPG. It used chromium ore to make paint pigments. Although burying industrial wastes was then common and accepted practice in the chemical industry, PPG has been already ordered to pay $31.5 million for cleanup at just a few sites. Total costs are estimated at $200 to $300 million.

The Commerce Department's National Oceanographic and Atmospheric Administration sued eight unrelated firms for alleged pollution to coastal waters off Los Angeles and Long Beach. The suit alleged the firms dumped DDT and hazardous PCBs into sewers that emptied into Los Angeles and Long Beach Harbors. The contamination dates back to the 1940s! The price tag for *restoring* the coastal waters is estimated at tens of millions of dollars.

But the great granddaddy of all proceedings against manufacturers must be asbestos. Used for decades in hundreds of applications including brake finings, insulation, and interior tiles, there are two types of asbestos. The type mined in the U.S. and Canada, and used for the overwhelming majority of applications, probably poses no health risk. Although the other type, imported from South Africa, was used almost exclusively in the ship building industry, the government-imposed asbestos hysteria insists that all asbestos must be removed everywhere, even where it physically can't be released into the environment. Civil suits against producers of asbestos products have piled to incredible heights: eighty *thousand* law suits against Celotex, sixty-eight *thousand* claims against Raymark, Manville Corp. in bankruptcy. The Green Giant is on a roll.

A so-called task force of 30 state attorneys general sued in the U.S. Supreme Court to force manufacturers of asbestos products to pay for removing it from public buildings. That removal would increase exposure to asbestos some *100,000 times* (that is, by ten million percent), at an estimated cost of $16 *billion*. Happily, the Supreme Court dismissed the suit, but we have not heard the end of it.

No-Fault Liability?

Manufacturers and distributors of toxic chemicals may be looking at liability for cleanups, even where they aren't at fault for any accident at all.

As the Wall Street Journal (May 25, 1990.) reported:

Preliminary rulings in a handful of cases suggest that courts may be heading toward the conclusion that, with cleanup costs skyrocketing, the burden must be shared more broadly. [*Remember the lightning bolt theory?*] Under the Superfund Law, companies that generate, transport, store, or dispose of hazardous waste are liable for its cleanup. Chemical suppliers who played no role beyond manufacture or sale of their products had assumed until recently that they could escape such liability...

So far, most courts have required that a supplier can't be held liable unless it played at least an indirect role in disposal of the product. In the latest case, the EPA acknowledged that the companies hadn't actually created or disposed of the waste. But the agency argued that the companies should still pay for the cleanup because the generation of waste was an inherent part of a company they hired to mix and package their chemicals into finished pesticides.

Polluters may even sue manufacturers in an effort to shift their own blame. Facing huge damages for ground water contamination in Michigan, Gelman Sciences sued seven companies that made or sold the chemical in question, alleging they failed to disclose its dangers adequately and should therefore bear the cleanup costs.

Lenders

The long "clenched fist" of environmental legal terror even extends to those who finance projects or property. Maryland Bank and Trust was held liable for hazardous waste cleanup costs on property acquired through foreclosure. In fact, not foreclosing seems to be the only way for the lender to avoid the liability.

Now, a federal appeals court has ruled that Fleet Factors Corp., a commercial financing company, may be liable for the cleanup of hazardous waste at a site owned by a company to which it lent money. No appeals court had previously ruled on the scope of the Superfund law exemption that supposedly shields lenders, but not owners and operators, from liability.

The majority of courts have ruled that lenders who *foreclose* on contaminated property are no longer covered by that exemption. This court said in addition that lenders *who are able to affect hazardous waste disposal decisions* are liable under Superfund. The appeals court found that the lower court had erred when it ruled that lenders must be involved in the day-to-day operations to incur liability.

Now hear this: the appeals court said that lenders must INSIST that debtors comply with environmental standards as a requirement for continued and future financial support!

Fear of these risks has led more and more banks to require "environmental audits" before financing properties. The threat of lender liability even has some banks avoiding foreclosure on overdue debts.

A few years ago Robert Wallace and Jack Hensley bought a scrap yard in Houston from Charter National Bank. When they tried to sell the business six months later, an environmental audit revealed widespread PCB contamination. The EPA condemned the lot and said the place needed a $10 million cleanup. The men stopped payment on their loan and sued, claiming the bank knew about the pollution but had kept them in the dark. So far, the bank hasn't foreclosed, and its lawyer won't discuss the case. (*Wall Street Journal*, April 2, 1990.)

Legal Extortion

Along with extended liability, business also faces terror by legal extortion. Corporations face potentially bankrupting, interminable litigation, adverse decisions, injunctions, and civil and criminal penalties. The result is not only compliance, but the avoidance of any project, no matter how economically attractive, which might carry environmental risk.

Individuals, including corporate managers and directors, are subject to this same extortion. They fear adverse publicity, public humiliation, civil penalties, fines, and even the stigma of criminal sanctions or jail time. Is it any wonder that so many of them cave into legal threats from environmental bureaucracies and legal action groups? In November 1990, the mere threat of bad environmental publicity forced fast-food giant McDonald's to switch from foam to paper hamburger packages. Now, in almost a comedic scramble of Max Sennett proportion, they are trying to make sure that the paper has been "recycled."

Expanding Legal Standing

Until recently, "standing" (the right to bring a law suit) depended on the existence of clear legal rights. Only people with direct and particular harm could sue. Through radical legal advocacy groups this concept has been stretched like a rubber skin across the legal horizon and beyond.

As L. Gordon Crovitz puts it:

Environmentalists are pushing the Supreme Court toward this choice: (1) Get ready for animal, vegetable, and mineral plaintiffs, or (2) make sure only real people with real cases can get into court. This is no joke, at least not to legions of "public-interest" lawyers who, with any luck, could be out of work. (*Wall Street Journal*, April 18, 1990, p. 23.)

Under the extension of standing, these radical "public- interest" lawyers are free to bring all sorts of obstructionist law suits. In one 1973 case, *U.S. vs. Students Challenging Regulatory Agency Procedures* (SCRAP), the Supreme Court allowed five students in what was essentially a law-school project to sue because each of SCRAP'S members "breathes the air within the Washington metropolitan area."

If this sounds like a trivial requirement to get into court, at least it required that the plaintiffs have lungs. Since at least 1972 the radical legal community has been pushing for legal rights for natural objects. Absurd? Not to the late Justice William O. Douglas, who in a dissenting opinion agreed that standing "would be simplified and also put neatly in focus if we...allowed environmental issues to be litigated...in the name of the inanimate object about to be despoiled, defaced, or invaded."

Overseas, standing has not only been extended to live animals: the dead may also qualify. In Sweden, a man went hunting, bagged a squirrel, and was slapped with a wrongful death suit which accused him of "the senseless murder of a helpless creature." It seems Sweden's new animal-protection laws say any citizen can sue on behalf of an injured or abused animal – and someone did.

They've Taken Over the Cockpit!

A cowardly Congress and brainwashed public has left the American legal system hostage to legal terrorists. Supported by Establishment foundations, government grants, and the federal judiciary and bureaucracy, radical environmentalists and other revolutionaries have hijacked American jurisprudence.

The list of casualties is long: presumption of innocence, due process, punishment only *after* conviction, liability only for your own acts, corporate limited liability, trial by jury, understanding the charges against you, objective law, separation of powers – these are all dead or wounded.

Monstrous fines and "civil penalties" inconceivable a few years ago, pre-trial seizures, and criminal penalties for environmental wrongdoing *which can't be defined or avoided beforehand* have created a reign of environmental terror. Under the threat of this terrorism, businesses and individuals around the country are knuckling under to the environmentalist program which will radically transform our present system into a socialist command economy staffed by terrified yes-men.

The hallmark of the new system will be former eco-czar Reilly's "clenched fist." That far-seeing American thinker and philosopher, Al Capone, might have described our new green "legal" system this way:

"You can get a lot farther with a smile and a gun than you can with a smile alone."

CHAPTER 15

THE NEW GREENMAIL

Green is not only the color of environmental activism – it's also the color of money. American marketers, supersensitive to every kind of consumer sentiment, real or contrived, have not been slow to smell the dough.

"This is the feel-good issue of the decade," says Joel Makower, a co-author of *The Green Consumer* about the coming green revolution in marketing. (*New York Times*, April 21, 1990.) The drive to appear green is being fueled by the rising environmental consciousness of American consumers. "Just as the '80s saw a proliferation of 'lite' products designed to meet growing health awareness, the '90s will be the decade of 'green' products," said Dorothy MacKenzie, head of product development for the Michael Peters Group, a package design firm.

Eco-Extortion's Vicious Circle

For consumer goods producers, the threat of eco-greenmail may be unavoidable. Under the attacks of green propagandists and pseudo-scientists, yesterday's universally popular product can become today's environmental nightmare. Aerosol-propelled cans once stocked every American's home, but under the threat of "global warming," manufacturers have scurried to return to more primitive methods of packaging.

Worse yet, the eco-threat may not only arrive indirectly as generalized propaganda, it may come knocking directly in the form of an organized boycott. As the *Wall Street Journal*, November 8, 1990, reported, "[Boycotts] have become increasingly common (300 in 1990 vs. 39 in 1984) as more and more groups have targeted individual companies...And, facing embarrassing publicity, many companies have changed their policies to pacify the boycotters...Opinion Research Corporation reported in June 1990 that 27 percent of consumers say they have boycotted a product because of the manufacturer's record on the environment." More bad news: those likely to boycott come from the most valuable demographic group: two-income families, college degrees, and from the big-spending thirtyish crowd. Is it any wonder that companies will go to great lengths to avoid such controversy?

Another direct form of eco-extortion is the newly-emerging environmentally-safe labeling movement. In some countries – Germany, Canada, and Japan – government panels certify products that reduce waste and pollution or promote recycling. In Germany the so-called "Blue Angel" shows up on about 2,500 products. In America, private interests are scrambling for the business of rating consumer goods, and the financial rewards are huge.

Contenders include Scientific Certification Systems, Inc. ("Green Cross") of Oakland, Good Housekeeping, and Green Seal, Inc. A private, profit-making laboratory, Scientific Certification Systems, charges companies from several hundred dollars to $10,000 for its certification. *Good Housekeeping* magazine, mindful of the success of its "Good Housekeeping Seal of Approval," wants to market a "Good Earthkeeping" seal as well. Green Seal, a private, non-profit organization, has a leader with a reputation: Denis Hayes, the chairman of Earth Days 1970 and 1990.

In June 1989, Green Seal, Inc. announced a board studded with environmental stars. Headed by Denis Hayes (of whom more later), the board also includes Alice Tepper Marlin, executive director of the Council on Economic Priorities; Esther Peterson, a long-time consumer advocate; Joan Claybrook, president of Public Citizen, the activist group founded by Ralph Nader; Henry Hampton, TV producer; and finally, Hubert H. Humphrey III, Attorney General of Minnesota.

Humphrey has been most visible of late issuing legal challenges to companies such as Mobil for making "false" environmental claims about their products. It was Humphrey who helped organize a "strike force" with nine other state attorneys general to attack this "problem." In a production worthy of the Rev. Al Sharpton, H.H.H. III plays both sides of the pavement and the middle of the road. He makes a national name for himself by prosecuting the innocent for manufacturing the innocuous, while serving on the board of Green Seal which stands to profit most by promoting environmental labeling.

But Three H's altruism is no more questionable than that of environmental activist and instant expert Denis Hayes. Hayes probably qualifies as the prime example of environmentalist cronyism at its most rewarding. In 1979, Hayes, at 35 and lacking any substantial scientific credentials (his only graduate degree was in law in 1985), was appointed head of the quasi-governmental Solar Energy Research Institute. SERI, the "spearhead" of the government's efforts to develop renewable forms of energy, had a staff of800 and a research budget of more than $120 million. Somebody convinced Energy Secretary Schlesinger that Hayes was the "leading environmentalist of his generation." The appointment was loudly supported by then-acting chairman of the Council on Environmental Quality, Rhodes Scholar, Natural Resources Defense Council co-founder, and now Clinton's eco-chieftain, Gus Speth.

As reported above, Hayes was one of the originators of Earth Day 1970 and helped found the Solar Lobby in 1978. Absent any scientific credentials, he was also a Visiting Scholar at the Smithsonian Institution, 1971-72, Director of the Illinois State Energy Office, 1974-75, and a senior researcher at Worldwatch Institute, 1975-79.

"Partnership"

The only way enough money can be "wasted," as the Iron Mountain report prescribed, is for the environmental movement set up a "partnership" among government, eco-groups, and business. Reporting on corporate sponsors for The Nature Conservancy, in the

January 1991 *Eco-Profiteer*, I wrote, "Lest you believe that the champions of American free enterprise are going to fight back, [we are fisting] major corporate sponsors of The Nature Conservancy (TNC), taken from TNC's 1990 annual report...These companies are spending tens of millions of dollars each year on behalf of The Greening." They don't intend to oppose The Greening – they intend to cash in on it. The list reads like a who's who of the Fortune 500.

In an outwardly ironic turn of events, businesses seek advice from groups which seem to be their natural enemies. As *Newsweek* reported November 19, 1990:

> Increasingly, companies are joining forces with environmentalists. McDonald's turned to the Environmental Defense Fund to help clean up its "McToxics" image [dumping its foam wrappers for paper]. "We listened to our customers, we listened to environmental experts," says McDonald's U.S.A president Edward H. Rensi.

Fundis Versus *Realos*

But there's never peace where money is at stake. The Big Bucks have divided the Greenies into what their German counterparts call "Fundis" and "Realos" – no-compromise "fundamentalists" and limousine "realists." The great divide offers plenty of scope for environmentalist pharisaism as each side curses the other for abandoning the True Faith.

The bias of many greens is so red that they can never forgive free markets, even when they grant everything the eco-maniacs want. They accuse business of "greenwashing"; for these true believers, every effort the free market makes is hypocrisy. Spokesmen for the environmental movement characterize manufacturers' moves to meet environmental concerns with their products as "merely window dressing."

"The nature of American business has not changed," said Alan Hershkowitz, a senior scientist at the Natural Resources Defense Council (Gus Speth's alma mater). "Right now the environment is a marketing trend they have to respond to. Three years from now, they will be doing something else as socioeconomic issues change." (*New York Times*, April 19, 1989.) [Don't we hope.]

In the aforementioned issue of *Newsweek*; "One business leader in the waste industry grumbles that 'it's to [the environmentalists'] advantage...to keep the problem alive to force societal change.'" After all, if we solved the so-called environmental problems, what would we do with all the excess eco-activists?

It's not even easy to satisfy the "realos" who carp at every attempt at environmental labeling. They complain that things are labeled "recyclable" but sold where no recycling facilities exist. Mobil added a chemical to its Hefty Trash Bags to promote their degradation in sunlight, but the Greenies griped that burying them in landfills kept them from decomposing. That's when Hubert the Third jumped on the funeral procession, filing suits with the six other top cops.

Greed ads and promotion have brought the eco-pharisees running to anathematize green groups who allow their names to be used for advertising. Coca-Cola, Sears, Ben & Jerry's Homemade, Patagonia, the Body Shop, and even Moosehead Beer, Tanqueray Gin, and Absolut Vodka have used environmental ads. What an opening! The eco-righteous at American Rivers, Friends of the Earth, and the Environmental Action Fund rushed to announce that they would not take part in promotions with companies that produced alcoholic beverages or – Eco-horrors! – tobacco.

Sometimes green activists are caught in their own trap. Since many if not most of their complaints have no basis in scientific fact, they are forced into hilarious Orwellian flip- flops in order to "good-think." Yesterday they hated plastic bags and loved paper bags, but today somebody points out the overlooked fact that plastic bags generate 70 percent less solid waste, so tomorrow they have to chuck their paper and buy plastic. "Science by fad" is a strain on the green budget.

To avoid these hysterical flip-flops for the Faithful, some environmentalists are promoting the "cradle to the grave" concept of environmental cost assessment. Unfortunately, this technique only re-emphasizes the impossibility of the task.

What's "cradle to the grave?" The *New York Times* (September 22, 1990.) provides the answer:

> Scientists are struggling to devise a way to help consumers, regulators, and others choose among competing products...based on their environmental impact. But researchers say that despite a spate of studies that make such comparisons, a valid method is not likely to be found for years. "Right now, it is impossible to make these kinds of decisions for 95 percent of the products out there," said Dr. Alan Hershkowitz, a senior scientist at the Natural Resources Defense Council.
>
> At issue is an increasingly popular research technique known as "product life cycle" analysis, [which] tries to measure the environmental impact of a product on a 'cradle to grave' basis. It looks at...the resources used to make the product, the pollutants released during that process, and the problems associated with the products disposal.

What's a True Green Believer to do? Remember the classic psychology experiment with cats? They were trained to push a particular lever to get food. Once the cats had broken the code, the psychologists changed signals on them. Sometimes when they pressed the lever, the cats still got food; other times, they got a powerful electric shock. The infelicitous felines responded by curling up in the corner of their cages in a – we can't resist – catatonic state. Pavlov deranged dogs with a similar process.

"'The result of all this is that people are going to assume that they can't do anything right,' said Linda Lipsen, a legislative counsel for Consumers Union. We're going to guilt-trip them into lethargy.'" (*New York Times*, April 21, 1990.) With environmental marketing, "can't win for losing" can also apply to businesses.

Right in time for Earth Day (April 1990), McDonald's had also announced that it would spend $100 million on recycled construction materials used in building and remodeling its restaurants. A lot of good all the eco-groveling did: in late October a group called the Earth Action Network broke the windows and scattered supplies at a McDonald's restaurant in San Francisco to protest the company's environmental policies. Paying off blackmailers doesn't pay, not even for McDonald's. Nothing less than complete de-industrialization will satisfy the eco-fringe. (Who knows, maybe they wanted to, as one Jack-in-the-Box ad says, "set the burger free.")

The Bottom Line

While in some polls, seventy-plus percent of American consumers say they'll pay more for "environmentally safe" products (if they knew what that meant), the facts suggest they won't. On November 11, 1990, The *Wall Street Journal* reported:

Despite the hype surrounding Earth Day, less than one-fourth of Americans can be considered true environ-mentalists. A study conducted by [The] Roper Organization...classified Americans into 5 types based on their environmental attitudes and behavior. Eleven percent are more likely to be involved in a wide range of pro-environmental activities. Another 11 percent are willing to spend money, but not time, on environmental activities. Both groups are better educated and more affluent than average. Fully 26 percent are average Americans who form a swing group: pro-environment on some issues, anti-environment on others. Over half of Americans fall into the last two groups. Twenty-four percent are not very involved in the environment, largely because they feel no one else is, either. Twenty-eight percent are uninvolved, apathetic, and believe that their attitude is main stream. They tend to be disadvantaged in terms of education and income.

Newsweek (November 19, 1990.) laments:

Yes, consumers say they are willing to pay as much as 10 cents more on the dollar for environmentally safe products, but at the same time voters are striking down major environmental initiatives across the country, including California's...Big Green package.

Consumers are also confused by eco-claims. A recent survey by the Council on Plastics and Packaging in the Environment, an industry trade group, shows that fewer than 25 percent of consumers even know what 'environmentally friendly' means.

Humphrey the Third and his attorneys' general "strike force" aren't helping matters. Their November report and a separate one from ad agency giant J. Walter Thompson conclude that consumer confusion over environmental claims is mounting. Because they don't understand what most of the terms mean, "people don't have a lot of faith in green labeling," says Lois Kaufman, president of Environmental Research Associates, Princeton, New Jersey pollsters on environmental issues.

The attorneys' general task force convened last year with much fanfare, vowing to police misleading environmental ads and craft uniform marketing standards. But their first report (November 8, 1990.) is filled with broad generalizations and few special recommendations... The task force asks the federal government to draft national standards, an effort that has already begun...The report wants companies to avoid vague phrases such as "environmentally friendly" and clarify whether a claim is for a package or a product.

Because of such confusion, the J. Walter Thompson report finds, corporate environmental messages aren't getting through. Most consumers would stop buying a product they know to be environmentally unsafe, according to the nationwide survey by the agency...but only 14 percent of the 1,000 Americans polled could recall environmental advertising for a particular company, while 56 percent said they knew about companies whose actions have hurt the environment... "advertisers are still struggling [to determine] what should be the right 'green' advertising message." Those that succeed 'will have a positive halo for the 1990s.' (*Wall Street Journal*, November 8, 1990.)

Consumers, like juries, vote not-guilty when they are confused. According to an ERA report in November 1991, 47 percent of consumers have come to dismiss environmental claims as mere gimmickry.

Industry has responded with lack of interest, ambivalence, and fear. In the fall of 1991, the Florida-based Environmental Institute announced a conference for environmental groups AND business styled "Eco-Glasnost!" (eco-freaks love exclamation points), but by November the two-day forum had to be cancelled for lack of interest.

Businesses are ambivalent about environmental labeling because they are afraid it might backfire in their faces. No one is quite sure, consumer or manufacturer, what terms such as "recycled," "recyclable," and "degradable" are really supposed to mean. Frustrated and confused consumers might just reject the whole thing as hype and hypocrisy.

Businesses hear and can't forget what happened to Mobil over its environmental claims for Hefty Trash Bags. Mobil was accused by seven states in the summer of 1990 of exploiting popular misconceptions by making environmental claims for Hefty Trash Bags that it allegedly knew were false.

Finally, the environmental labeling and marketing movement is beset with conflicting goals. We've already noted the near – impossibility of assessing so-called "environmental costs." Worse yet, recycling some materials may help the solid waste "problem" while they worsen energy consumption. Some recycling can cost more than producing new products, and, after all, cost is the best measure of resource use (for everybody but a Greenie).

Dr. Petr Beckman noted in *Access to Energy*, (July 1990.) "Recycled paper is of lower quality than virgin paper and more expensive...That market soon saturated when recycling became fashionable, and while at first paper recyclers would pay as much as $40 a ton for used newspapers, [now] in New Jersey it has plummeted to minus $40, which is what you have to pay to have it taken off your hands. That is what the market thinks of recycled paper.

"Recycling paper does not make any environmental sense, either. It saves trees that do not need saving, for they are grown for that purpose by companies who are the world's best environmentalists...The used paper could be burned for electric power...if the Green Church did not condemn it as sinful."

The Philosophical View

After we strip away the hype and hysteria, green labeling and marketing doesn't promise to serve consumer, business, or even the environment very well. It does offer unlimited opportunities for the Environmental Industry of professional activists, lobbyists, advocacy groups, and opportunists of every shade of green. Green labeling flies in the face of that great wisdom from Pearl Bailey: "If ya have to wear a sign that says ya are, ya ain't."

CHAPTER 16

THE SPOTTED OWL
CRUSADE

While the media focuses America's attention elsewhere, to the latest "crisis" of the month, the Greening juggernaut rolls merrily along. The Greening Revolution is designed to do two things: (1) control people, including all their activities and (2) control natural resources, the basis for all wealth and productivity. The stakes in this warfare are colossal, but too few people, even those who consider themselves well-informed, are aware of just how far these two authoritarian goals have been advanced in the name of "preserving the environment." The Spotted Owl Crusade offers a case study in Green strategy and tactics. In it they have combined their considerable propaganda sophistication, media leverage, and organizational efficiency with legal terrorism.

On the other side, founded in 1970 with six loggers, the Washington Contract Loggers Association (WCLA) now represents about 600 members. Most of these are small outfits, with an average of 12 employees and about $1 million a year gross income. Similar industry organizations exist in Oregon, California, Idaho, Montana, and Alaska, but the WCLA has been the logging industry's point man against the environmentalists' Spotted Owl Crusade.

In 1976, the U.S. Forest Service chose the spotted owl as an "indicator" species for the health of the old growth eco-systems. Since many loggers have worked in the woods 25 years without ever noticing a spotted owl, they contend it is nothing but a political indicator.

The spotted owl was first singled out by the environmentalists in a seminar held at the University of Oregon – the Eugene

Environmental Law Clinic. Resource Analyst Andy Stahl of the Sierra Club Legal Defense Fund in Seattle made an interesting, if cynical, confession there on March 5, 1988:

"The northern spotted owl is the wildlife species of choice to act as a surrogate for old growth protection, and I've often thought, thank goodness the spotted owl evolved in the northwest, for if it hadn't, we'd have had to genetically engineer it."

"The perfect surrogate" equals the perfect excuse to halt timber harvesting. Several of these "crusade" species are spotted around the country: the red cockaded woodpecker in the South, the grizzly bear in the West, or the desert tortoise in Nevada and Utah. You name it, the eco-monitors are ready to protect it, no matter what it costs – you.

This tactic really dates from blocking a Tennessee TVA dam project for the sake of the snail darter, a tiny fish. Ironically, the Northwest timber folks thought the spotted owl issue was so clearly a farce that it would fool neither the public nor the politicians. Remember the snail darters? Congress overrode that, built the dam, and then snail darters were found everywhere.

Timbermen contend the same holds true for the spotted owl. Although they are now finding owls everywhere, the bird has already been declared a threatened species protected under the Endangered Species Act, so now the timber industry faces a whole new set of rules.

Before the 1988 conference in Eugene, there was no movement to lock up the so-called "ancient forests." When the Greenies found out they had a usable tool, they started using it. For the cost of a stamp, environmentalists could appeal any timber sale in the old growth forests, the Forest Service would issue an injunction, and logging would stop. For the loggers it became a nightmare bottleneck. At a negligible cost, environmentalists could force the logger to cease all operations and bear the expense of hiring attorneys to try to hit the injunction.

In most cases, the appeals were obviously frivolous. In 1987, practically no appeals were filed, but in 1988 filings skyrocketed into the hundreds overnight. In 1989, the WCLA learned that students from some Ivy League colleges were filing appeals on forests in Washington and Oregon that they had never seen or even visited.

These legal tactics cost American taxpayers tremendous sums. For every appeal, the Forest Service has to jump through a whole series of hoops – along with the loggers. Loggers are either shut down and can't operate, or have to move out of the area until the appeal has been resolved.

The legal bottleneck devastates lumber mills as well. A mill needs to know how much timber will be available for cutting. If there's no timber, the mill owner shuts down. Several weeks or even months of shut-down can put him out of business for good.

Just how endangered is the spotted owl? In 1986 the Audubon Society called on their top ornithological experts for a study of the owls. They said that if the bird population fell below 1,500 pairs they should be declared endangered, but at that time they concluded the population was at least 2,000 pairs. In a lengthy interview which ran in the Sunday edition of the Tacoma *Morning News Tribune*, September 8, 1991, former Washington State Governor, Atomic Energy Commission chairwoman and college professor Dixie Lee Ray, made some very telling points. The interview was conducted by Art Popham of the *Tribune* staff and centered around Ray's book *Trashing the Planet* which is very critical of the environmental movement. At an early point in the piece, the former marine biologist and zoology professor is asked:

Popham: Now you have written a book, called *Trashing the Planet*. What is the basic thesis?

Ray: ... I think there has been so much misinformation – sometimes simply misguided because of ignorance, sometimes rather deliberate – on questions that affect the way we live. In this whole area that we would call "environmentalism," there has been so much in the way of scare tactics and unnecessarily frightening hyperbole, that I've been speaking out on these issues...*Trashing the Planet* is a little bit of an ironic twist because I consider the trashing that's being done is being done by the rabid environmentalists who are crying "wolf" all the time.

Pogham: Is that happening with the northern spotted owl/timber industry conflict?

Ray: No question, no question. Of course, the whole Endangered Species Act thing is a vast overreaction. When we look at what constitutes a species, and if one is going to be at all accurate, the northern spotted owl is not a species, it's a subgroup of a species of spotted owls. That's why they always, and should always, refer to it as the northern spotted owl because it's only a variant of the spotted owl species...There's no limit to the spotted owls. But the variant of the species, called the northern spotted owl, is claimed by some, mainly from the more radical end of the environmentalist movement, to be totally dependent upon old-growth forest and in danger of being wiped out if there's not enough of the old-growth left.

Now, the fact is, most of the old growth – not all by any means, but most of it – is in national parks, and that's never going to be cut anyway. And the fact is that the northern spotted owl doesn't have to live in old growth, it has to live in old snag. And you know what a snag is – it's a tree that the top has been blown off, therefore the top of the snag itself is kind of rotted. And that's where the northern spotted owl nests.

It can't build its own nest, and it must have a snag to nest in. Now, usually the nests are found in the old growth because the trees do get blown down every once in a while because they're old and decayed and so that's a good place for nesting. But when timber has been cut and if snags are left, that leaves them a nesting place.

Popham: So, in other words, this subgroup, the northern spotted owl, doesn't need protecting at all?

Ray: I don't believe so, no. And many of the people from the group that have brought the issue forward have freely admitted that it's not the owl that they're interested in, it's to prevent timber from being cut. They want to save forests. And you can get people much more emotional about a bird than you can about a tree.

Popham: Was there a time in your career as a zoologist that you belonged to or supported the Audubon Society, the Sierra Club, or organizations like that?

Ray: No question about that – clear up until about the middle '60s, and it was about that time when those organizations and their leadership changed and they were taken over by the radical wing. [Considering our premise about what kicked the environmental movement into high gear, Dr. Ray's "middle '60s" comment is very significant.]

Thank you, Dr. Ray - you can now move to the top of the environmental groups' hate list if you aren't already there.

Nonetheless, the timber industry is now intensively counting birds. Their lowest population figure is 3,000 pairs. On the high side, loggers believe there are at least 5,000 pairs. In fact, a new study last year counted approximately 2,000 pairs in California alone. The feathery bottom line is that there are certainly more owls than anybody suspected, with more being found every day.

How many acres of forest land are now set aside for this bird, which may or may not be "endangered?" Not counting the owl set-asides on Washington State lands, there are already five million acres preserved forever in parks, wilderness areas, and other parcels. That equals the size of Massachusetts!

There's no logging permitted on that land and probably never will be. Of that area, 1.4 million acres are considered low-elevation old growth, which is "spotted owl habitat." If you use the halfway credible Forest Service figures, the total old growth in Washington State is 2.6 million acres. More than half of that is already preserved, so we're only arguing over the 1.2 million acres left. The environmentalists want to lock up all the land in Washington and take it away from the people.

In fact, Sierra Club chairman Mike McCloskey has a great idea. "Why not make the sequoia groves a World Heritage site? That would give them protection under international treaty and remove them from any commercial timber category." (*National Geographic*, September 1990, p. 114.) The United Nations World Heritage Convention, adopted in 1972, ostensibly aims to preserve great natural and manmade landmarks around the earth. However, it actually transfers control of the land to the World Heritage administrator, UNESCO (United Nations Educational, Scientific, and Cultural Organization). The nature and extent of that jurisdiction is still a deep legal question. In effect, Mr. McCloskey thinks that some western forest lands should be taken out of United States jurisdiction and put under United Nations jurisdiction.

Are the forests really endangered? Consider these facts from the American Forest Council. "Today America has over 20 percent more trees than it had just twenty years ago... Trees are being replenished faster than they are harvested in every region of the country. Private landowners and America's forest products companies...plant over six million trees a day, re-seed entire forests, and use other forest management techniques to promote natural re-growth."

Measuring the Cost

What has the spotted owl escapade done to the price of timber? On the stump it has skyrocketed by as much as 200-300 percent. Buyers are speculating they might not be able to buy old growth again. At one sale in Oregon, timber appraised for about $300 per 1,000 board feet was actually knocked down at $900.

Although the price for timber has skyrocketed, the price for finished products has risen more slowly. When that catches up, the price of a 2x4 in your local lumber yard will probably climb 33 percent to 50 percent, and that will be reflected in housing as well as all other areas where forest products are used – paper products, film for your camera, ice cream, you name it.

How many jobs will the Owl Crusade destroy? The American Forest Resource Alliance says that 102,000 jobs could be lost, but no one knows for sure because of the multiplier effect. Since businesses depend on each other like a chain of dominoes, logging lay-offs will cause lay-offs in a multitude of dependent industries, from heavy equipment to groceries.

What will it cost the logging industry? That's fairly easy to calculate. Just multiply the total acreage to be set aside (8.4 million acres) by the average sales from that acreage. Tracing the cost from timber to mill to store to home, the WCLA figures roughly $95 million per pair of spotted owls, compared to these birds, the snail darter was a bargain.

That figure only accounts for the loss due to timber taken out of production. There are more costs to the taxpayer on the government's side of the ledger – the agencies, the legal bills, and the Forest Service won't get any smaller. Even though less revenue will be generated, past experience shows there will be ever increasing budget allotments to the various agencies involved. The taxpayer gets a double whammy: lost revenue and more spending.

Who Benefits?

Many mysteries can be solved by asking the simple question, *"Cui bono?"* – Who benefits? In Washington State about one-fourth of the land is owned by big corporations such as Weyerhaeuser, Georgia Pacific, and Plum Creek Timber, a Burlington Northern spin-off. Another fourth is owned by small companies, mom-and-pop operations from a few hundred acres down to only twenty or thirty.

In the past three or four years these small grassroots companies and the workers out in the brush have borne the brunt of fighting the Owl Crusade. The big companies haven't helped a lot. Of course, if more national forest land is locked up, the large owners will see the value of their own holdings soar. In fact, Jack Creighton, Weyerhaeuser president, has said that the decrease in available timber would definitely increase the value of Weyerhaeuser's products, raw timber, and land. That may help explain why Weyerhaeuser and Georgia Pacific are major contributors to such organizations as the Sierra Club. Boise Cascade, to their credit, doesn't play the game.

Still, it's hard to get in bed with the devil without eventually getting bitten yourself. The corporations have been assuring themselves that this log export ban on state lands was never going to affect them because it would never apply to private lands. Now, however, the people who received those donations are biting the hand that feeds them. A total ban on all exports is more than probable in the next few years, because that's what the environmentalists are seeking.

Redefining Property Rights

The line between public and private land is blurring and dissolving. As far as the owl is concerned, he can't tell whether he's on Forest Service land or private land. Ominously, neither can the public.

The enviros know this, and use it very effectively. They don't want any trees cut, period. They're going to do their utmost to stop the cutting of trees – and it doesn't matter whose land they're on. Obviously, this is going to have a tremendous impact on private land ownership: they want to see private land totally controlled.

Already in Washington State, laws have been proposed to control the rate of harvest on private lands. After President Bush signed a virtual ban on exporting logs from public lands in the Northwest, Rep. Peter DeFazio (D-OR) argued recently that private lands should not be treated differently.

These are just the first steps toward total control of private land. The environmental movement is now gearing up toward the private land issue right now in California. In the name of preserving "endangered" species from desert turtles to whooping cranes to woodpeckers to owls, private property could ultimately become extinct – all under the cover of environmental preservation.

Whoever controls the land controls the people. They're starting to control the land subtly now, through zoning and through other regulations which are not so obvious, and people are buying it. They think it's great to pay a few dollars so people won't cut trees, but they don't realize they're just opening the door to further regulation.

This is a battle between the not-so-jolly Green Goliath and little logger David. The WCLA's total annual budget totals about $1 million, but most of that is required for other purposes. To educate the public and fight against the Greenies' Owl Crusade, they can only spend $80,000 to $90,000. Even counting the other six or seven loggers' associations, they don't have over $500,000 to fight with, while the environmentalist have hundreds of millions of dollars (literally).

Dollars are important, because dollars buy media time, and this battle will be won or lost in the media. The loggers may be slowing turning the public around at the grassroots level, but they haven't even entered the fray in the urban areas, and that's where the big fight takes place.

A Pattern Emerges

Two other examples of the "endangered species" strategy, particularly as it relates to timber, are also worth noting. In Tennessee and the south, it's the red-cockaded woodpecker that must be "protected" by closing off access to their nesting sites. Curiously, as was the case with the spotted owl, these unassuming little birds seem only to thrive in mature woodlands.

With the owl, it is "ancient forests" of Douglas fir. The woodpecker, according to environmental "experts," nests only in "old-growth pine forests." As the Memphis *Commercial Appeal* (May 20, 1990.) reported, "The problem is one of numbers. Fewer than 10,000 of the woodpeckers remain – and the old-growth pine forests that provide the trees they need for nests are rapidly giving way to even-aged tree farms..."

In its efforts to protect the red-cockaded woodpecker, the government has restricted timber harvests in 16 national forests in nine states. No cutting is allowed within 3/4 mile of every known red-cockaded woodpecker nest – a rule that places 1,100 acres of trees around every site "off limits."

The Memphis newspaper commented:

Timber interests say the policy will be ruinous for individual sawmills, some of which depend on national forests for 90 percent of their lumber...Timber officials say the fight "is only beginning." They fear the Forest Service—prodded by environmentalists – will place more federal land off-limits as more woodpecker sites are identified. So far, protection plans apply only to federally owned forests, but timber interest say private landowners could be next.

Next, we have the case of the marbled murrelet. In August 1990, the Associated Press reported:

Researchers in the Walbran Creek watershed on the west coast of Vancouver Island claim to have discovered the first nest in British Columbia of the threatened marbled murrelet.

The find is expected to fuel efforts to conserve remaining old-growth forests in the province.

Discovery of the nest [was made] recently on a mossy limb about 132 feet up an old-growth Sitka spruce...*Biologists have suspected the marbled murrelet, a small diving seabird, requires old-growth forests for nesting in B.C.* [Emphasis added.]

So let's add it up. Millions of acres of "ancient forests" for northwest owls, millions of acres of "old-growth pine" for southeastern woodpeckers, and millions of acres of "old- growth spruce" for Canadian diving seabirds. Do you get the feeling that there just might be a pattern here? One question I've never seen answered anywhere is, "Who pays whom how much to count the birds, and who keeps score?"

Many of these same battles are being waged throughout the U.S. and the world. Wolves, bears, elephants, rodents, turtles, eagles, whooping cranes, birds of every color, fish of every stripe, are all being used in The Greening grab of natural resources. Most Americans still don't see it, and won't believe it until it hits them in the pocketbook. It's already hitting the loggers, and they're responding with anger and fear – fear of the unknown. They can't see down the road, and they've got a lot invested in their businesses – not only their lifestyles, but also their life's savings.

More Battles, More Allies

The loggers are beginning to network with other groups outside the timber industry: the cattlemen, the builders' association, raining, and other land-user groups. They are trying to band together on this issue, but they still need more allies. They need to alert hunters and fishermen, who don't realize that once the environmentalists grab control of a resource, it may no longer be available for their favorite hobby.

The tragedy is that well-financed professional environment groups using guile, deception, and legal manipulation can mislead the public into locking up 8.4 million acres of public land. It's the ultimate sting operation. Amazing, isn't it? Our government protects a flag-burners right to free speech, while at the same time it strips private landowners of their property rights – for a bird.

CHAPTER 17
SOCIALISM IS DEAD: LONG LIVE SOCIALISM!

We live in an age of illusion. For a hundred years, in politics and advertising, manipulators of every stripe have honed "the art of human engineering." Goebbels or Ivy Lee, Pennsylvania Avenue or Madison Avenue, they've all learned the art of persuasive illusion.

In the building of the great one-world plan, the future holds the corporate state: fascism. And fascism, as any careful reader knows, is nothing but corporate socialism. But if socialism is a discredited economic disaster, how is it to be made palatable? Simple. Call it something else. While socialism supposedly wheezes out its last outdated breath in Eastern Europe, Greenies worldwide are preparing the way for a new, improved, and more potent version under the guise of "environmental consciousness."

Invariably, the "solutions" offered to the various environmental threats are only more socialism: centralized planning, price controls, fascist "partnership" between industry, government, and environmental elitists, and an end to private property. "Global environmentalism requires global planning, global regulation, and, inevitably, jobs for global bureaucrats." (*Wall Street Journal*, November 8, 1989.)

For suffering mankind, the worst part is the anti-development mentality that colors all these proposals. As pitifully inefficient as it is, at least socialism *claims* the goal of production. The new radical environmental socialists oppose production and development, *for the sake of opposing it alone.* One man who is using the Greening to fill his pockets with green is also one of the movement's most outspoken critics. Joseph Jacobs is the 75-year-old founder and CEO of an engineering firm which bears his name. The *Wall Street*

Journal reported on September 17, 1991, "Pollution policies exemplify, in Mr. Jacob's view, how the U.S. is being choked by bureaucratic restraint."

The nerve center of a capitalist economy is the price system. Through the price system, consumers "vote" on the plans and output of producers. Those producers who obey the voice of consumers continue to produce; those who don't, don't.

It was the refusal to bow to the delicate mechanism of free prices in free markets which, more than any other technical mistake, left the Soviet Union incapable of rational industrial production or even self-sufficient agricultural production after 70 years of central planning.

Now enter the Greens with a new proposition to make pricing impossible and to divorce prices from the realities of the marketplace and consumer wishes: the Green GNP. The "Green GNP" proposes to assemble a Gross National Product figure which takes into account environmental costs in the national economic statistics, to show the costs of using, or misusing, the environment. Because such costs can be at best only educated guesses and at worst pure imagination, this is a statistician's nightmare and a bureaucrat's fantasy comes true.

The questions posed in formulating a Green GNP are almost unanswerable. According to the *International Herald Tribune*, (July 4, 1989, p. 9.) German "officials say that the already daunting task of assigning a monetary value to existing resources and to steps taken to protect them is relatively easy compared to the greater challenge of assessing how much it would cost to restore the environment or compensate those who suffer in the meantime.

"This search has already led some West German researchers into such areas as noise pollution, aesthetic pollution [sic], and even smell pollution." The result will be the arbitrary assignment of non-quantifiable "costs" to the price of everything, in order to account for a supposed, presumed, or imagined "cost" of its production to the environment. Users' fees?

GNP statistics are questionable at best, since even the vast economic activity of a small nation can hardly be accounted for in its totality. But at least this is an objective quest that seeks to deal with facts. The Green GNP would interpose subjective factors, arbitrary "costs" chosen out of thin air, resulting in numbers completely useless from a scientific standpoint. Further, this elitist undertaking presupposes that consumers are incapable of making such choices themselves and have not already figured in all the costs in the prices they are willing to pay.

But the purpose is not scientific or objective – the purpose is to shoehorn the economy into the environmentalists' pipe- dream of the eco-millennium. The *International Herald Tribune* article further notes, "The [German] Greens...are especially anxious to have such calculations for use in steering resource and taxation policies." In other words, down the road, after the perfection of the Green GNP, special taxes will be levied to make sure prices reflect their "true environmental costs."

Nor are the German Greens the only environmentalists calling for inclusion of environmental "costs" in the economic calculation. In his book *After the Crash: The Emergence of the Rainbow Economy*, British "Green" Guy Dauncey predicts that "instead of justifying their operations solely in terms of profit, businesses will have to become 'holistic' – responsible to their employees and customers for personal, social, environmental, and planetary goals." (*Vancouver Sun*, September 16, 1989.)

Of course, our Native American socialists in Congress have extensive experience as social engineers. Their major instrument is tax policy, and the internationalists have taken a leaf from their book with a proposed *carbon tax*. In order to force the public into their green notions of personal righteousness, they need a means to force energy conservation.

Their answer is a tax on every barrel of oil, and its equivalent in other forms of energy, beginning at $3 a barrel and rising by the end of the century to $10 a barrel. That translates into about 25 cents a gallon at the gas pump. The bureaucracy of the European Commission has already tried to adopt a *carbon tax*, and the green hordes at the Rio Earth Summit could hardly stop drooling over it. Not only would it force conformity to their green agenda, it would also establish an *international tax* for the first time.

The *Atlanta Journal* (July 14, 1989) reports that "growing numbers of corporate planners and financial analysts are trying to forecast the business climate in a world transformed by global warming, rising seas, and shifting rainfall...Global climate is starting to figure into investment decisions."

Two recent items in the financial pages of the *New York Times* announced that Disney and General Electric had just created Departments of Environmental Policy and appointed men to the positions of vice president of same. Other major companies are quickly jumping on this bandwagon.

In an Australian TV interview, environmentalist Steven Schneider asserted, "Right now the current price of coal, oil, and gas doesn't include the disruption it does to the environment...If we're going to ever have the right market incentives [sic] to solve the problem...we are going to have to have the right prices on energy. We've got to include environmental costs." (Quoted in *Greenhouse Hokum*, R.J. Long, Dominion Data, GPO Box 1467, Brisbane, Queensland, Australia 4001, p. 28.) Let me assure you that when Mr. Schneider talks about "market incentives," he is not talking about privatization of the power industry or removal of subsidies and government-controlled energy prices.

What does all this mean to us? The *International Herald Tribune* article gives a clue. "Mr. Schultz [of the German Federal Environment office in Berlin] noted that gasoline is available at roughly one Deutsche mark (50 cents) per liter (0.26 gallon) in West

Germany, but he said that some studies show it should be as much as 5 DM [*Five times the present price!*] to pay for the effects of noise and air pollution, and the cost of accidents."

The costs won't stop there. Consider just one item the Green Industrialization will eliminate, chlorofluorocarbons (CFCs). Not only do CFCs power aerosol sprays, they are also the most effective refrigerant known. Chlorine produced from CFCs is the much-touted culprit behind the "ozone-hole" at the South Pole. Yet volcanoes emit 36 million tons of chlorine gas a year, while only about 750,000 tons per year are attributed to CFCs, or about 2 percent of the total. For their 2 percent, CFC producers are being forced to develop alternatives. Du Pont, the largest producer, "estimates that retrofitting and shifting all the world's processes to alternative compounds will cost the world between $50 billion and $100 billion by the year 2000." (*Forbes,* October 30, 1989, p. 225.) Alternatives will cost three to five times that of CFCs presently being used.

Environmental safety won't come cheap, and you must pay.

Partners in Crime

The chief distinction of fascism is the "partnership" between business and government. In practice this amounts to a government-sanctioned price-fixing scheme, with a side-benefit of locking out the competition forever. As evidenced by the 600 corporate exhibitors at Globe '90 in Vancouver, the environmental movement thrives on "partnerships." To the fascist corporate socialist state of the future will be added a new partner: NGOs, or non-governmental organizations. These NGOs are private, un-elected tax exempt foundations and environmental groups. While many people with a sincere and well-founded concern for stewardship of the environment may be connected with these organizations, they are also the major supplier of radical environmentalists. From the UNESCO Heritage Treaty to the Fourth World Wilderness Congress to the Earth Summit in Rio, environmentalist declarations and official documents call for the participation of these un-elected

NGOs in the planning and administration of national environmental policies. This is like giving a kleptomaniac the keys to Macy's.

Fascism is, by its very nature and practice, elitism, and this tendency is reinforced by the appointment of these un-elected radical environmentalists to positions of great power over the destiny of national economies. Of course, this is sold under the guise of "scientific or professional expertise," but the threatening result is a world governed by persons unaccountable to the public.

It's not the spotted owl or elephant which is the endangered species: its man and his liberty.

Good-Bye Small Business

Socialist central planners like to plan, and nothing throws a wrench in the planning like an entrepreneurial small businessman. Every time the bureaucrats look around, there they are, mucking up the Five Year Plan, building factories and businesses, making jobs for people, and using up precious resources that should have been left "natural."

Increased regulation for the economy means increased overhead for business, and it is small business that can least absorb increased costs, whether in buying capital equipment for regulation compliance or merely in the cost of complex record-keeping. But there is another face of eco-socialism that threatens small businessmen, farmers, ranchers, and developers alike: the legal axis and the eco- land grab.

The Eco-Land Grab

Armed with a new federal Court of Appeals ruling, environmental groups in the Pacific Northwest now have standing to sue the Bureau of Land Management because of their "recreational interest" in these lands. (*U.S. News & World Report*, July 3, 1989, p. 16.) This means that environmental groups without any economic interest in government lands can block development, mining, or, as noted in the last chapter, even logging on those lands in long, costly legal battles.

"If there was no such thing as the owl, you might not have this crisis to the current extent, but you'd have it eventually, because you're up against a group of people who don't like logging and who at the very minimum don't want any logging of old growth," says Washington's Senator Slade Gorton.

For the logging industry, this is only the beginning:

A powerful, reinvigorated environmental movement is going to *revolutionize* the management of public and private forest lands, former U.S. Senator Dan Evans told the Washington Forest Protection Association yesterday...Curt Smitch, director of the Washington Department of Wildlife, said that overwhelming public pressure is growing to manage forest and other lands for the protection of all wildlife, not just for the propagation of game animals. *'And that means private lands,' according to Smitch.* [Emphasis added.]

The difference between public and private land is slowly dissolving in the name of "environmental protection."

To the south in Nevada, the desert tortoise is the cause celebre. Since a federal listing of the tortoise as an endangered species, disruption of the animal's habitat is prohibited. That threatens not only off-road races and some cattle grazing on federal land, but also land development.

"If you have ungraded land that has tortoises on it, it basically stops you dead," said Jim Ley, a Clark County administrator. "There won't be any impact for 6 to 9 months because of the projects already under construction, but after that, you'll see a definite lull." (*Investor's Daily*, September 15, 1989.)

Current U.S. legislation threatens not only the control of private property by the rightful owners, it even threatens title. The American Heritage Trust Act of 1989 (HR 876) was reintroduced in the 1991 session of the U.S. Congress. Among other things, the Act creates a gigantic land trust, independent of Congress, and provides for funding states and private organizations in the acquisition and management of wilderness areas. (Remember the NGOs and "partnership" mentioned above?) This is in a country where already 740,885,157.6 acres are already being administered by federal agencies: 31.9 percent of all U.S. territory!

National Cattlemen's Association President Dale Humphrey commented on the first defeat of the Act in 1988:

> [This Act] would have given federal and state agencies and local land trusts hundreds of millions of dollars every year to buy up private land, and could have led to restrictions on livestock grazing and other multiple uses on surrounding federal lands. (*Beef,* December 1988.)

There is no satisfying the appetite of the environmentalist land grab. In a plaintive letter to the editor of *Agri View,* (February 9, 1989) a threatened Wisconsin farmer pleads his case:

> For three years, myself and others have been trying to get the Department of Natural Resources (DNR) and the legislature to listen to our concerns as landowners and to treat us as the constitution guarantees. Sadly, we are finding out that because our numbers are small in comparison to the environmentalists and others with great political pull, we have few, if any, rights. With the proposed legislation now being pushed, people...will lose local control...Did you know that 5,300,000 acres of our state is now owned by the DNR, U.S. government, and county and local governments? Did you know that DNR is working on 137 more projects that will involve buying land?

Think about what's been happening to our rights as Americans and then ask yourself: Am I really free? The free landowner is becoming an endangered species.

But no farm is so humble, no ranch so huge, that the environmentalists are willing to leave its owners in peace. In fact, Deborah and Frank Popper, professors at Rutgers University in New Jersey, are environmentalists who can really think big. Their plan is to return most of Montana, Wyoming, Colorado, New Mexico,

North Dakota, South Dakota, Nebraska, Kansas, and half of Oklahoma to – not the Indians, but the buffalo!! According to the Poppers, "The only way to keep the Plains from turning into an utter wasteland, an American Empty Quarter, will be for the federal government to step in and buy the land – in short, to deprivatize it." A few years ago the Poppers and their proposal would have been the subject of deserved ridicule, but nothing, and I mean nothing, seems beyond possibility anymore.

There is a real partnership between government and NGOs in the eco-land grab. "The National Park Service has secretively surveyed the entire U.S., territories, and possessions, sorting through millions of properties, public and private, without the knowledge or consent of private owners."

In a frightening expose, the highly reliable *Daily News Digest* reported on January 4, 1990:

The program is called National Natural Landmark Program. It has no organic basis in legislation. For a private landowner, being singled out by the Program is the property rights equivalent of being Jewish and having your name, address, photo, and fingerprints on a fist safely in the hands of the Nazi party. Secrecy is a necessary part of the process, to wit:

"The question of secrecy and of publicity is a hot topic which will undoubtedly come back to haunt us over the years if this document ever becomes generally available to the public." [1]

Daily News Digest editorializes:

What it amounts to is the National Park Service has been caught dead to rights in a corrupt process of swindling private owners out of property rights...Presented as innocuous, the National Landmark Pro-

---

1 Potential Ecological and Geological Natural Landmarks of the New England Adirondack Region, Thomas G. Sicama, Ph.D, Yale School of Forestry and Environmental Studies; for the Department of Interior, Division of National Natural Landmarks, 1982. A Theme Study, a survey.

Program is tied into every conceivable form of land use regulation. It is the foundation of de facto federal zoning, mostly, but not exclusively, enforced by other jurisdictions (state, county, municipal). If your property appears in a Theme Study survey (33 regions; 6 volumes, each the size of a metropolitan phone directory), then the Environmental Mafia (federal, state, and local agencies, The Nature Conservancy, the National Parks and Conservation Association, etc.) feel entitled to develop plans for your property which you know nothing about...

If your property is geologically, ecologically, or scenically remarkable, this Program, working in tandem with the environmental consortium, is out to stick it to you...Theft of rights by bureaucratic means is a well-oiled process, and the Environmental Mafia owns the system like a lynch mob owns the courthouse...Functionally, their maxim is that if you cannot hold onto your property rights, you deserve to lose them.

What we are witnessing on an international level threatens the end of private ownership of property with control and title in private hands, and the beginning of a new feudalism under government and corporate landlords.

Why do so many environmentalists hate and fear mineral and logging development? One suspects the genuine reasons differ vastly from those proffered, obscure perhaps even to the conservationists themselves.

The wealth of the world consists in the things men dig from the ground. If mineral exploitation can be prevented, vast wealth will not be brought into existence, and whole populations can be kept dependent. When new mineral wealth is suppressed, existing developments become more valuable, and the status quo of wealth distribution and power is preserved and strengthened. The key to the survival of monopolistic economic power is the ability to keep out the competition. Or, as John D. Rockefeller expressed it with characteristic cogency, "Competition is a sin." The "partnership" will know who is "suitable" and who isn't.

In an interview I held in January of 1993 with Robert Friedland, a venture capital provider to the mining industry, he explained how the industry within the U.S. was untenable. When asked to give a political resh analysis, ten being the highest, one the lowest, he said without hesitation, "The U.S. is a ten." The result of course, is the flight of industry to South America, Southeast Asia, and elsewhere. Friedland's view is that within five to ten years the mining industry will be gone and our nation's dependence on metals of every kind will be from foreign sources.

Indicative of how the environmentalists have viewed mining can be summarized in their oft-repeated and long-standing slogan: "Mine Free by '93." They have almost succeeded.

CHAPTER 18

A NEW RELIGION FOR A NEW AGE: THE DARK SIDE OF THE ECO-CULT

[I]t is difficult to generate a balanced discussion about the greenhouse effect, indeed about almost any other environmental issue. It has been removed from the rational sphere into the religious dimension. The environmental movement has developed a thoroughgoing theology, with its own demons and deities and, most significantly, it's intense sense of guilt. [Emphasis added.]

-Australian Financial Review, June 21, 1989.

If the eco-movement were small or localized, we might quickly dismiss its transformation into a *religion*. But it is growing rapidly worldwide, forcing itself into every political and economic discussion with a zeal and fanaticism that can only be described as religious. Whatever your religion – or lack of religion – this religious direction of environmentalism, more than any other trend, concerns you. It threatens the very roots of Western civilization. The eco-cult has a theology of sin and salvation, apocalypse and millennium, god and man – or perhaps more aptly, god(dess) and wo/man – some new, but most very ancient, and very dark.

From the aging hippies at its ratty fringes to the limousine liberals at its Gucci'ed center, all the shades of the radical environmental spectrum share an outlook fundamentally hostile to the teachings of Judaism, Islam, and especially Christianity. The Western religions (in which Islam must be included because of its Biblical roots) all presuppose the *transcendence* of God – God is the

Creator, personal, above and outside his creation, although also active in that creation.

Immanence Versus Transcendence

Against this teaching of transcendence, the environmental movement poses the immanence of God – God is not personal, but dwells everywhere and in everything. God is not the Creator in the creation, He/She is the creation. This is *pantheism* – the ancient pagan religion which identifies the Deity with the various forces and workings of nature. The New Age magazine *Gnosis* put it very plainly in its Issue No. 13:

> The material world...is now, according to present conventional wisdom, being recognized as Divine. We are clearly in the middle of a historical swing away from transcendental spirituality...toward immanently spirituality...In other words, it is more socially acceptable right now to say that God is in and of the material world than it is to say that Divinity transcends what can be seen and measured... [T]he trend toward pantheism is more or less associated in the collective mind with the "return of the Goddess."

Put more baldly, secularism has for several centuries denied the existence of any transcendent God, yet man, created in the image of God to serve and worship Him, is inescapably religious. This yearning for God has now brought the secularists to make creation a divinity. If there is no God outside creation, then He must be within the creation, or indeed, He is the creation itself. Science has become its own religion.

The great Christian writer, C.S. Lewis, who perhaps among all modem writers had the keenest understanding of evil, discusses this materialistic naiveté in *The Screwtape Letters*. The book is supposedly a series of letters written from a senior demon, Screwtape, to a junior tempter, Wormwood, on the battle lines, struggling to mislead and devour just one man's soul ("the patient"):

My dear Wormwood: I wonder you should ask me whether it is essential to keep the patient in ignorance of your own existence...Our policy, for the moment, is to conceal ourselves. Of course this has not always been so. We are really faced with a cruel dilemma. When the humans disbelieve in our existence we lose all the pleasing results of direct terrorism, and we make no magicians. On the other hand, when they believe in us, we cannot make them materialists and skeptics. At least, not yet. I have great hopes that we shall learn in due time how to emotionalize and mythologize their science to such an extent that what is, in effect, a belief in us (though not under that name) will creep in while the human mind remains closed to belief in the Enemy [*i.e.*, *God*]. The "Life Force," the worship of sex, and some aspects of Psychoanalysis may here prove useful. If once we can produce our perfect work – the Materialist Magician, the man, not using, but veritably worshipping, what he vaguely calls "Forces" while denying the existence of "spirits" – the end of the war will be in sight. But in the meantime we must obey our orders. I do not think you will have much difficulty in keeping the patient in the dark. The fact that "devils" are predominantly comic figures in the modem imagination will help you. If any faint suspicion of your existence begins to arise in his mind, suggest to him a picture of something in red tights, and persuade him that since he cannot believe in that (it is an old textbook method of confusing them) he therefore cannot believe in you.

The Greening of the Churches

This paganizing view is not confined to the followers of secularism or occult mysticism; it has its voices within the Christian church. The pharisaical environmental movement has long since invaded Protestantism. On May 25, 1992, the *New York Times* reported on the Greening of the Churches.

The [environmentalist] work of the Hamburg [NY Presbyterian Church] congregation is part of a movement some are calling the "Greening of the Churches," an awakening to environmental issues in churches and synagogues across the country. Congregations that once took the lead on issues of poverty, homelessness, civil rights and peace are now composting, testing the pH of local waterways, serving meatless church suppers, conducting energy conservation surveys and praying for endangered species as well as people.

Paul Gorman, a speechwriter for Eugene McCarthy's 1968 race for President, is a convert to the new religious environmental ethic. "This is not just religious people finding yet another social issue," he said from his office at the Cathedral of St. John the Divine in upper Manhattan, where he runs an interfaith environmental organization, "but rather religious people experiencing a very profound challenge to faith and to what it means to be religious."

The despoiling and exploitation of the earth is seen as "a violation of God's creation," Mr. Gorman added. "There is a very instinctive reaction out of a religious conscience. People experience it in their gut."

Mr. Gorman is the executive director of a non-profit group called the Joint Appeal by Religion and Science for the Environment...His group has brought together scientists and an array of religious organizations, from Roman Catholics and Evangelicals to Jews and mainstream Protestants who have committed themselves to the environmental cause. Representatives of the groups met May 10 [1992] in Washington, where they adopted a statement that declared the environment "an inescapably religious challenge."...

Not everyone is enamored of the new religious focus on the environment. Some religious conservatives say it is a distraction from church-centered practices like liturgy and sacraments as well as from social programs that help the poor. They also warn that it runs the risk of becoming a sort of religion in itself, and argue that it has more to do with new age, holistic approaches than with the Judeo-Christian tradition...

On the other hand, some environmentalists are not enamored of religion. They say Judaism and Christianity have led to the exploitation of the earth, by giving man, in the words of Genesis 1:28, "dominion over the fish of the sea and over the fowl of the air, and over every living thing that moveth upon the earth."

Environmental theologians emphasize another verse from Genesis, 2:15, that talks about man's responsibility to "work and keep" the land, a concept known as "stewardship."

From the often muddle-headed evangelical Protestant journal, *Christianity Today*, came this less-than-theologically-astute editorial on May 18, 1992, "It's not easy being green, but the time has come for evangelicals to confront the environmental crisis." This piece parrots mindlessly the standard Green line about environmental problems being "irreversible." Then, apparently forgetting for the moment the "Christianity" in its name, the editor opines, "And as we [evangelicals] have done in the past, we must stand with all – whether atheist, Buddhist, or New Ager – who support the work of preserving God's handiwork as long as we are not forced to compromise our beliefs or allegiance."

Of course, it's hard to believe that any Christian could swallow this sort of comatose theological word-salad, but its appearance is a measure of how thoroughly the Greening has already penetrated our culture. Environmentalism has become the primary vehicle for the repaganization and de-Christianization of the West, and the theological naiveté of Protestants puts no hurdle in its way.

The Greening goes farther. Franklin Sanders charged in the October 1989, *Moneychanger* that:

If you think this is just a Protestant problem, think again. Ever since Teilhard de Chardin, the Jesuit paleontologist and mystic, this conscious repaganization has surfaced over and over in Roman Catholic circles. Consider this article which documents the damage in both confessions:

"A New Story of Creation: It's the season for a theology of ecology...Now, amid signs and warnings of impending ecological crisis, religious scholars are searching their Scriptures for a theology of ecology that can guide and inspire the burgeoning environmental movement. [In March 1989, there was a World Council of Churches seminar on the environment in Basel, and then another WCC conference in San Antonio] and next weekend the United Nations Environmental

Program [UNEP] is sponsoring an Environmental Sabbath, which all the clergy of North America...have been urged to celebrate with appropriate prayers and sermons on the soil, water, and air.

"The most provocative figure among this new breed of eco-theologians is Father Thomas Berry, a solitary American monk whose essays have aroused environmentalists...If religious leaders want to know what God thinks about nature, he says, books like the Bible and the Koran are the wrong places to look. The universe itself is God's 'primary revelation,' Berry declares, and the story it tells of its own evolution from cosmic dust to human consciousness provides the sacred text and context for understanding man's place in God's creation. The natural world is the larger sacred community to which we all belong,' Berry writes...We bear the universe in our being [*the doctrine of immanence*] even as the universe bears us in its being.

"'The same atoms that formed the galaxies,' Berry likes to remind audiences, 'are in me.' In short, God may be our father but earth is truly our mother.

"Among some enthusiasts, the ecology movement itself has become a kind of religion, in which cosmic piety replaces worship of a transcendent God and anthropocentrism [*man-centeredness*] becomes the deadliest sin. The movement has also inspired a form of competition among the world's religions to see which is most capable of valuing nature for itself, *apart from its ability to satisfy human needs.*" [Emphasis added.]

Sanders concludes:

In this sweepstakes, not surprisingly, Taoism and the religions of the American Indians surpass all other rivals...Where the Bible enjoins man to five in covenant with a transcendent God, Berry emphasizes a new covenant with his creation. Moreover, unlike the book of Genesis, which is designed to desacralize nature [i.e., to remove the animism and pantheism], Berry's new cosmology imposes certain values on its human offspring.

According to the Bible-based Western religions, Earth was created for man to rule and use to God's glory. In the eco-cult, the Earth and its beings are divine while man is the intruder and destroyer. This helps to explain the religious zeal the environmentalists display in their opposition to development of any kind. Nature is not to be used, but *worshipped* – it's not nice to *use* Mother Nature.

The Goddess Comes

In the emerging eco-cult, "Mother Earth" is more than just a comic reference to nature: she is the divinity on which we live. This also accounts for the identification of the eco-cult not only with radical environmentalism, but also with radical feminism. Franklin Sanders writes:

The increasing practice of witchcraft and repaganization both arise *from and give rise to* radical feminism and radical environmentalism. How? Both paganism and witchcraft are already pantheistic and occult. From these beginnings, the pagan will inevitably express his pantheism more explicitly by identifying the environment with "god." Beginning from radical environmentalism or radical feminism, the search for justification [religious assurance and freedom from "sin"] will lead finally to pantheism and the mother earth cult. It is but a brief step, and a greater consistency, to move from the *admiration to the worship* of nature, and thence to belief in some sort of "world soul" that inspirits all matter. Witchcraft and paganism are next, since they are congenial to this conclusion...

These concepts build and fit into the environmental movement. If the Earth and all creation are God, then 'she' is holy, along with everything in or on it: trees, mountains, streams, even the animals. Being holy, it must be left in its pristine condition untouched by profaning man. The step into the irrational and mystical is the next logical one for the "scientific" person as an unchallengeable, i.e., religious, rationale for the non-development of the environment. It is the *greater consistency* inevitable for those who reject a Biblical worldview. Repaganization of Western society dovetails with the re-introduction of goddess worship.

The Scientific Worshippers

The impulse toward worship of Mother Earth was given a "scientific" push by the work of Dr. James E. Lovelock with his "Gaia [pronounced GUY-uh] hypothesis."

"Mother Earth is alive," said the *Atlanta Constitution* on July 12, 1989. The item reports:

For James E. Lovelock, maverick scientist, inventor, and philosopher, that is the only explanation...When Dr. Lovelock proposed his hypothesis a decade ago, he called it "Gaia," after the Greek earth goddess...Despite the new-found respectability, Gaia still makes many scientists uneasy. They say it smacks more of religion than science. Most scientists are uncomfortable with the idea of Earth as a self-conscious creature...

Dr. Lovelock believes the scientists have it backward. He says the Earth maintains its chemical balance by marshaling its living matter, from whales to viruses, to manipulate the environment, to him, Gaia is a "complex entity involving the Earth's biosphere, atmosphere, oceans, and soil...which seeks an optimal physical and chemical environment for life on this planet." Without it, Dr. Lovelock says, Earth's climate would be out of control and Earth itself would be an inert chemical ball.

"People think there is a force out there that will take care of these problems for them," says [Joseph C.] Farman [the British researcher who "discovered" the Antarctic ozone hole]. "That's not really Lovelock's view at all. *The human being is an irrelevance as far as Lovelock is concerned. If Gaia needs to kill man off, it will.* That's his view." [Emphasis added.]

Speaking on the religious program *Compass*, Australian legislator Richard Jones was much more blunt: "Gaia is nature, is God; God is nature, is Gaia." Get the point?

In the January 11, 1993 issue of *Christianity Today*, Tod Conner reported, "James Morton is dean of the Cathedral of Saint John the Divine in New York City...Morton created the Gaia Institute; he commissioned Paul Winter to compose a full-blown choral mass entitled *Missa Gaia;* and he even had Lovelock, an avowed agnostic, preach at a Sunday service."

Of course, this Gaia hypothesis fits right in to pagan concepts of the mother earth goddess. For the "ratty fringes" seeking to extend their "spiritual knowledge," the next logical step moves toward the oldest nature religion, witchcraft. In a June 8, 1988, *New Zealand Herald* interview with several New Zealand witches we read:

> The *New Zealand Herald* spoke to women belonging to two other [witchcraft] groups with a more formal approach – Cone and Aurora. The same thread ran through the conversations. They were older women who had once been part of orthodox religion but who found their churches lagging behind the fast pace of social change in the '70s and '80s. *The growth of feminism, the upsurge of interest in environmental and racial issues left many of the churches, more than other institutions, grasping unsuccessfully for relevancy* [sic]. As the awareness of the women grew they became increasingly dissatisfied with the way the churches were catering for their spiritual needs.
>
> The [witchcraft] rituals affirm that we are all part of the Earth and cosmos and that we must each be caretakers of our bodies and environment, says [witch Audrey] Sharp. "Rather than relying on a God or Supreme Being to solve our problems, it's our responsibility and *within* our power. I am the goddess and you are the goddess." [*This isn't terribly original. Look at Genesis 3:5*]
>
> As she and other women explain it, the use of pre- Christian ritual provides a spiritual dimension [sic] to present-day issues of conservation, sexual politics, and the peace movement....Holford [a teacher of "women's spirituality"] looks overseas to conservationists, the peace movement, and those trying to deal with poverty in the

Third World. 'I see women's spirituality as just part of a commonality [sic] which has at its heart the concept that the Earth is sacred and needs our help.

In the October 1989, *Moneychanger*, Sanders also quotes another mystic who reveals the inevitability of environmentalism's progression to paganism.

"Not only did [Tim Zell of the Church of All Worlds] state that the earth was a living organism, but that it was a feminine deity, and that all life was a part of this single, living, feminine organism. Here was the first expression of a theory now central to all of modem paganism and goddess worship – the belief that we are all interconnected, and that this interconnection requires us to incorporate ecological principles into our philosophy." (Quoting *Gnosis*, No. 13, p. 30.)

This new pagan religion requires the worship of animals as well.

"The ecological imbalance which we are experiencing today is a result of a culture based on immediate gratification which has forgotten the Goddess as a living entity, Earth, and has forgotten the animals as beings who know how to live peacefully with one another in a balanced eco-system [*This writer has apparently never witnessed the peaceful coexistence of the lioness and the wart-hog in the wild*]. By reclaiming the ancient wisdom, the animals again may become sacred. As the goddess is respected and honored, her animals too become respected, for the two are inseparable." (Quoting *Gnosis*, No. 13, p. 46.)

Gathering the Materialist Magicians

On February 5, 1990, *Christian News* ran a lengthy two-column article about a Moscow gathering. The lofty title for this get-together was Global Forum of Spiritual and Parliamentary Leaders on Human Survival. I also have in my files a lengthy (seven-page) promotional letter and brochure signed by the Executive Coordinator Akio Matsunura which extols the virtues of what took place in Moscow.

A few quotes will give you an idea of the spiritual overtones which dominated the discussions.

Environmental destruction has deep roots in the spiritual un-fulfillment of the people and the decay of social relations as well as in economic, legal, and technical explanations... Our approach is to reconstitute the political, spiritual, and scientific in an attempt to address the whole issue...It is unlikely that such an event could have taken place at any previous time in history. Equally amazing is the fact that a group as diverse as this one actually could collaborate to produce a comprehensive document on reversing the global destruction of our natural environment.

The letter then makes the call to action.

Now that the success of such a gathering has been proven, we would like to encourage similar meetings and discussions in as many places as possible... Spiritual people, politicians, students, scientists, and others need to join hands in every community, on every college campus, and in every town hall in order to help speed the changes in attitude and in awareness that are sweeping the world.

This was no gathering of also-rans. Speakers included Gorbachev (yes, he is spiritual – just ask him), then-UN Secretary-General Javier Perez de Cuellar, Gro Bruntland (of course), Episcopal Bishop James Parks Morton, the Grand Mufti, Sheikh Ahmed Kuftaro, Franz Cardinal Koenig, plus representatives from Buddhism, Jainism, Sikhism, Shinto, and the much-revered Native American Indian.

The Green tide is rising higher and higher. Late in July 1990, Archbishop of Canterbury Robert Runcie, titular head of millions of Anglican believers worldwide, announced that Queen Elizabeth II had just appointed Dr. George Carey to succeed him January 31, 1991. Shortly before his appointment Carey had received much media attention with the assertion that "God is green."

Apocalypse and Millennium:
Disaster and the Golden Age

Any religion worth its incense has an *eschatology* – a vision of the way the world will end. The eco-cult is not lacking here, either. In the eco-apocalypse, the final battle between man and the environment lies just around the comer, the grand ecological disaster in which either global warming, a new Ice Age, add rain, overpopulation, the death of the ozone layer, rising sea levels, or some combination of all will sweep most of mankind away to start all over again.

But the Apocalypse will be followed by a millennium – a golden age which the environmentalists, by good eco-works and clean living, can help to bring about here and now. "There are 'environmentalists' in Australia and elsewhere who are clearly attracted not merely to alternatives to present energy sources and land uses but to a wholesale retreat to what they see in their millennial terms as 'the simple life.'" (*Australian Financial Review*, June 21, 1989.)

This is part and parcel of the "small is beautiful" theories and the "earth is running out of resources" mentality that cropped up in the '70s. But for American environmentalists, the millennial vision, shifting back and forth from the religious to the secular arena, has deeper historic roots. From her beginnings, Americans have viewed themselves as a people chosen by God to bring deliverance to the rest of the nations – oft times whether they want it or not. When American Greens transform their environmentalism into a millennial religion, they are simply following an ancient American tradition.

The American Millennial Mentality

Writing in the *Southern Partisan*, (Second Quarter, 1989) Ludwell Johnson notes:

Evangelicals of Lincoln's generation believed that the United States, established by God far from the corruptions and Antichrists of the Old

World, was evidence of the coming of the millennium and was itself to be the Redeemer nation, destined to bring Protestant Christianity and American institutions to benighted humanity. They believed, moreover, that "only the labors of believers" would bring the millennium, "and if they proved laggard in their task, the millennium would be retarded." [*Compare this to the pharisaical zeal of today's Greens*]

The first order of business if America was to fulfill its divinely ordained role was self-purification... [Then] as Methodist Bishop Matthew Simpson said, the American flag would eventually fly "over the whole western hemisphere," and then "we must take the world in our arms, and convert all other nations to our true form of government." [*How many times has America heard this one!?*]

The political side of the millennialist movement can be seen in the belief that the American republic was both a harbinger of the millennium and a necessary instrument in redeeming the world. The true gospel could flourish only where our form of republican government also flourished. So political conversion was indistinguishable from religious conversion... [*This is the pattern the Greens are following today, confusing their political ideas with religion*]

Such a view of things blended smoothly with what might be called *secular millennialism*, a way of looking at the world rooted in the 18th century enlightenment rather than in St. John's Revelation... [Emphasis added.]

As one American senator, flushed with the imperial acquisition of the Philippines, said in 1900:

We will not renounce our part in the mission of the race, trustee, under God, of the civilization of the world...And of all our race, He has marked the American people as His chosen Nation to finally lead in the regeneration of the world. This is the divine mission of America...

Americans have a long history of combining religious, secular, and national millennial aspirations which are very easily carried over, whole cloth, into the new eco-cult. "Self-purification" and the "labors of believers" are the only works needed to bring on the ecological golden age. And for these green religious fanatics, it is only logical that if he will not volunteer, mankind must be coerced into the millennium are we too extreme in predicting the environmental movement will take this course? Judge for yourself.

Saddling Up the Four Horsemen

Whether in the hands of Robespierre, Hitler, Stalin, or the Ayatollah Khomeni, the millennial dream has often been used to justify lawlessness and inhumanity – always in the name of some "greater good." In fact, listening to some of these "religious" leaders, we are struck by the fervor of their rhetoric. It is taking on the characteristics of an Islamic Jihad or "Holy War." As it develops, the new eco-cult will drive its devotees to greater and greater zeal, perhaps even to violent means "justified" by the great good of their "ends." As the true believers become more and more impatient for the golden age, saving the whales vicariously with a check may no longer suffice. This turn to violence already appears in a *Newsweek* report of February 5, 1990: (p. 24.)

Eco-guerrillas, radical environmentalists...have turned to outrageous – and sometimes illegal – tactics in their war against "greedheads" and "eco-thugs." Militants vow not just to end pollution but to take back and "rewild" one-third of the United States.

They call us the Kaddafis of the movement, but we feel like cornered animals," says Jamie Sayen, a member of Earth First!, one of the best-known groups of radical environmentalists, which claims 15,000 members. "We feel like there are insane people who are consciously destroying our environment and we are *compelled* to fight back." [Emphasis added.]

In practicing what Earth First! co-founder Dave Foreman calls 'a form of worship toward the Earth,' eco-guerrillas pour sand in the fuel tanks of logging equipment and drive spikes into the trees of old-growth forests, potentially ruining expensive lumber mill saws. They tear down power lines and pull up survey stakes; they sink whaling ships and destroy oil-exploration gear. Even the upcoming trial of Foreman and three others on conspiracy charges hasn't dampened the militants' fervor. In just the last six months, radicals have conducted blockades on the big island of Hawaii to stall development of a geothermal plant on the flanks of the Kilauea volcano, and chained themselves to the tops of cranes on a China-bound freighter to protest the export of timber.

The militant faction of America's environmental movement is growing rapidly. Many mainstream environmentalists, impatient with their own leadership, are defecting to the radical ranks. A large contingent of environmental scientists, some of them involved in the very government agencies that militants despise, are also aligning themselves with groups like Earth First! 'The more you study ecology, the more radical you be-come,' explains environmental biologist Jeff Elliot. "You develop for all living organisms the affection that you have for your relatives, and you don't have any choice but to be as effective as you can against people who are at war with your family."…The FBI alleges that [Earth First!], with financial help from Foreman, planned ultimately to cut lines to three nuclear power plants...

What unifies radical environmentalists is their adherence to a philosophy of biocentrism. Earth First!, the Wolf Action Network, the Rain Forest Action Network, Virginians for Wilderness, Preserve Appalachian Wilderness – scores of small groups across the country *endorse the belief that every species has equal, intrinsic value and that the planet cannot be viewed solely as a resource for humans.* Though still considered an eccentric and impractical theory by some mainstream environmentalists, the concept of "deep ecology" is finding increasing grassroots support... [Emphasis added.]

"It's like the early days of the civil-rights movements," says Denis Hayes, coordinator of Earth Day 1990.   "People didn't send money to the NAACP to see if they could get a new law passed. They got up, walked to the front of the bus, and sat down."

Mike Roselle, a founder of Earth First! and supporter of Greenpeace, spends much of his time organizing new militants around the country. "I think we've got so many more people out there who are willing to do things," he says, "and yet there are fewer groups that are actually asking anything of these people other than to send a check." But, he adds, "with groups like us nipping at their heels, mainstream groups are going to take stronger positions." [Emphasis added.]

Totemism Resurrected

Totemism, the worship of animals, accompanies pantheistic paganism. Not surprisingly, it crops up in the new eco-cult. We've already read that biologist Jeff Elliot says that "you develop for all living organisms the affections that you have for your relatives." Also, radical environmentalists are unified by their adherence to a "philosophy" of biocentrism and "endorse the belief that every species has equal intrinsic value." But some animals have more "equally intrinsic value" than others. The spotted owl, grizzly bear, timber wolf, red-cockaded woodpecker, whale, and porpoise, among others, each have their enthusiastic totem-cult.

Those eco-cultists who have bridged the whole gap be-tween science and religion, progressing all the way to Mother Earth worship, say, "By reclaiming the ancient wisdom, the animals again may become sacred. As the goddess is respected and honored, her animals too become respected, for the two are inseparable." In fact, according to many radical environmentalists, the only creature which is *not* sacred is "the destroyer," "the up setter": *man*. All of this cultish nonsense is part of what C.S. Lewis prophesied in a book by the appropriate title *The Abolition of Man*.

This strange self-hatred and misanthropy, wound about tightly with an unfocused and inexpiable guilt for all the eco-sins of the world ("we're all responsible"), runs like a blood-red thread through environmentalist pronouncements. It is a categorical rejection of the Western Biblical concept of man as the crowning glory of creation, made in the image of God and therefore worthy of respect, dignity, and human rights. Eco-cultists grudge a profound suspicion and sour distrust toward any man who appears to be enjoying himself by using God's creation – the obvious evidence of his immoral refusal to accept the collective guilt. These eco-killjoys make the much-maligned Puritans look like Falstaff on a spree. Under their assumed mantle of "tolerance" they allow any belief – as long as it agrees with their own.

This diseased loss of balance in the eco-view of man can only be explained as religious fanaticism run wild. How far will it run? Ingrid Newkirk, director of People for Ethical Treatment of Animals (PETA), intones, "The smallest form of life, even an ant or a clam, is equal to a human being." In an interview on the Australian religious program, *Compass*, Richard Jones, said, "I think an ant is as much a part of God, as a polar bear, or a koala, or you and me or a priest. *I think they're all spiritually equal.* So if I save an ant from drowning, that's as equal as [sic] saving anything else from drowning. And I think we can be taken seriously. When people get this connection, when they finally get the connection that we are all interconnected." [Emphasis added.]

Conclusion

Long, long ago the Apostle Paul explained this very sickness: "Professing themselves to be wise, they became fools, and changed the glory of the incorruptible God into an image made like to corruptible man, and to birds, and four-footed beasts, and creeping things." (Romans 1:22-23)

Footnote: As crazy and implausible as all of the above appears to any normal person, there is a "method to their madness." The last time western civilization was subjected to such anti-religious religion, was during the frenzied height of the French Revolution. Much of the "bio-sphere" nonsense has its origin in those who, like Rousseau, were the "inspired" high priests of 18th century pantheism. Yet even then their antics caused Lord Acton to comment "midst the tumult there is too much design."

Epilogue

As I write these final thoughts, it is January 19, 1993. Tomorrow Bill Clinton will be given the Oath of Offices for President of the United States. So too will Albert Gore, Jr. be administered the oath for Vice President. The world will change but the architects for the power that makes those changes will, in large part, remain the same.

At the outset of tins volume which, incidentally, was started in 1989, my collaborator, Franklin Sanders, and I stated right up front that we intended to prove how the Greening was created and controlled by the Insiders of the Establishment. Nothing contained in these pages can possibly make the case for our contention any better than the people who make up the new Clinton Administration. From the President himself, throughout his Cabinet, down to his second-level appointees, the one consistent thread is membership in the Council on Foreign Relations, the Trilateral Commission, or both.

The very same institution which directed the creation of modem environmentalism, via the George F. Kennan article in *Foreign Affairs* of April 1970, is now once again in full working control of a team who pledged to the electorate, "We will finally make an environmental presidency a reality." I must take them at their word, and so should you, gentle reader.

And if Messrs. Clinton and Gore implement only a modicum of what they advocated during the campaign or in their books, we will watch the face of America change forever. The "change" they promised and are now about to implement will, in practice, affect every man, woman, and child in this country.

If they have their way, as oft-stated by themselves, by the time their first term has run its course, our sovereignty, our right to property, our economic well-being, even our very liberty will have been "changed" beyond recognition. Most of this will come in the name of "preserving the environment."

The only question which remains is, will the American people allow it to happen?

The answer to that one, my friend, is in your hands.

THE VIEW FROM IRON MOUNTAIN (PLANNING GLOBAL ECO-WAR)

By Brooks Alexander

(Ed. Note: Certain elements of the following article are repeated elsewhere in this volume, but the information is so important we felt it should be reprinted in its entirety.)

Did a secret government think-tank meet in the early 1960s to find a substitute for war? Did they conclude that peace is possible only by replacing war with something else that serves the same functions? And did they think environmentalism was an excellent substitute for war because the eco-threat could motivate people credibly, globally, and sacrificially? *The Report from Iron Mountain* says that they did. Your view of Iron Mountain will depend on your view of the information that follows.

The book's full title is *Report from Iron Mountain on the Possibility and Desirability of Peace*. The author is identified only as "John Doe," an obvious pseudonym. Leonard Lewin, author of the book's forward, describes Doe as in internationally known professor in one of the social sciences at a large university in the Midwest. Lewin met with Doe in a New York restaurant and later transmitted Doe's manuscript to the publisher, Dial Press.

According to Lewin, Doe telephoned him unexpectedly (they were previously acquainted) and asked if they could meet over lunch to discuss a matter of some importance. After a half-hour of uncomfortable and self-conscious small talk, Doe asked Lewin what were his views on "freedom of information." On receiving an answer that apparently satisfied him, Doe abruptly began to explain that several years previously, he had been recruited as part of an extraordinary governmental "Special Study Group." The purpose of the Group was to investigate the problems that would arise from a condition of general peace.

After several years of study, the Group rendered the sum of its collective wisdom. However, its conclusions were so radical that, contrary to Doe's own convictions, its report was suppressed – both by the Group, and by the committee to which it had been submitted. Doe's involvement with the Group began in August, 1963, when, he said...

...he found a message on his desk that a "Mrs. Potts" had called him from Washington. When he returned the call, a man answered immediately, and told Doe, among other things, that he had been selected to serve on a commission "of the highest importance." Its objective was to *determine accurately and realistically, the nature of the problems that would confront the United States if and when a condition of "permanent peace" should arrive, and to draft a program for dealing with this contingency.* The man described the unique procedures that were to govern the commission's work and that were expected to extend its scope far beyond that of any previous examination of these problems...

Doe entertained no serious doubts of the bona fides of the project, chiefly because of his previous experience with the excessive secrecy that often surrounds quasi-governmental activities. In addition, the man at the other end of the line demonstrated an impressively complete and surprisingly detailed knowledge of Doe's work and personal life. He also mentioned the names of others who were to serve with the group; most of them were known to Doe by reputation. Doe agreed to take the assignment – he felt he had no real choice in the matter – and to appear the second Saturday following at Iron Mountain, New York. An airline ticket arrived in his mail the next morning.

The cloak-and-dagger tone of the conversation was further enhanced by the meeting place itself. Iron Mountain, located near the town of Hudson, is like something out of Ian Fleming...It is an underground nuclear hideout for hundreds of American corporations. Most of them use it as an emergency storage vault for important documents. But a number of them maintain substitute corporate headquarters as well, where essential personnel could survive and continue to work after an attack...(pp. viii-ix, emphasis in the original).

The Group and Its Work

Including Doe, the Special Study Group consisted of fifteen men from a variety of disciplines, each a recognized authority in his field. Their areas of specialty included history, international law, economy, sociology, cultural anthropology, psychology, psychiatry, mathematics, and astronomy – among others. Members were assigned individual research projects between meetings. Doe said that...

...a lot of it involved getting information from other people...Among the fifteen of us, I don't think there was anybody in the academic world we couldn't call on if we wanted to, and we took advantage of it... (p.xxv)

Their meetings were held all over the country – at hotels, universities, summer camps, private estates, and elsewhere, but never in Washington or on government property. At the end of its labors, the Group recognized that it had a "hot potato" on its hands – it strongly recommended that its findings not be released for publication. In the "Letter of Transmittal" that accompanied its report, the Group said [that]...

...such action would not be in the public interest. The uncertain advantages of public discussion of our conclusions and recommendations are, in our opinion, greatly outweighed by the clear and predictable danger of a crisis in public confidence which untimely publication of this report might be expected to provoke. The likelihood that *a lay reader, unexposed to the exigencies of higher political or military responsibility*, will misconstrue the purpose of this project, and the intent of its participants, seems obvious, (p. 4, Emphasis added.)

Doe balked at that decision. For whatever reason, he thought the American people were entitled to know what was being planned for them, and who (in a general sense) was doing the planning. Doe evidently thought the overall plan was too large to be identified politically (much less targeted) and far too along to be slowed down. He scoffed at the idea that the public reaction could have a lasting effect on long-range measures to implement the Group's proposals. (p. xiv)

Whatever Doe's motives, he eventually decided to go public. According to Lewin,

...after months of agonizing, Doe decided that he would no longer be a party to keeping (the Report) secret. What he wanted from me was advice and assistance in having it published. He gave me his copy to read, with the express understanding that if for any reason I was unwilling to become involved, I would say nothing about it to anyone. (pp. vii-x)

After reading the report, Lewin wrote that "the unwillingness of Doe's associates to publicize their findings became readily understandable."

In accord with its mandate, the Special Study Group had approached its subject with a calculated detachment from ethical standards and a profound rejection of moral considerations. Its moral nihilism ultimately endorsed war as the cornerstone of social order and the foundation of social institutions. Equally cynical – but more manipulative – were its proposals for long-range social engineering. The *Report* directly affirmed (for our society) or indirectly endorsed (for other societies):

war...human sacrifice, slavery, genocide, racist eugenics (including the substitution of artificial insemination for normal human procreation), a planned economy, fascist partnership between business and government, planned government waste, official opposition to medical advances, globalism, environmentalism, and even the new pagan Mother Earth religion. (Sanders, 1992; p.4)

Lewin (in a considerable understatement) said of the *Report* that "the general read...may not be prepared for some of its assumptions." Finally, he stated "for the record" that he did not...

...share the attitudes toward war and peace, life and death, and survival of the species manifested in the *Report*. Few readers will. In human terms, it is an outrageous document... (But) it explains, or certainly appears to explain, aspects of American policy otherwise incomprehensible by the ordinary standards of common sense, (pp. xiv-xv).

Seeing to the Bottom of War

The Group did not begin with its "outrageous" attitudes in mind, but the more they studied the case, the more they became convinced that the structure of society as we know it depends on what they called the "war system."

They concluded that some outside threat or conflict is needed to maintain the social cohesion and political organization that we call a "nation."

The war system makes the stable government of societies possible. It does this essentially by providing an external necessity for society to accept political rule. In so doing, it establishes the basis for nationhood and the authority of government to control its constituents (p.64).

That inversion of conventional thought gives the *Report* much of its shock value. The general public is not prepared to deal with a total reversal of its "common knowledge." The *Report* declares that nations are stable internally *because* they are in conflict externally. National sovereignty implies international discord. Nationhood breeds national enmities, and national enmities need one another to define their national identities. Without the unifying pressure of some external danger, societies would be torn apart by the competing interests within them. *The elimination of war therefore implies the elimination of national sovereignty.*

The Special Study Group understood that the coming of peace would mean much more than deciding how to spend the money freed from military budgets. Abolishing war will change more than the government's accounting system.

It is surely no exaggeration to say that a condition of general world peace would lead to changes in the social structures of the nations of the world of unparalleled and revolutionary magnitude. The economic impact of general disarmament, to name only the most obvious consequence of peace, would revise the production and distribution patterns of the globe to a degree that would make the changes of the last fifty years seem insignificant. Political, sociological, cultural, and ecological changes would be equally far-reaching (p.8).

The "traditional" view is based on the twin concepts of national sovereignty and national interest. It is distilled in the saying of Clausewitz that "war is merely politics, pursued by other means." The Special Study Group began with that classical, "instrumental" view in mind. To them, war was just another "instrument" of national policy, distinguished only by the fact that it uses lethal and military means.

However, as the Group studied various disarmament scenarios, it was struck with "the miasma of unreality" that surrounded them all. Eventually they decided that most thinking on the subject was irrelevant and wrong-headed because of "one common fundamental misconception; 'namely, *the incorrect assumption that war, as an institution, is subordinate to the institutions it is believed to serve* (p.28, Emphasis in the original).'"

Within its calculatedly amoral framework, the Group came to understand that "war itself is the basic social system, within which other secondary modes of social organization conflict or conspire. It is the system which has governed most human societies of record, as it is today (p.29)." The *Report's* conclusion declares that:

> war is not, as is widely assumed, primarily an instrument of policy utilized by nations to extend their expressed political values or their economic interests. On the contrary, it is itself the principle basis of organization on which all modem societies are constructed (p.79).

The Looking-glass World

That is the primary insight behind the *Report*. We don't *resort to war, we depend* on war. We don't go to war, we stay at war – because nationhood implies it, social structure demands it, and economic control depends on it. Society claims to abhor war, but in reality is focused on war. With that revelation, we pass through the looking-glass. Suddenly, opposites switch places. Left is right, up is down, and right is wrong. It is a dizzying and disorienting experience. Dualities are not just reversible, they are interchangeable. Clausewitz is turned on his head, and now "politics is merely war, pursued by other means." As the *Report* says:

> Wars are not "caused" by international conflicts of interest. Proper logical sequence would make it more often accurate to say that war-making societies require – and thus bring about – such conflicts (p.30).

The collective realization was central to the Group's further thinking. Having concluded that some form of external conflict is basic to social order, the Group made the further and obvious point that this fact must be taken into account by anyone who tries to bring about peace. To them, the question was not whether peace could be arranged, but whether it was a good idea to begin with. The Special Study Group understood very well that peace was possible, but questioned if it was worth the dangers and dislocations that the process of transition would involve.

At our present state of knowledge and reasonable inference, it is the war-system that must be identified with stability; the peace-system with social speculation, however justifiable the speculation may appear, in terms of subjective moral or emotional values (p.90).

It is easy to read the *Report* and conclude that it endorses war without reservation and dismisses peace without reprieve. But that is not the case. The *Report* affirms that war has pragmatic drawbacks, and it affirms that peace could be the basis for an alternative system of human governance. It simply warns that getting there could cost more than the prize is worth. The changes required would be revolutionary, and might well become chaotic. Nations would cease to exist as such, economies would be thrown into disarray, and societies would experience upheaval.

The Group understood that peace would upset everything, and for that reason thought it unwise. But they recognized that we would be even more unwise if we failed to plan for peace anyway.

It seems evident that, in the event an important part of the world is plunged without sufficient warning into an inadvertent peace, even partial and inadequate preparation for the possibility may be better than none. The difference could even be critical...our government must...be ready to move in this direction with whatever limited resources of planning are on hand at the time – if circumstances so require (p.92).

The Functions of War

The bulk of the Report is devoted to describing the various functions of war, and speculating on what might replace them.

The *Report* identifies seven non-military functions of war: "economic," "political," "sociological," "ecological" (the *Report* uses that term in the sense of "human ecology," especially referring to the effect of war on human numbers – in other words, it means "malthusian.") "cultural and scientific," and "other." In every case they concluded that the war system functions to create and maintain a stable society.

The order of listing is not random. The "economic" function of war tops the list for the obvious reason that the war-system (via the "military-industrial complex") is a major part of the economic engine. War expenses affect the economy as a whole (including the civilian sector), by acting, at various times, as brake, throttle and rudder:

> Military spending can be said to furnish the only balance wheel with sufficient inertia to stabilize the advance of (those) economies. The fact that war is "wasteful" is what enables it to serve this function. And the faster the economy advances, the heavier this balance wheel must be (p.35).

To put it simply, a nation's economy (that is, a nation's system of managing its resources) is its national power. And the "wasteful" demands that war makes on a nation's resources is the most effective means of controlling that power. But *war works as a form of economic control only as long as it works outside of a nation's "normal" economic life.* The economic extravagance of war is only half the point; the other half is that war's extravagance is imposed on the economy from outside of it. If military spending just turns into civilian spending, it just sinks into the general economy, and thus becomes useless as an instrument of economic influence.

The "political" functions of war are even more basic and pervasive than its economic ones. The main political contribution of the war-system is to create the "nation" itself, as a focus of collective identity and a motive for collective purpose.

> The war system not only has been essential to the existence of nations as independent political entities, but has been equally indispensable to their stable internal political structure. Without it, no government has ever been able to obtain acquiescence in its "legitimacy," or right to rule its society. The possibility of war provides the sense of external necessity without which no government can long remain in power. The historical record reveals one instance after another where the failure of a regime to maintain the credibility of a war threat led to its dissolution, by the forces of private interest, of reactions to social injustice, or of other disintegrative elements. The organization of

a society for the possibility of war is its principle political stabilizer (p.39).

War also serves politically as the "last great safeguard against the elimination of necessary social classes (p.40)

All societies need "hewers of wood and drawers of water." All functioning societies exhibit some form of class divisions in the name of national identity, and enforces them in the name of national survival.

That is not a new function of war, but it has become a more critical one in recent years. The affluence of our society has tended to blur social boundaries. As we rise further beyond economic subsistence, and as technology displaces rote labor, social instability increases.

The arbitrary nature of war expenditures and of other military activities make them ideally suited to control these essential class relationships...Until (a substitute) is developed, continuance of the war system must be assured, if for no other reason, among others, than to preserve whatever quality and degree of poverty a society requires as incentive, as well as to maintain the stability of its internal organization of power (pp. 40-41).

Plainly, the Group put a high value on stability. But beneath its fondness for stability lies a collective obsession with control. The prospect of peace is unsettling to them because it would unleash vast and rapid changes. In modem bureaucratic jargon, the transition to peace would be "destabilizing;" that is, it would set events in motion that could not be predicted or controlled by conventional means.

The Group takes a position so radical that it becomes reactionary. The Group's radical amorality (they call it "moral objectivity") finally boils down to the refrain of every entrenched regime: "don't rock the boat." The genius and novelty of the *Report* is that it adds this proviso: "...unless you are moving to another boat."

Replacing the Functions of War

The *Report* is based on a two-fold insight into human affairs, namely: (1) despite appearances to the contrary, war is a system of order, not an outbreak of disorder; (2) therefore, war cannot simply be abolished, it has to be replaced.

The Group recognized that international peace was feasible, but they considered it a risky and difficult proposition at best. At worst, they feared the end of hostilities would create anarchy. To prevent that descent into chaos, a strong surrogate for war is needed.

By now it should be clear that the most detailed and comprehensible master plan for a transition to world peace will remain academic if it fails to deal forthrightly with the problems of the critical nonmilitary functions of war. The social needs they serve are essential; if the war system no longer exists to meet them, substitute institutions will have to be established for the purpose (p.57).

The most intriguing aspect of the *Report* is its recommendation that we begin immediately to prepare for peace by preparing an effective replacement program for war. In its function as a blueprint for policy-development, the *Report* displays an urgent determination to set some kind of planning into motion, and to translate that planning as quickly as possible into active preparation. The preparation they had in mind specifically consisted of creating war-surrogates (economically, politically, and otherwise) that could be engaged when and if they were needed.

The *Report* defines what an ideal war-surrogate should do. Most of all, a war-surrogate should present a serious, believable, external threat. The threat should be of a scope and magnitude that demands both social organization and material extravagance to combat it.

A viable political substitute for war must posit a generalized external menace to each society of a nature and degree to require the organization and acceptance of political authority (p.83).

The planned response to the substitute threat should be "technically feasible, politically acceptable, and potentially credible to the members of (society)... (p.82)."

In other words, if we want to achieve peace (or cope with "accidental" peace), we must: (1) come up with an alternative threat that people can believe in, then (2) mobilize society against it in ways that people think will work, and finally, (3) reorganize society around it.

Conventional thinking becomes irrelevant at this point. In the looking-glass world of the Special Study Group, it is not enough to replace the war on the Evil Empire with a war on Poverty. Quite apart from the fact that domestic crusades lack the motivating power of an external jeopardy, their expenditures soon sink into the general economy and thus become useless as an instrument of economic control. Both politically and economically, a believable external threat is required.

Which Replacements?

What could stand in for the war system? The Special Study Group auditioned numerous candidates for the role, including "a comprehensive social-welfare program...a giant open-end space research program, aimed at unreachable targets...an omnipresent, virtually omnipotent international police force, an established and recognized extraterrestrial menace, massive global environmental pollution, fictitious alternate enemies...new religions or other mythologies, socially oriented blood-games (and) combination forms (p.84)."

The Group emphasized that all its potential substitutes were flawed in one way or another. The "conservatism" of the *Report*, and its obsession with stability reflect the fact that its authors had examined the available replacements for war and found every one of them wanting – at least in the short run. Even the best of them were possibilities to be cultivated, not (yet) opportunities acted upon.

In the long run, the Group decided that *if no workable substitute for war can be found or created, then the coming of peace means the coming of chaos and dissolution.*

However unlikely some of the possible alternate enemies we have mentioned may seem, we must emphasize that one must be found, of credible quality and magnitude, if a transition to peace is ever to come about without social disintegration. It is more probable, in our judgment, that such a threat will have to be invented, rather than developed from unknown conditions (p.67).

Of all the possible substitutes for war that the Group surveyed, it thought environmentalism to be among the most credible and effective. However, while an eco-threat served the functions of war very well, it was (as of 1964) not fully credible yet, and thus not ready to be invoked. *Iron Mountain* stressed that our environmental problems needed more time to mature, and to reach a more obvious danger point:

It may be, for instance, that gross pollution of the environment can eventually replace the possibility of mass destruction by nuclear weapons as the principle apparent threat to the survival of the species. Poisoning of the air and the principle sources of food and water is already well advanced, and at list glance would seem promising in this respect; it constitutes a threat that can be dealt with only through social organization and political power. But from present indications it will be a generation to a generation and a half before environmental pollution, however severe, will be sufficiently menacing enough, on a global scale, to offer a possible basis for a solution... (However), the mere modifying of existing programs for the deterrence of pollution could speed up the process enough to make the threat credible much sooner (pp.66-67).

The Special Study Group understood that the problems of peace would be severe, and exhorted the Government to lay plans immediately for coping with them. Specifically, it recommended that the President act by executive order to create "a permanent War/Peace Research Agency (WPRA) ... organized along the line of the National Security Council, except that none of its personnel will hold other public office or governmental responsibility (p.95)."

The main responsibility of the WPRA would be to process information – to "determine all that can be known...that may bear on an eventual transition to a general condition of peace (p.96)." The activities of the WPRA would include "the creative development of possible substitute institutions for the principle nonmilitary functions of war." Various substitute institutions would be proposed and evaluated, then developed and tested, "with the eventual objective of establishing a comprehensive program of compatible war substitutes suitable for a planned transition of peace (p.97)." In the meantime, a major function of the WPRA would be to maintain and improve the effectiveness of the war system, and to keep peace from happening accidentally.

The War/Peace Research Agency probably never existed as such. But we have no way of knowing if the Special Study Group managed to create some other successor in its image. Official secrecy and byzantine bureaucracy conspire to conceal that information. If there is a successor, it might not even have an identifiable form. The functions of the proposed WPRA could easily be distributed among an interagency network.

The Riddle of Iron Mountain

The above information takes Iron Mountain at face value, and simply presents it as what it claims to be. But that claim is by no means universally accepted. The Report stirred sensation and controversy from the day it was put into print. U.S. News & World Report called it "the book that shook the White House," and said that its appearance...

...set off a blazing debate...cries of "hoax"– and a "manhunt" for the author, or authors. Sources close to the White House reveal that the Administration is alarmed. Those sources say cables have gone to U.S. embassies with stern instructions: Play down public discussion of "Iron

Mountain;" emphasize that the book has no relation whatsoever to Government policy.

But nagging doubts fingered. One informed source confirmed that the "Special Study Group" ...was set up by a top official in the Kennedy Administration. The source added that the report was drafted and eventually submitted to President Johnson, who was said to have "hit the roof" – and then ordered that the report be bottled up for all time (11/20/67, p.48).

The hunt for "John Doe" produced gossip, guesswork, and denials, but very little else. A number of candidates were named, including Dean Rusk, Walter Rostow, Robert McNamara, Kenneth Boulding, Noam Chomsky, and Amatai Etzioni. All disclaimed responsibility, some of them indignantly (Boulding, a professor of economics at the University of Colorado, said "I regard the suggestion that I wrote it as very close to being an insult"). Having little hard evidence to go on, the manhunt soon broke up, leaving only patterns of speculation in its wake.

Many considered John Kenneth Galbraith to be the chief suspect and probable culprit. In typical impish style, the Harvard economist had reviewed *Iron Mountain for Book World* (a newspaper supplement) under the pseudonym of Herschel McLandress [Galbraith had written a book about Herschel McLandress under the pseudonym of Mark Epernay]. The review was headlined *"News of war and peace you're not ready for."* The full-page article was illustrated by an electronically distorted photograph of Galbraith, captioned "Dr. McLandress looks through a psychometric screen."[1] Despite the distortion, he is easily recognizable. In the review itself, he didn't exactly own up to authorship, but he did acknowledge being involved in the project, saying that "as to the authenticity of the document, it happens that the reviewer can speak to the full extent of his authority and credibility."

According to Galbraith, he had never been recruited to join the group, but was forced to decline because of a previous commitment (he was scheduled to attend a conference in Italy on the date of the Group's first meeting). But, he said, members of the Group consulted him later in preparing their *Report*. As to the ultimate credibility of the document, Galbraith wrote: "the public would not be more assured had I written it myself."

Galbraith's pseudonymous review took the Report for what it claimed to be. But beyond factual issues, he raised another question – the matter of validity. Galbraith stressed the relevance of *Iron Mountain's* outlook, regardless of where the book came from. The Report's conclusions, he declared, were "thoroughly sound." He especially affirmed the Group's calculated a moralism:

> The reaction to war, hitherto, has been moralistic, emotional and even oratorical. This is the first study of its social role to be grounded on modern social science and buttressed by modern empirical techniques as extended and refined by computer technology...As I would put my personal repute behind the authenticity of this document, so would I testify to the validity of its conclusions. My reservations relate only to the wisdom of releasing it to an obviously unconditioned public.

With such statements in view, it is not surprising that much early speculation identified Galbraith as "John Doe."

Iron Mountain as "Satire"

But many of those who reviewed the book named Lewin himself as the likeliest source of the manuscript. *Time* magazine summarized a common surmise:

> (Lewin), after all, contributed political satire to the *New Yorker* and anthologizes it as well. Since he bears a longstanding grudge against think-tanks and their war games, he may have decided to counterattack with some peace games...the book implies that there are conspiracies afoot in the Government to perpetuate war. Lewin is indulging in a little conspiracy for peace (11/17/67; p.44).

Beyond the question of authorship looms the question of authenticity. Regardless of who wrote or transmitted the *Report*, what does it really represent? Is it the product of a government think-tank? Is it satire – a biting parody of bureaucracy gone mad? Or could it be an accurate summary of policy thinking – a "leak" of classified counsels in the form of a fictitious "secret report?"

Publicly expressed opinion has been about equally divided between those possibilities. But we see patterns of attitude. The think-tanks were quick to discredit the book. Henry Rowen, President of RAND Corporation, treated the *Report* dismissively, saying that its statements "are not ludicrous versions of serious views, they are merely ludicrous (Rowen, 1968; p.9)."

Especially, the academic community, many believed that the *Report* was "a hilarious hoax – a kind of dead-pan parody of the studies emanating from the nation's 'think tanks' (*U.S. News & World Report*, 11/20/67; p.48)." The "satire theory" likened *Iron Mountain* to Jonathan Swift's *Modest Proposal*, in which Swift suggested that cannibalism was the most economically sensible solution to Ireland's problem of too many people and too little food.

The parallel is appealing. Swift wrote his satire to express disgust with the social callousness of his day. He attacked the system of unbridled economic greed by exposing its ultimate implications. He discredited the purely economic ethic by pursuing it to its final, grotesque conclusion. If nothing matters but the bottom line, then cannibalism does indeed "add up" in Ireland's dire circumstance. In the same way, says the "satire theory," *Iron Mountain* lampoons Government think-tanks by taking their logic to the level of outrageous.

But the comparison is superficial and misleading. Swift's satire "worked" because his jump from the normal to the grotesque was a quantum leap. The satirical gap between the ordinary and the outrageous is what creates black humor. The moral insult of the *Modest Proposal* is critical to its satirical effect. If Swift had suggested mass deportations instead of cannibalism, the reader's sense of ethical shock would have been "muted," to say the least.

"Swiftian" satire depends on a maximum gap between what is accepted and what is being suggested.

And therein lies the weakness of the "satire theory." *Iron Mountain* isn't funny, because there is little if any difference between what it proposes and what is under discussion or already underway. The *Report's* way of thinking is not new; it is not even unusual. In 1962 we were shocked to find that Herman Kahn and others (under government auspices, in a state of "moral objectivity") had seriously considered policy options that involved sacrificing millions of lives in a nuclear exchange. That kind of amoral calculus came to be called "strategic thinking." Once the beast was named, we adapted to it – after a brief spasm of public indignation.

The arguments which shocked an earlier generation of scholars, such as those set forth by Kahn, Brodie, Ikle, *et al*, have become so absorbed into the general consensus that the shocking has become the commonplace. What was once distinctive is now part of the American operational code book (Horwitz, 1968; p.27).

Report from Iron Mountain is written with altogether too straight a face to be amusing. As one reviewer said:

How can one tell the hoax from the real thing these days? ...what is there in the *Report* that stretches credibility?

Recall that when (Herman Kahn's) *On Thermonuclear War* first came out, the late James R. Newman refused to believe in its authenticity. Now we know better. The barrier of the Unthinkable has been breached once and for all (Rapoport, 1968; p. 10).

Iron Mountain looks like a parody only to the naive. Its "humor" is evident only to those who are unaware that the "satirical gap" has been permanently closed by our policy planners. The *Report* gives moral offense only to those who are "out of the loop," and still believe that Government exists to serve the interests of its citizens.

We have come a long way when...think tanks can plan for levels of genocide matter of factly and with only an occasional need even for secrecy. The Report stirs revulsion only in those who play the game in which people count (Pilisuk, 1968; p. 16).

"Strategic thinking" is a parody of pragmatism to begin with. Kahn and his kind of leap satirical gaps without laughing and embrace holocausts without flinching. Therefore, any exercise in "strategic thinking" will look like a sick joke to some extent, and the more consistently it is pursued, the more it will look like an elaborate sick joke. It is interesting in that, in contrast to the ivory tower world of academics,

> ...those who take the book seriously tend to be Government officials...(one) informant, who works at the highest levels in strategic planning within the Pentagon, asserted after reading the *Report* that he saw no reason to consider it a hoax, since he often comes upon reports that read in much the same way. Yet (another) person – a recent alumnus of the defense Establishment – found the Report quite credible (Trans-Action, Jan-Feb 1968; p. 8).

Answering the Sphinx

What is *Report from Iron Mountain?* Is it a leak, a hoax, a satire? The early reviewers had almost nothing but internal evidence to go on, and they predictably disagreed over that. Some thought the language of the *Report* supported its authenticity because it was the "flat metallic jargon of the U.S. bureaucrat;" others claimed that the language exposed it as a fraud, because it "doesn't fit the authentic jargon of a government research report." James Morey of Columbia University wryly remarked that "the book has proved in some ways a kind of Rorschach test for social scientists (Lewin, 1968; p. 2)." To paraphrase Churchill, *Iron Mountain* comes to us as a riddle wrapped in a mystery inside an enigma.

But whatever else the book may be, it is certainly not satire. It has nothing to do with Jonathan Swift, his ethical purposes, or his literary methods. When Swift's *Modest Proposal* came out, the British Government did not react with nervous confusion, or send a flurry of dispatches to its embassies, telling them to downplay the book and deny that it reflected official policy. *A Modest Proposal* was not "the book that shook the Crown," and it produced no "blazing debates." On the face of it, *Iron Mountain* is in a different category of literature.

But what category is it in? Is the book what it claims to be – the official report of a committee of incognito geniuses assembled by the government? That question is simply unresolvable on the basis of evidence available to us. More importantly, the question itself is beside the point.

> Whether this book is a hoax or not is irrelevant. What is important is the fact that it exists, and that it reflects a particular style of thinking (Duhl, 1968; p. 18).

Twenty-five years have passed since *Iron Mountain* was published (almost three decades since the Group was convened). That historical distance gives us an advantage over early reviewers of the book. Specifically, it gives us a quarter-century worth of evidence toward answering two basic questions: (1) does the *Report* describe ideas that actually shape our government's policy planning, and in particular, (2) is the so called "plan to replace war" an actual, long-term, policy objective? We can begin to answer those questions by looking at what has happened since 1966 (the year that the Group submitted its report).

The ideas broached in *Iron Mountain* soon broke the surface in mainstream publications. The issue of *Foreign Affairs* for April 1970, (just in time to coincide with the first Earth Day), contained an article entitled "To Prevent a World Wasteland – a Proposal," written by George Kennan, an eminent government policy planner. Kennan's article made three points: (1) the eco-crisis is a global threat so great that it endangers life on earth; (2) the crisis should be controlled by a partnership between government and business, operating under a central, international Super-Agency to regulate environmental issues; and (3) the new crusade "must proceed at least to some extent at the expense of the...immensely dangerous preoccupations that are now pursued under the heading of national defense." In other words, the military threat will be phased out, and the eco-threat phased in, while national sovereignty is whittled away. Kennan's "Proposal" does more than "echo" *Iron Mountain's* precepts - it turns them into a concrete program.

Somewhat later, during the 1970s and 1980s, the themes of globalism, peace, and environmentalism began to be finked in the popular media. *Iron Mountain's* agenda was increasingly thrust into public view, both in part and as a whole. The key part of that thrust has been to create acceptance of the eco-danger as a credible threat. It would be redundant to document the media's rising chorus of environmental anxiety. Anyone who reads the newspaper or watches TV endures the barrage on a daily basis.

But the interesting development has been that, *precisely as the Soviet Empire was unraveling and a new world peace, order and cooperation was being hailed, opinion- molders and policy-makers began to suggest very specifically that the cold war should be replaced by eco-war.* The *New York Times* provides a typical and recent example. On March 27, 1990, the *Times* ran an "Op-Ed" article headlined "From Red Menace to Green Threat." The article said that "as the cold war recedes, the environment is becoming the number one international security concern."

A Generation Later: Earth in the Balance

Remember, *Iron Mountain* had said that the eco-crisis was a suitable substitute for war, but also said that it would be "a generation to a generation and a half before (it would) be sufficiently menacing, on a global scale," to offer a solution. And recall that the Group was coming to these conclusions in 1963-1965. According to *Webster's New World Dictionary*, a "generation" equals thirty years. According to arithmetic, the *Report's* transition from war to environmentalism should be ready to happen right about...now.

And now comes Al Gore. Gore's bestselling book, *Earth in the Balance*, has been praised and damned on various grounds. It has been called "farsighted," "visionary," and "wise." It has also been called "dangerous," "demagogic," and "deranged." It has even been called "irrelevant." But it has not been called an "offspring of *Iron Mountain.*" It should be. Gore rubs our faces in the ecological crisis as a credible threat. The bulk of his book is devoted to that purpose. Then he offers his answer to the emergency, in the section he calls "Striking the balance."

Gore gets right to the point. By his second paragraph he is telling us *"we must make the rescue of the environment the central organizing principle for civilization* (Gore, 1992; p. 269)."

The hard part, of course, will be securing a sufficient measure of agreement that difficult, comprehensive changes are needed. Fortunately, there are ample precedents for the kinds of pervasive institutional changes and shared effort that will be necessary. Though it has never yet been accomplished on a global scale, the establishment of a single shared goal as the central organizing principle for every institution in society has been realized by free nations several times in recent history (p. 270).

Gore gives two examples of using a common goal to unify and organize society, and they are: the cold war against communism, and the struggle of World War II against fascism – both based on the war system. Gore never says directly that his eco-crusade will *replace* war, but he makes it plain that the new "central organizing principle" will do what the war system has done before it.

And now, Gore says, global eco-war must play that organizing role on a larger stage. The old, outmoded threat gives way to the new, updated threat. The (nationalistic) functions of military danger give way to the (globalistic) functions of eco-danger.

What does it mean to make the effort to save the global environment the central organizing principle of our civilization? For one thing, it means securing widespread agreement that it should be the organizing principle, and the way such a consensus is formed is especially important because this is when priorities are established and goals are set. *Historically, such a consensus has usually been secured only with the emergence of a life-or-death threat to the existence of society itself;* this time, however, the crisis could well be irreversible by the time its consequences become sufficiently clear to congeal public opinion...It is essential, therefore, that we refuse to wait for the obvious signs of impending catastrophe, that we begin immediately to catalyze a consensus for this new organizing principle (pp. 273-4, Emphasis added).

In other words, Gore's message is, "we can't wait for evidence – we need believers now, for the sake of the global welfare." We might ask if his urgency and disdain for proof are connected to *Iron Mountain's* admonition that "It is more probable, in our judgment, that such a threat will have to be invented rather than developed from unknown conditions (p. 67).

Gore's *Earth in the Balance* essentially promotes *Iron Mountain's* program for transition from war to peace. It adds some detail, but otherwise takes the *Report's* purposes for granted – especially its globalism and its assumption that national sovereignty is expendable. Yet we need not assume that Al Gore has turned a single page of *Iron Mountain*. Its way of thinking has come to be so pervasive that he could have picked up the same ideas by reading *Foreign Affairs* or, for that matter, *Time* magazine.

On the other hand, Gore probably is familiar with the *Report*. Given his political sophistication, it is more than a plausible assumption. Certainly his book exhibits a remarkable, point-for-point adherence to the *Report's* strategic agenda.

The Ultimate Question

In any case, the fact that the question comes up is a measure of *Iron Mountain's* importance and impact on policy thinking. The Report was the first publication to draw together themes that have been linked together ever since. It is the source document for a key constellation of ideas, namely: (1) that the threat of war must be replaced by another threat, preferably global in scope, (2) that the eco-threat is the best of several possible replacements, and, finally, (3) that the threat must be cultivated and the populace prepared before the "solution" to the threat can be applied.[2]

As early as 1968, some reviewers suggested that the *Report* might be a Teak" that was both genuine and fictitious – a creative conflation of real think-tank discussions and real policy recommendations.

The fact is that the *Report* could have been compiled entirely from authentic sources. There are many social scientists doing this kind of investigation; there are members of the Defense Department who think like this. As one reader has observed, "This provides a better rationale of the U.S. Government's posture today than the Government's official spokesmen have provided (*Trans-Action,* 1968; p.8)."

It is appropriate, somehow, that this modem Machiavelli remains faceless and collective. In the bowels of bureaucracy, the buck never rests. *Iron Mountain* is a child of the bureaucracy, and it exhibits all the arrogance and moral evasion of its parent. Behind a cloak of anonymity and expertise, it decrees the fate of the multitudes. Plans are laid, decisions are made, and actions proposed are taken. The public is not consulted, nor is it asked to ratify. In the view from *Iron Mountain,* the citizenry is a rabble, not the source of Constitutional authority.

In the long run, the question of who wrote *Iron Mountain* is dwarfed by larger considerations. The real issue today is not where those ideas came from, but where they have gone since then. Plainly, one of the places they have migrated to is the heart and mind of Al Gore. Never mind who wrote *Iron Mountain* – we know who wrote *Earth in the Balance.*

Professor Mark Pilisuk of U.C. Berkeley went beyond the tantalizing issue of authorship to define the ultimate question:

My great hope, however dim, is that it was done by some dropout from the RAND corporation as an overture to his reentry into the family of man. My great fear is that the strategic framework of thought is so prevalent and so compatible with the competitive advantages of an affluent society that the *Report* describes a process of controlling the future that is too far along for warnings to be of value (Pilisuk, 1968; p. 16).

1 *Book World* identified "Herschel McLandress" as a "psychometrist." Psychometry is a field of psychology that measures the relative strength of mental faculties. But Galbraith may have used the term as a symbolic title for a symbolic person. Its basic meaning combines the Greek word for "soul" (*psyche*) with the Greek word for "measure" (*metron*). Thus, a "psychometrist" is one who "measures the soul." And measurement, of course, is an indispensable prelude to control and manipulation.

2 Professional cynics might wonder if the EPA's dismal record of actually protecting the environment is linked to the *Report's* observation that "the mere modifying of existing programs for the deterrence of pollution could speed up the process enough to make the threat credible much sooner."

Resources

Bayron, Ricardo, (1990) "Ecology vs. Economics: Time to Reconsider" *World Press Review*, August, 1990.

Boulding, Kenneth, (1968) No Title *Trans-Action*, Jan/Feb 1968.

Carman, John, (1991) "Tarzan No. 19 Swings into View" *San Francisco Chronicle*, August 8, 1991.

Cort, David, (1967) "The Ultimate Joke" *Nation*, December 11, 1967.

Duhl, Leonard J., (1968) No Title *Trans-Action*, Jan/Feb 1968.

Gore, Al, (1992) *Earth in the Balance – Ecology and the Human Spirit* (NY, Houghton Mifflin).

Horowitz, Irving Louis, (1968) "The Americanization of Conflict: Social Science 'Fiction' in Action" *Bulletin of the Atomic Scientists*, March, 1968.

Huyser-Honig, Joan, (1992) "A Green Gathering of Evangelicals" *Christianity Today*, October 12, 1992.

Kennan, George, (1970) "To Prevent a World Wasteland – A Proposal" *Foreign Affairs*, April, 1970.

Lear, Norman, (1990) "Nurturing Spirituality and Religion in an Age of Science and Technology" *New Oxford Review*, April, 1990.

Lewin, Leonard, notes and intro, by, (1967*) Report from Iron Mountain on the Possibility and Desirability of Peace* (NY, Dial Press, also: Esquire, December, 1967; NY, Dell Books, 1967; Hammondsworth, Penguin Books, 1968; and London, McDonald and Co., 1968).

Lewin, Leonard, (1968) "Feedback From Our Readers" *Trans-Action*, April, 1968.

"McLandress, Herschel," aka J.K. Galbraith, (1967) "News of War and Peace You're Not Ready For" *Book World*, November 26, 1967.

Petit, Charles, (1992) "Earth Summit' Organizers Hope For a Revolution" *San Francisco Chronicle,* January 30, 1992.

Petit, Charles, (1992) "Earth Summit Could Be a Turning Point for the U.N." *San Francisco Chronicle*, June 16, 1992.

Pilisuk, Marc, (1968) No Title *Trans-Action*, Jan/Feb, 1968.

Rapoport, Anatol, (1968) No Title *Trans-Action*, Jan/Feb, 1968.

Rowen, Henry S., (1968) No Title *Trans-Action*, Jan/Feb, 1968.

Sanders, Franklin, (1992) "The Three Legs of the Beast" *Moneychanger*, January, 1992.

Time (1967) "Peace Games" *Time*, November 17. 1967.

Trans-Action, (1968) "Comment-Social Science Fiction" Jan/Feb, 1968 [Note: *Trans-Action-Social Science and Modern Society* (now called *Society*) is published by Rutgers University. Its Jan/Feb 1968 issue contains reviews of *Report from Iron Mountain* by a prestigious array of scholars and government officials].

U.S. News and World Report, (1967) "Hoax or Horror? A Book That Shook The White House" November 20,1967.

Viets, Jack (1991) "Costeau's Deadline for Earth" *San Francisco Chronicle*, November 22, 1991.

(Reprinted from *SCP Journal* by permission; SCP, Inc., P.O. Box 4308, Berkeley, California 94704, (501)540-0300.)

Index

304

New reality, 19, 25, 48, 49, 51-54, 56
New World Order, 22, 29, 36, 39,
    47, 49, 56, 180, 183, 185, 191,
    199
New York State Council of Parks
    and Outdoor Recreation, 92
New York Times, 29, 36, 47, 48, 58,
    63, 103, 104, 106, 108, 109,
    117, 119-121, 125, 157, 174,
    175, 178, 179, 184, 190, 192,
    198, 219, 223, 224, 244, 255,
    291
New York Zoological Society, 92
New Zealand, 49, 154, 176, 261
Newman, Paul, 40
Newsweek, 78, 83, 117, 198, 222,
    223, 225, 266
Non-Governmental Organizations
    (NGOs), 19, 164, 167, 169,
    176, 181, 191, 245, 246, 248,
    249
Nitrogen oxide, 157
Nitze, William A., 174, 178
Nixon, Richard, 10, 93, 95, 96, 102,
    103
North Cascades Conservation Coun-
    cil, 68
Nunn, Sam, 3

O

Olympic National Forest, 176
Operation Husky, 71
Operation Overload, 71
Oppenheimer, Michael, 48
Orwell, George, 24, 129, 188; *1984*,
    24, 80, 83, 129, 188, 207, 219
Ortega, Daniel, 42
Overpopulation, 10, 12, 22, 48, 75,
    91, 92, 114, 133, 138, 139, 145,
    146, 153, 162, 164, 167, 192,
    264; Overpopulation Industry,
    91
Ozone Depletion, 48, 63, 112, 116,
    157, 158
Ozone hole, 22, 89, 121, 157, 158

P

P3, 124, 125
Pacific Gas & Electric Co., 81

Pacific Science Center Foundation,
    94
Palisades Interstate Park Commis-
    sion, 92
Paris, 48, 174
Partners for Livable Places, 86
Paul, the Apostle, 269
PBS, 102, 111-113, 121
PCB, 89, 216
Peace 1, 3-7, 10, 20, 32, 35, 58, 71,
    74, 137, 163, 186, 222, 248,
    256, 261, 271, 272, 275-278,
    280-286, 290, 291, 293, 295,
    296
People for Ethical Treatment of Ani-
    mals (PETA), 269
People's Bicentennial Commission,
    89
People's Business Commission, 89,
    90
Perestroika, 41, 185
Petit, Charles, 296
Philip Morris, 96
Phillips Petroleum, 162
Physicians for Social Responsibility,
    72
Piedmont Environmental Council,
    86
Pilisuk, Mark, 288, 294-296
Planned Parenthood, 26, 90, 137,
    143, 145, 150, 168, 170
Player, Ian, 54
Poindexter, Admiral, 33
Poland, 35, 148
Polar ice caps, 155
Politicians, 2, 3, 22, 29, 85, 125,
    173, 174, 230, 263
Pollution, 9, 10, 14, 74, 88, 95, 103,
    112, 116, 156, 160, 164, 167,
    170, 178, 180, 181, 183, 193,
    197, 200, 212, 213, 216, 220,
    242, 245, 266, 282, 283, 295
Pollution Enforcement Agency
    (PEA), 180, 183
Population, 2, 20, 23, 70, 71, 74-76,
    90, 91, 114, 116, 121, 133, 134-
    136, 138-151, 164, 206, 231,
    233

CPSIA information can be obtained at www.ICGtesting.com
Printed in the USA
BVOW08s2148031215

429310BV00001B/33/P